AF328534

I SUFFER THEREFORE I AM

PASCAL BRUCKNER

I Suffer Therefore I Am

Portrait of the Victim as Hero

Translated by Stephen Muecke

polity

For Caroline Thompson, of course

For Patrice Champion, in memory of Belgrade and Krakow

For Olivier Nora, who stood firm

One does not ask of one who suffers: What is your country and what is your religion? One merely says: You suffer, that is enough for me.

Louis Pasteur

Man is a pupil, pain is his teacher and no one knows himself until he has suffered.

Alfred de Musset, *Lorenzaccio*

Contents

Contents

Prologue: An inverted Pantheon

On 8 December 2015, the Élysée Palace announced that President François Hollande planned to award the Légion d'honneur to the 130 victims of the 13 November attacks in Paris at the Bataclan theatre and in the surrounding streets. The Chancellor of France disagreed. Since its creation on 19 May 1802 by Napoleon Bonaparte, the Légion d'honneur has rewarded military personnel and civilians who have rendered outstanding services to the nation. The 130 innocent people who had the misfortune to be in the wrong place at the wrong time and were mown down by jihadist barbarity, deserved the nation's esteem, but in a thousand other ways.

In 1999, Spain created a special decoration for those killed in terrorist attacks. The United States built a monument to the 9/11 dead. But the Légion d'honneur is awarded neither for being involved in a tragedy, nor for mourning. It is supposed to be an acknowledgement of merit. It is one thing for the country to pay homage to the victims, but quite another to give them a medal reserved for heroic deeds. It's as if we wanted to exorcize the tragedy by pinning republicanist baubles on the murdered men and women. To be decorated, you have to have fought, and with valour; being randomly shot down does not suffice.

In the end, the Élysée gave up on the idea and on 12 July 2016 created the National Medal of Recognition for Victims of Terrorism, the fifth most important decoration in the order of protocol, ahead of the Resistance Medal and the Croix de Guerre. But the creation of this medal got a frosty reception in some sectors of the public and the army. Was just suffering some outrage or being murdered by fanatical individuals more important than paying tribute to armed combatants? Everyone was a child of the nation, it seems, but some more than others. Since 1990, medallists for terrorism have been considered 'civilian victims of war' and their children are eligible to be wards of the state. These are all significant symptoms of an ongoing confusion that had already given rise to a debate in the aftermath of the Second World War between resistance fighters and deportees: does the torture inflicted on someone deserve more consideration than actual accomplishments? Is an unfortunate person more heroic than a valiant one?

Introduction: Thucydides and Jesus Christ

In *The History of the Peloponnesian War*, an account of the conflicts between Athens, Sparta and the other Greek cities, the Athenian historian Thucydides (460–395 BCE) states the following law: 'Justice does not enter into the reasoning of men unless the forces on both sides are equal; otherwise, the strong exercise their power and the weak must yield to them.' This is a law of the ages: the powerful rule, the wretched bow down. It was a Christian revelation, heralded by Judaism, that reversed this paradigm, much to the dismay of the pagans, who were appalled by this exaltation of a God who allowed himself to be crucified like a slave in order to save humankind. 'Was it fitting for God to allow himself to be tied up and dragged away like a criminal? Much less was it fitting that he should be abandoned and betrayed by those closest to him, who followed him like a messiah, the Son and messenger of God himself', exclaimed the Roman philosopher Celsus in the first century.[1] For a man of antiquity, it made no sense for Jesus to pronounce the commandment to love one's enemies and to enjoin believers to give precedence to the sick, the poor and the dispossessed. It's an anthropological upheaval that puts the low above the high, the ignoble above the noble, and against which Friedrich Nietzsche, the great worshipper of strength and aristocracy, never tired of railing.

A common homeland

In the Passion narrative, Jesus offers his suffering as a common homeland to all the downtrodden and brings them the cross as an aid. This is Christianity's stroke of genius and its absolute singularity, the new agreement proposed to the human race: the invention of a man-god who has the weaknesses of the former and the transcendence of the latter. Contemporaries were astonished that this obscure sect should have succeeded among the cohort of fanatics, zealots and healers who populated Galilee at that time. The Son of Man did not preach for the rich or the righteous, but for sinners, loose women, thieves and the fallen. He made himself humble among the humble. His intransigence was not of this world and it put a bomb under every institution, even the Churches. With the mixture of gentleness and aggression that characterizes the Gospels, his call for an insurrection against the powerful would shape the whole of the Western world, including the great secular doctrines of modernity. What is the working class in Marxism if not the body of Christ constituted as a revolutionary bloc to overturn History and establish the perfect society? What are minorities in 'wokeism' if not so many Christ-like effigies to be revered, no matter what? Is it not their misfortune that legitimizes them, especially when that misfortune is written in the plural through Kimberlé Crenshaw's 'intersectionality', the crossroads of various oppressions?[2] Christianity inverts hierarchies and gives pre-eminence to the vanquished over the brutes. The language of the victor consists of saying: I am right because I am the strongest. The language of the victim, on the other hand, says that my weakness is my weapon and my right. There is a transcendence and almost a sanctity to it; I share their pain; their destitution makes it incumbent on me to come to their aid.

We know that this quasi-divinity of the vulnerable is the prerogative of civilization. For better or worse, we are the heirs to this Christian revolution. Over the last two millennia, and often against the advice of the Churches, it has given consistency to the rights of women, of children, of the exploited, of slaves and the colonized. But a derivative strategy has been grafted onto this invention: the attitude of victimhood, which can be found at both the State and the individual level. It seems to be stronger in rich countries, devoted to material pleasures and structurally dissatisfied with their lot. Our pantheon is made up only of the downtrodden and the crushed. They are the only ones eligible for our sympathy, and we find new ones every day. This is our great democratic passion; even the privileged want to play the victim. Freedom, the ability of each individual to lead their life as they see fit, is above all permission to lament their own fate.

Respect my suffering

The word victim has many meanings even though being subjected to robbery, rape, accident or torture are not the same thing. But in this area there is an escalation to extremism and confusion reigns. Everyone aligns their condition with that of the person most affected. 'Respect my suffering', individuals demand. 'Prove to me that you are suffering', demands the State, insurance companies, public opinion and the media. But what can be done about those who suffer neither enough nor too little – in other words, the majority? Traditionally, the status of victim was obtained from historians or the courts. The historian described the reality of a massacre, and the courts recognized this reality and drew out the consequences. This process of recognition took a long time, and was often enshrined by the State or governments in official ceremonies. But these days, in an age of impatience amplified by social media, people want to speed up the process of crowning themselves martyrs. For instance via 'grievance studies'[3] in the USA, where university departments specialize in grievances affecting all sorts of categories: fat people, women, minorities, queers, lesbians, trans people, etc., and who grant themselves this title from the outset, so to speak. Armenians, deportees, slaves, colonized people, Harkis and homosexuals all had to wait a long time for recognition. We no longer have the courage to wait; we want the title of oppressed immediately.

What is victimization? It's a narrative identity that we ascribe to ourselves and expect others to confirm. It is a *pathology of recognition*, a desire to be identified without having to come forward.

The nineteenth and twentieth centuries' dominant dreams of heroism have been replaced, in the twenty-first, by intense dreams of victimhood. This is the result of three reversals: the frenzied quest for happiness is flipped into a frenzied obsession with misfortune. Suffering is annexing ever-expanding territories to its empire, including areas that were previously outside its jurisdiction. Lastly, the promise of democracy, always a disappointment, exacerbates dissatisfaction and puts complaint at the centre of the contemporary psyche. In a word, the ideology of victimhood sins three times over: it discredits the spontaneous stoicism of each individual in the face of evil. It distorts priorities: under the guise of protecting the vulnerable, it smuggles in false victims who obscure from view those genuinely in trouble. Finally, it becomes the alibi for the killers who use this false flag to commit their crimes.

Promotion of the damned

In the past, the victims, whether male or female, were sacrificed by fire, hanging or lynching in order to repair a fractured community. They were sacrificed and sometimes sanctified. Nowadays, it's the other way around: first we sanctify, then we sacrifice. After 1945 and the Holocaust, the figure of the Jew was put on a pedestal, then pulled down when it became that of the Israeli, accused of all the evils of colonialism, racism and imperialism. The prime position has become damned: from being a model, the figure of the Jew has become a rival to be eliminated in order to take its place.

On a global scale, there is a complaint competition, with each trying to howl the other down. The fraternity of the fallen is matched by the cacophony of complainers, who hoist the figure of the martyr on high, while feeding the two great passions of revenge and resentment. White or black supremacists, radical Islamists, bitter masculinists, angry neo-feminists, furious ecologists, revanchist Slavophiles, vindictive neo-Ottomans, each cashes in on a past glory or disaster to blame their enemies. How many defeated empires – Russia, Turkey, Iran, China – dress themselves up in the trappings of the doomed to then dive headlong into the hubris of reconquest? How many independent states invoke the former colonial metropolis to continue exploiting their peoples? The natural inclination of any persecuted person, once in power, is to metamorphose into a persecutor. *Victimism is warmongering*: the more people feel sorry for themselves, the more they feel justified in punishing those they see as their enemies. Their tears are heavy with rage and enmity.

Concern for the humiliated is humanism's strong point. But blackmailing with victimhood is the flip side of this progress. Its final stage is the erasure of the truly unfortunate in favour of carnival pariahs whose only distinguishing feature is that they possess the networks and notoriety that allow them to promote themselves. They seize the language of the oppressed to usurp a position. They enter into a war of words, taking them hostage, kidnapping them. From one end of the social ladder to the other, each brandishes their hard-luck certificate that raises them above their fellows. This character, this strange kind of professional sufferer, is on the march through every country, cutting across all social classes. So how do we distinguish the counterfeiters and cheats from the others?

This book has three parts: the first examines how the message of the Enlightenment and the Revolution, of a better world free of fatalism and fanaticism, leads to a society of fragility and tears – in other words, of resignation. In the second part, we look at how the status of pariah potentially gives people every right, especially the right to accuse and oppress in the name of their injury. The final section looks at the figures of the executioner and the hero. Both the hero and the victim create unity, each in their own way: the first reassures societies subject to doubt, while the second reshapes the torn fabric of the social contract. Both need an audience to endorse them. We gorge ourselves on the unfortunate, just as we exalt the brave, who bolster our image. But horrified as much as fascinated, we also gorge ourselves on the monsters who kill out of sadism or disguise themselves as martyrs to perpetrate their abominations.

Why are the breeding grounds of victimhood so fertile? Paradoxically, in the hedonistic West, suffering has become a new, meditative sacred. Once a common feature of the human condition, it is now a passport that you flaunt to impress your contemporaries. It provides you with a borrowed identity, transforming you into an exceptional being who can show off on the public stage at little cost. This is the message of our age: you are all disinherited and entitled to feel sorry for yourselves. The ultimate dream would be to become a martyr without ever having suffered anything other than the misfortune of having been born.

Facing Misfortune

'One day all will be well, so runs our hope'[1]

No one suffers needlessly.

SAINT AUGUSTINE

The classical age was hard going, at least if we are to believe its leading lights. In the sixteenth and seventeenth centuries, there was plenty of misery to go around; people had to put up with it and would even flaunt it. The whole point of life, which was short at the time – thirty-five years for princes and the nobility of the robe, twenty-seven for the rest of the population, with remarkable exceptions depending on the individual (Louis XIV lived to be nearly seventy-seven) – was to prepare for death. In other words, to face the Supreme Judge and wash away one's sins. When Europe was predominantly Christian, the fear of damnation had to take precedence over the fear of dying: death had to be a path to divine bliss or the flames of hell. The seventeenth century abounded in admirable texts on the need for believers to welcome misfortune as a trial of internal purification, and to prepare for the Great Departure. Whereas for the Greeks and Latins suffering was an inevitable fate, for the early Christians it was the price of the Fall, the wages of original sin. Fate is unjust, evil strikes the innocent and children at random but, as in the Book of Job, God will provide for the happiness of the deserving.[2] Death is not an end, but a bridge to the unknown of the Last Judgement.

The wages of sin

Fortunately, God gave his only Son to deliver humanity from evil and death. The passion of Christ becomes the founding narrative of faith: each believer, in their own sorrow, can play a part in this story and find in Jesus a guide and a friend to help them. On his cross, strung up like a thief, the Son of God looks death in the face and overcomes it with the hope of Resurrection. On this condition, suffering becomes an ally; it is the failure that leads to victory, says Martin Luther; it is the sign of our downfall and our possible elevation.

Christianity rejects both aristocratic heroism, which is contemptuous of the poor, and Stoic morality, which recommends enduring grief and misfortune without complaint. The latter goes so far as to invite the wise man to undergo torture and dismemberment with a smile: even in the Phalaris bull in Agrigento, Sicily, a hollow, red-hot bronze sculpture in which the tortured were locked up, the wise man was supposed to remain happy and overcome the atrocious pain. Blaise Pascal castigated the insolence of Epictetus and Marcus Aurelius and saw in them a major crime: the affirmation of a human freedom unaware of its penury. In his view, we must confess our ordeal and, from the depths of this degradation, go back to the Creator. 'In Thy sight none is pure of sin, not even the infant whose life is but a day on earth', wrote Saint Augustine in his *Confessions*. The Churches developed a very real concern for the unfortunate, along with their appetite for misfortune. This is evidenced by the aesthetics of torture and blood in a certain form of Catholicism, particularly in Spain, the love of the dismembered body and the ability of this monotheism to be one of the greatest manufacturers of martyrs (it has now been surpassed by Islam, which churns out a whole string of them, the Shahids,[3] also known as terrorists).

But in the Gospels, misfortune loses its worst feature: gratuitousness. It has a meaning, and all religions are saturated with meaning; they exist only to make grief, mourning and death bearable by giving them a higher purpose. Buddhism itself, through the notion of karma, makes present misfortune the result of faults committed in previous lives. As the saying goes, the arrows we fired in the past come back at us as a just retribution for our past sins. A cruel concept (we all deserve our fate, especially the poorest), but eminently consoling. Immanent justice sanctions the division, from birth, between the disadvantaged and the advantaged. In Hinduism and Buddhism, which are very different (the latter does not recognize castes), there are two kinds of salvation: an intramundane salvation that we earn as we reincarnate and that allows us to improve from generation to generation, and an extramundane salvation where we escape the cursed cycle of rebirths. With Christianity, suffering became a mystery brought to light and deciphered in the course of one's own suffering. And theologians competed in casuistry to legitimize the existence of pain, illness and the death of children without undermining the goodness of God.

Vale of tears, valley of roses

It would appear that this justification for our misfortune was not all that convincing, since over time it has become a breviary of resignation. Advances in agriculture, the diversification of diets, even among the poorest, and the discovery of alkaloids and opiates to soothe physical torments, which gave rise to the first controversies on opium among doctors,[4] swept away the priest's fabulations about pain as a necessary divine punishment. As the Middle Ages drew to a close, a fierce desire to live and escape the inevitability of torment began to emerge in Europe. If a few drops of laudanum could banish an intolerable ache or induce a beneficial torpor, then sermons on just punishment would resound in the void. Christian algophilia was rejected via action. The greatest benefactor of humanity remains John Collins Warren, who invented ether anaesthesia in the United States in 1846.

At the turn of the seventeenth and eighteenth centuries, the Enlightenment set itself a simple ambition: to replace the obsession with salvation with a concern for happiness, to tear itself away from the inexhaustible leprosy of misfortune and arbitrariness that characterized the Ancien Régime. Life is not just a vale of tears; it is possible to transform this world into a fertile, cheerful garden. Evil may persist, but we can abolish many of the pointless evils that have crushed mankind for centuries. The idea of progress replaces that of eternity, the future becomes the refuge of hope, the place where man is reconciled with himself. 'One day all will be well, so runs our hope; all is well today, that is the illusion', says Voltaire. This shift in sensibilities was also extended to animal suffering in public debate with the theory of the 'chain of being', which postulated a kinship between all living beings. Condillac's sensualist philosophy gave beasts a common destiny with man: 'Let us conclude that if beasts feel, they feel as we do.'[5] The torments caused by animal fighting, the castration of horses, the brutality of slaughterhouses and hunting, and the wild beasts caged in menageries would gradually awaken a genuine religion of compassion towards our inferior brothers and sisters, especially as humans became attached to some domestic species and devoted genuine affection to them, as they did with other members of the family.

The concept of progress brings together individual and collective happiness, as exemplified by Anglo-Saxon utilitarianism, which claims to place happiness at the service of humankind. The calamities that befall us will disappear tomorrow if we put some work into them. The forward march of the human spirit can be slow or fast, but it is always infallible. But the promised land of the future remains, for the long term, a land compromised by the old world, which it strangely resembles. Progress is an equivocal ambition; it nurtures the hope of succeeding where previous generations have failed, but it postpones Eden. Misfortune doesn't disappear, it shifts its location. Tomorrow, once again, becomes hope's eternal category. There are countless secular doctrines that recommend patience before the advent of the perfect society. There can be no triumph of the spirit for Hegel, no proletarian revolution for Marx, without a long period of bloody tribulations and wars of all kinds. The chaos of History gives rise to the Better, and violence is the great midwife of the future. Nietzsche was not to be outdone, extolling cruelty and savage hordes to improve the human race by selecting the strongest. These are all doctrines for which evil is a necessary moment of good; in every calamity there is a secret reason at work. The worst horrors that humans inflict on each other are supposed to end up in a collective flourishing. The secular heirs of Catholicism are staging their noisy revival on the altar of pain. Our societies believe themselves to be de-Christianized, but our passions remain those of Christianity. Religion is not coming back; it has never disappeared. It smoulders like an ember beneath our secular assertions.

The beginning of the twenty-first century in Europe has seen a proliferation of bloated promises. Each era boasts of its ability to resolve the crises of the previous one. The digital age, with its billionaire prophets and its high priests of immortality and artificial intelligence, is no exception. It was a regenerated and purified humanity that was to enter the third millennium, certain that it had hunted down the last germs of hell. Death, disease and old age were to be swept away as archaisms. But the intoxication of transhumanism was followed by the hangover of Covid and the excessive morbidity of this period, highlighting the limits of medicine. The end of History, combined with the progress of democracy and the benefits of the market, was to propel the human adventure to new heights. Europe would be the only place where tragedy would no longer take place, in the profound words of Susan Sontag, uttered at the time of the war in ex-Yugoslavia. Every decade, the same drunken oaths and the same hopes return, mirrored since the beginning of the twenty-first century by the apocalyptic announcements of millenarian groups about the end of the world. The drunkenness of the utopians is matched only by the panic of the catastrophists.

The pea syndrome

The optimism of the great philosophies of History has been swept away, at least in the West, by a growing number of conflicts, genocides and mass exterminations, which have made people more hesitant about the ultimate end of History. Humanity has become disenchanted because of all the abominable crimes and no longer has confidence in its own resources. It seems to be moving simultaneously towards the worst and the best. Faith in the future is wavering, at least in the West. All the more so since democracy is the ultimate regime of legal insatiability: it intensifies a thirst it cannot quench, spikes fevers and exacerbates rivalries. It feeds indignation and revolt, but also envy and jealousy. It makes each of us a citizen more tormented by what we don't have than by what we already have. The prosperity of some feeds a permanent jealousy based on comparison, including among the advantaged. Marx wrote: 'A house may be large or small; as long as the surrounding houses are equally small it satisfies all social demands for a dwelling. But if a palace arises beside the little house, the little house shrinks into a hut.'[6] Frustration is heightened by the fact that a certain level of comfort is already assured in wealthy nations, an advantage that people fear losing at any moment. What we thought had been eliminated continues to taunt us: new epidemics decimate us, wars reappear, extreme climatic phenomena ravage the countryside, and the impoverishment of citizens resurfaces in societies that we thought had settled down.

We Europeans and Americans of the twenty-first century have become hypersensitive to the slightest annoyance. We have all been struck by the princess and the pea syndrome, the Hans Christian Andersen heroine who spends a sleepless night because of a tiny hard pea slipped under her mattress.[7] Our emotions are heightened as medicine softens the conditions of our existence. Victim mythology is usually explained by the gap between the promises of modernity and its results. But what if the opposite were true? What if it were the undeniable successes of science and industry that have exasperated our impatience? So many evils have been vanquished, so many injustices abolished, that we are surprised that they cannot all be done away with immediately. In spite of itself, the state of civilization creates as much suffering as it relieves. It produces a telescoping between aspirations and realities that can generate disenchantment. By establishing well-being and health as minimum standards, it makes their lack more intolerable. Anything that thwarts our appetites becomes a source of discomfort; we aspire to better things all the time, at the risk of raising our petty miseries to the level of intolerable deprivation. Our allergy to worries grows as the prospect of overcoming them increases.

Unlike Christianity, which never set out to eradicate evil on earth – 'it is in vain, O men, that you seek in yourselves the remedy for your miseries', said Pascal – the American and French Revolutions, guided by human rights, aimed to regenerate the human race through the combined efforts of knowledge, industry and emancipation. It was supposed to be possible to overcome almost all ills – hunger, poverty, superstition – with time. Alas, there is no one progress, but rather localized progresses, themselves equivocal, producing regression and considerable damage. How can we still take communion at the high mass of productivism and scientism, whose ravages are obvious, without mentioning the 'accidents' that were the crises of mad cow disease, asbestos, contaminated blood, levothyroxine and fentanyl? Our undeniable progress over the last three centuries has come at the price of terrifying setbacks. Every conquest is also a defeat, every show of strength an admission of weakness.

But it would be a mistake to believe that our faith in progress is dead and buried. Even the most ardent opponents of this idea swallow a painkiller as soon as they feel pain, or submit to the surgeon's scalpel if their life is in danger. The best remedy for the pains of progress is yet another advance that will correct the effects of the previous one. Both the submissive Christian and the arrogant modernist have been replaced by contemporary perplexity. We have become moderate believers who aspire to a progress that is controlled or localized.

Eradicating evil?

The Moderns have sometimes toyed with the mad desire to abolish disorders of all kinds, to treat suffering as null and void, or to sweep it under the carpet. The philosopher Alain, in his 1925 book on happiness, saw hygiene and gymnastics as the best remedies for pain.[8] He mocked Pascal for being frightened by the silence of infinite space, saying that he had probably caught a cold at his window.[9] In his view, fatal illnesses, and even wars, stem from a failure in education: we must learn to be happy, it's a polite duty. Serenity is an obligation that is sometimes disrupted by evil geniuses; thus the hostility between Germany and France, 'robust children, pestered and finally exasperated beyond endurance by a mere handful of spiteful boys'.[10] As for the man on his way to the guillotine, all he has to do is count the bumps in the road to distract himself from the fatal deadline! The historian Philippe Ariès has remarked that, in the post-war West, mourning and grief have become solitary activities like masturbation.[11] While the disappearance of our loved ones continues to devastate us, the funerary customs that provided a framework for survivors have disappeared. Death is no longer a life event, except when it strikes a great person like Queen Elizabeth II in September 2022. The whole world was moved, including France; for three weeks, we literally borrowed Great Britain's queen to rediscover the splendour of the monarchy. The obituaries in the magazines are devoured all the more avidly because they are a quasi-taboo. We no longer go into mourning or wear dark clothes; we can follow funerals on the Net. Grief remains private, the death of a close friend or relative must not disrupt the triumphant march of life. The aim now is to introduce a 'positive death', to make it more attractive, to banish glum funereal faces,[12] to shuffle off with a smile. Even palliative care, if the ads are to be believed, should be nice and friendly.[13] And why not compost yourself to reduce your ecological footprint, as suggested by the Humo Sapiens association?[14]

Our prevailing hedonism, in its attempt to avoid the negative, reinforces what it was trying to conceal: the omnipresent terror of pain, both physical and moral. *The society of compulsory happiness is also one that constantly speaks the language of distress.* In a perverse twist, it encourages the growth of unhappiness, spreading like weeds. While it may not be true that everyone seeks happiness, it is true that they all want to escape misfortune. The Epicurean and Stoic schools of antiquity sought to limit suffering by understanding its mechanism; Christianity exalted it with a view to redeeming the creature; we live on its denegation with the mad hope that it will dissipate if we deprive it of any public expression. The result: groups of the afflicted are multiplying exponentially, and public and private recriminations have never been so numerous. Young people in rich Western countries have been described as the 'snowflake generation' to reflect their extreme fragility.[15] Cohorts of the 'vulnerable' are gathering online to share their despondency and their fears.

Is well-being a cause of anxiety?

Have we all become softies? That's what many people nostalgic for bygone days thought. Nietzsche, horrified by the humanitarianism of his century, really pushed the hope of a human being shaped by the hammer, as clay is by hardness:

> The discipline of suffering, of *great* suffering – know ye not that it is only *this* discipline that has produced all

the elevations of humanity hitherto? The tension of soul in misfortune which communicates to it its energy, its shuddering in view of rack and ruin, its inventiveness and bravery in undergoing, enduring, interpreting, and exploiting misfortune, and whatever depth, mystery, disguise, spirit, artifice, or greatness has been bestowed upon the soul – has it not been bestowed through suffering, through the discipline of great suffering?[16]

It's like reading the rules of a reform school for wayward boys. In the same vein, the Hungarian-born British sociologist Frank Furedi mocks the setting up of medical and psychological emergency units for the slightest accident or difficult event, and points out that the people of South-East Asia, who fell victim to the 2004 tsunami, had no need of the experts rushed in by international bodies.[17] It also calls into question the new nosological entity of post-traumatic stress disorder (PTSD) developed by American psychiatry when Vietnam veterans returned home, and which is now applied to the descendants of the Shoah as well as to those of the former Yugoslavia and Rwanda.[18] As long ago as the 1930s, a pain manifesto was published protesting against 'the tyranny of the healthy' and the softening of medical care. Yet for a long time, in France, the medical world was reluctant to prescribe morphine, even in cases of serious illness. It was not until 2001 that this treatment became compulsory. This debate is absurd: we can both detest unnecessary pain and celebrate the fortitude of individuals in the face of adversity. Between the up-in-arms and the cowardly, there are other less extreme forms of behaviour.

But these days, many people see toughness, silence and solidity as a retrograde attitude: you have to sympathize and feel sorry for yourself. The slightest accident, especially one involving children, and we summon cohorts of psychologists for fear of irreversible after-effects.

Every time, emotion takes precedence over analysis, and identification with the bereft prevails. What has changed compared with previous centuries is not the sum total of the scourges we suffer from, but our disposition towards them. The classical age in Europe could be pessimistic, but it was content to confirm the dogma of original sin: crimes, horrors and atrocities followed as proof of our darkness redeemed by God. The tragedy began in the Renaissance, with the hope of a better world, the sole responsibility of man, who became accountable for his failures. This promise to build a reasonable Eden with the weapons of the welfare state, education and the law remains, by its very nature, unfulfilled and therefore disappointing. Whatever is done to support us, it is never enough; there are always obstacles, impediments. The more we try to make our lives easier, the more the residual difficulties seem like insurmountable walls. Particularly in France, where the welfare state is as obese as it is ineffective, we live with expectations that are constantly raised and then disappointed. We are never sufficiently fulfilled, loved, gratified. As Jean-François Laé writes, 'We suffer more and more from the effects of gencralised protection.'[19]

Did people suffer less in the past?

Our societies face a permanent dilemma. In the effort to eliminate injustice, they begin by naming it, thereby risking giving it undue weight. Our major issues, the promotion of disadvantaged groups and concern for well-being, must constantly be based on a state of imperfection that we recall the better to overcome it. We mentally contrast yesterday's deplorable state with today's preferable possibilities. And we look at poor or underdeveloped countries as embodying these archaisms that we no longer want.

Bad things generally had to be put up with, because the remedies were cruder and the medicine rudimentary. The remedies we now enjoy did not exist, and the threshold of tolerance has shifted. All the wisdom in the world ceases when faced with a toothache or a terrible pain. If we are writhing in agony, we insist on immediate relief. Knowing that the medicine exists but that we won't benefit from it is an indignity. A child dying for lack of care is an absolute scandal. People have always hated pain and, as the historian Roselyne Rey tells us, in the sixteenth century many people preferred to wait for death rather than undergo amputation or ablation (anaesthesia did not yet exist).[20] With any pain, it is the fine-tuned scale of what is inadmissible that must be taken into account. One person faints over a blood test, another allows herself to be butchered without batting an eyelid. Physical courage varies from one person to another and in each of us, depending on our stage of life. Despite the atrocities of war and epidemics, there is no evidence to suggest that societies of the past were hardier; they were more resigned and people died very young.

There have always been examples of superhuman endurance that have captured the imagination in every age. One such was a boy in Sparta, quoted by Montaigne, who preferred to have his liver eaten by a fox rather than confess to his theft (the education of young men implied mastery of theft), or the American mountaineer, Aron Ralston, who in 2003, trapped by a rock in Utah, amputated his forearm to free himself and was saved in extremis (he returned to the site six months later to scatter the ashes of his cremated stump). We have to distinguish between hardships we impose on ourselves and those we endure in spite of ourselves. Napoleon's soldiers on the run from Moscow, the deportees in Nazi Germany and the Zeks in the Gulag were subjected to abominations that leave us speechless, and rightly so.

In contrast to these ordeals, in liberal democracies the State looks after us, taking citizens under its wing and assuring them that the nation will not forget them. The caring society looks after us from birth to death, from morning till night, holding our hands, keeping us out of danger, showing us the right path. Especially in France, where the precautionary principle prevails, we need to minimize everyone's exposure to adversity. In other words, as Condillac wrote, to risk 'the chance of incurring a bad outcome, coupled with the hope, if we escape it, to achieve a good one',[21] is now suspect or restricted to specific activities. But fear increases as we seek to protect ourselves from all dangers. In the field of education, we know that children who are too well looked-after are incapable of dealing with the chaos of the world. At the first sign of trouble, they seek help from their mother or father and find themselves lost, unable to stand on their own two feet. Overprotection makes them more vulnerable. The little panics that disturb a child's soul are normal, and the duty of educators is to nurture boys and girls to help them mature. Children go from submission to separation, from obedience to progressive emancipation. They become masters of themselves as they learn about their newfound freedom. There is nothing more exhilarating at any age than overcoming one's apprehensions and testing one's limits.

Raising this sensitivity into a political principle can produce opposite effects: either 'I will work harder' Stakhanovists or daredevils. Private individuals subject themselves to inhuman trials, trekking to the Poles, sailing the Atlantic or the Pacific on a raft, impossible climbs on sheer rockfaces, crossing canyons or city streets on a wire, suspended above the void. Not to mention company boot camps designed to 'toughen up employees' who are put to the test walking on coals or bungee jumping in mad training courses that are reminiscent of the US Marines or the SAS. Or those reality shows where a naked man and woman are supposed to survive in a hostile jungle armed with a single knife, at the mercy of snakes, tarantulas and crocodiles.[22]

We choose 'good suffering' over 'bad suffering' as if one would cancel out the other, and we freely impose humiliations and challenges on ourselves that give us the illusion of owning and mastering our destiny. The only constraints we like are those we impose on ourselves in pursuit of a higher goal, as a challenge to our finitude. The fragility of a majority of citizens pampered by the public authorities is matched by the stubbornness of an intrepid minority. Between the two, the ordinary individual, man or woman, young or old, chooses the risks that suit him or her, without going in for madcap excessiveness. But misfortune always strikes unexpectedly and imposes its laws on us. Even a daredevil can be killed stupidly on the stairs after a lifetime of defying death. Misfortune is only accepted if we can give it meaning. It doesn't matter if it has the last word or not, at least we will have stood up to it until the end.

SMALL CONSOLATIONS

When there's a glitch, there's always one consolation: comparison. The accident from which I have just escaped could have been more serious. I could have lost both my legs or my life. Fortunately, the cancer that struck me is curable if it's caught in time, and so on. I compare the damage I suffered with the damage I feared and I'm almost satisfied with my fate. I've escaped the worst. This is what our loved ones try to tell us, with some restraint, in order to reassure us, and it is the story we tell them when they themselves are bedridden. The soothing word is the one that puts things back into proportion.

The media are another vector of consolation: through accounts of disasters, wars, floods, we verify with a sense of shame that others are more to be pitied than we are. Those who are depressed by bad news are unaware of this soothing function of the TV news: we need the dismay of others to verify that our fate is not so cruel after all. A petty but calming sentiment. Like those unhappy people who seek the ear of other unfortunates to feel less alone. Your happiness would offend them. This parallel can take bad taste to an extreme: witness the Indian film *Bawaal* by Nitesh Tiwari (2023), in which a young couple with relationship issues travels to Europe to find traces of the Second World War. They make up in Auschwitz by imagining themselves being gassed in the showers: 'Every relationship has its Auschwitz moment', says the actress in her moment of revelation.[23]

Our absolute pain is someone else's anecdote. Comparison is a psychological safeguard. When we curse our country, our political system, it helps to look at real dictatorships to understand the privileges we enjoy. Are we aware of how lucky we are? But the relief doesn't last, and as soon as this mental ping-pong is over, we go back to our litany of complaints. If joy is communicative and expands us to the dimensions of the universe, suffering locks us into our small tormented enclosures, impervious to empathy and pity.

CHAPTER 2

All kinds of awful

It is pleasant to believe one's self unhappy when one is only idle and tired.

Alfred de Musset, Confession of a Child of the Century

A century ago, in a republican and secular France emerging from the horrible Great War, pain and endurance were the norm for everyone. They represented the minimum discipline to which individuals, men and women alike, had to submit in order to succeed. To get by, one had to have strong character, especially among the working classes. Today, living conditions have become gentler for everyone, making us less tolerant of hardship. Effort, perseverance and even ordinary annoyances have become unpleasant. Is it not symptomatic that fentanyl, a cheap synthetic drug manufactured by Mexican cartels and originally created to relieve cancer patients, has become the most deadly narcotic in the United States – 71,030 deaths in 2021 alone – because it also combats unhappiness and depression?[1] It's as if the desire to do away with all worries has led to a fatal euphoria. This is the novelty of our new twenty-first century: the indeterminate distribution of suffering and non-suffering. Every day there are new afflictions which we find it hard to put up with. This difference is particularly noticeable between generations, with older people being more tolerant of injuries that younger people find shocking; this was already the case for baby-boomers in relation to their parents who had lived through the Second World War or the Algerian War. It seems that with each generation there are sensitivities that transmit and distribute pain and pleasure differently.

Effort is not pain

At least since Karl Marx and his son-in-law Paul Lafargue, author of the 1883 text *The Right to Be Lazy*, the left has been divided by a debate between those advocating work as emancipation and those denouncing work as alienating. For some, it is a 'right-wing' value, while for others, since the Enlightenment, it has contributed to freeing people from ignorance: work as transforming oneself by transforming the world. Many people object to this optimistic view, seeing skin colour or social origin as insurmountable obstacles to obtaining a good job. Even though it has been refuted by numerous studies,[2] this very Bourdieusian conception of the world is seen, as with the conservative right, as unrelenting. Pierre Bourdieu was not a professor of resistance but of fatality, and he said of himself that he was the best refutation of his own system. It's strange that a certain very vocal left has become, by a reversal of its premises, the fatalist camp. It denounces numerous injustices only the better to submit to them. Since we can't change everything at once, it's better not to change anything at all. The party of progress has turned into the party of renunciation, with incendiary rhetoric to boot.

This desire to eliminate difficulty at all costs runs the risk of aggravating it, obsessing over an evil that only starts spreading as soon as one begins to track it. A traditional category such as physical activity is rejected, except in its playful form of sport or fitness. Hard work in the building trade, roads, catering or the hotel industry, but also baby-sitting, security, home deliveries and housework are left to immigrants in our cultures. What is an immigrant? Immigrants are those who do the dirty work we no longer want to do.[3] When the younger generations in France and elsewhere ask for meaningful work, they forget, in this noble quest, to consider those humble tasks that keep things ticking over: our streets clean, our restaurants running and our children looked after. Difficult jobs are reserved for foreigners who don't calculate the pain they cause them. Spoilt children need slaves since the parents are reluctant to get their hands dirty while proclaiming their solidarity with the 'exploited', especially when this professional choice goes hand in hand with not having children at all, which would be giving up a lot of comfort. Cicero was already warning us not to confuse effort and pain, one consisting in the accomplishment of difficult work, the other in a brutal sensual shock.[4]

Allergies to constraints

What is the reason for our aversion to obligations, starting with work ones? The citizen of modern democracies is both a princeling who has benefited from a rather liberal education and a customer-king whose wishes are sacred in the commercial sphere. Our parents lived under a regime of expectation and deferred enjoyment. Since 1968, all we have known is multiple, instant gratifications, accelerated by the digital revolution. Democratic individuals no longer tolerate frustration or patience; these are an affront. Until adulthood, they remain 'Their Majesty the Baby', to whom we owe everything, right away, as Sigmund Freud put it. The right to have rights is inverted into the right to have all rights, and these are confused with 'whatever I want': any limitation or refusal makes me a victim and legitimizes my fury.[5] The ideal citizen, who is both 'legislator and subject', to use Kant's phrase, takes the divorce of rights and duties for granted. The latter, reduced to the bare minimum, are experienced as yet more mistreatment. The democratic formula, so beautiful and so vague, *Liberté, égalité, fraternité*, authorizes all hopes and fuels all frustrations.[6] We are restive old adolescents who get irritated by the slightest constraint and confuse restrictions with intolerable leg-irons. Hence the preference of our contemporaries, at least in France but the tendency can also be seen in the United States, for the maximum reduction in the working week, if possible with equal pay; and the spontaneous aversion to any policy that limits, for example, the speed of cars on the roads, or the introduction of low-emission zones in cities, penalizing older cars. The memory of the *Gilets jaunes* uprising in 2019 is too fresh for anyone to dare touch the means of transport that remains essential to a majority. In a democracy, putting a ban on something without a lengthy educational process beforehand is still akin to political suicide. People have forgotten how the compulsory use of seatbelts caused a furious controversy at the time.

Even studying is sometimes equated with oppression. After the 1970s, in an attempt to spare our little ones any vexation, schools often stopped teaching. Marks were tantamount to intolerable violence, and they were replaced by letters that were just as penalizing. Students should be helped to realize themselves, not be inflicted with useless knowledge. And when we teach them the classics, we have to spare them the language difficulties, the prohibitive anachronisms, the bombastic formulas, not forgetting the retrograde representation of women or minorities, so as not to wound their fragile souls. As a result, standards are falling, illiteracy is on the rise, and private schools that still focus on excellence and competition are flourishing. This suspicion of hard work stems primarily from a prevailing hedonism, which detests diligence. Those who struggle are seen as plodding and resistant to talent: the myth of the brilliant dunce has long been a ready-made excuse for bad pupils. They fail their exams but they'll end up with top honours. Finally, the culture of the easy way out is triumphing, encouraged by these new jobs on the Net – bloggers, youtubers, instagrammers, influencers – which require nothing more than an attractive physique, a sense of glibness and an ability to show up. This easy money devalues hard work and cutting-edge research that only gets a backlash as a reward. And yet, perseverance and concentration are the only way to progress. As Rousseau knew, we are imperfect beings, and therefore perfectible, always striving for self-improvement. In this respect, there is no form of education that does not involve pain, and the broadening of the mind through the experience of strangeness. Any teaching of a new subject – mathematics, physics, music, a foreign language – is still violence inflicted on a child who is being torn from the soft cocoon of ignorance. And if extending oneself reveals an intoxicating pleasure, it is at the price of incorporating whole swathes of an unknown universe.

To the puerile dream of an existence where the highest goals would be achieved effortlessly, we have to reply that when one takes away the spice of resistance, the pleasure is killed because it was all too easy. To complete one's satisfaction in life, one has to work for years, put a lot of time into one's projects, and avoid taking the easy way out. Let's not call what is incomplete suffering, let's call it a godsend, a happy surprise, a chance for everyone to work towards bettering themselves. We need trials that replenish our strength while at the same time upsetting us. The obstacle that discourages some galvanizes others. Ageing is an unfortunate inevitability, not a misfortune that merits compensation or even a lawsuit against the state (a Dutchman filed a lawsuit against his government in 2018 on the grounds that the age noted on his civil status penalized him professionally and in his love life). There has always been a code for pain in the various societies, but the code keeps changing with the times. The clarity of unhappiness, if it ever existed, has disappeared, and the boundary between the normal and the pathological continues to fluctuate. So we run the risk of losing our sense of proportion, of confusing one-off setbacks with unsurpassable calamities.

Self-pity

Instead of competing on the basis of excellence and talent, men and women in our societies all too often outdo each other in flaunting their disadvantages, making a point of saying that they are the object of appalling torment. In the United States, for example, there is a popular genre for entering university called the 'trauma essay'. Each student has to write an essay original enough to hold the attention of overworked assessors as they recount the ordeals they have overcome in the course of their studies, especially if they belong to a minority. On the face of it, it's a coming-of-age exercise that showcases skills and talents and turns everyone's life into a novel in which they are the hero, building a positive narcissism of ease and self-confidence. Many candidates, however, confess to racking their brains to dig up some devastating shock or event to highlight. They also don't like being reduced to their 'race', which would expose what is most impersonal about them, their ethnic characteristics or their skin colour, rather than highlighting their unparalleled uniqueness.[7] So, to be taken seriously, they have to amplify what is annoying them. A bit like in Catholic confession, where you invent sins to keep the priest happy. The consequence is that, instead of encouraging the candidates, they become beings marked by their tribulations rather than freely striving towards a goal. The good ego becomes a suffering ego, never a conquering ego. How can we draw new strength from ourselves if we are constantly forced to cultivate our vulnerabilities? The past rivets us to our determinisms; it is not a springboard or a stepping stone towards a future to be built. Pain has become an obligatory stage with people jousting with each other, exposing their sorrows.

Suffering sells more than sex. Just look at the 'misery memoirs',[8] these cry-baby autofictions where people compete with each other in tearful confessions about their own plight in order to attract attention. The authors, both men and women, describe the beatings, sexual abuse, poverty and the violent, alcoholic parents they had to endure. The genre is far from new, having emerged in Europe in the eighteenth century, in sentimental literature in England and France, which was already being mocked by the Marquis de Sade. The novel of child abuse had a huge following and influenced the courts. 'The art is to portray yourself as a victim while selling yourself as a survivor', as John Crace said. A terminal cancer will only have a chance of moving people if you die, but then you won't be able to enjoy your successes.[9] This tendency sucks the life out of literature. Reduced to confessions that are all the same, it is no longer creation, it is mere nosography, the nomination of sorrowful moods. Each person in their corner intones their own little lament. If suffering were enough to be talented, we would have noticed!

There is nothing, quite rightly, that our societies admire more than a man or woman who has been through great tragedies, flirted with death and risen to their feet again. Like the writer Sylvain Tesson, left for dead after falling from the roof of a chalet in Chamonix in 2014. The fall that disfigured him also transformed him. The American concept of 'resilience', now disputed, was first applied to physical materials, then it was reworked and extended in France by Boris Cyrulnik. It made such miraculous people exemplary: it is the only point at which victimism meets heroism, as we shall see. Victimology is a soteriology, a science of salvation; it is our worldly redemption that we also seek through the status of survivor, of death-cheater.

ILLNESSES TO A GOOD END?

In his 'Prayer Asking God to Use Illnesses to a Good End', published in 1664, Blaise Pascal rejoiced in the destruction of his own body if it saved his soul. He had abused his health and God had justly punished him for it.

We read it with dismay, especially when he confesses to a kind of secret joy at having been chosen by the Creator. Pain is an advance on Purgatory, the joy of being broken for the greater glory of the Most High. Our contemporary relationship with illness is no less ambiguous. When Nietzsche writes, not without provocation, that 'sickness is instructive ... *those who make sick* seem even more necessary to us today than any medicine men or "saviors"',[10] he is not far from Blaise Pascal, even though he also criticizes the war waged by the sick and the vindictive against the healthy and the robust.[11] Since the Romantics, morbidity has been a sign of distinction: Hans Castorp, the hero of Thomas Mann's *The Magic Mountain*, is 'consecrated' by the tuberculosis he contracted at the sanatorium. He goes from naive health to a reflective health that is aware of the fragility of the body and of peace, since in the meantime the First World War has broken out. For Dostoyevsky, his epilepsy was a mystical affliction to be treated with respect. Throughout his life, Proust cherished, as much as he hated, his all-consuming asthma attacks that also guided his writing. 'There are maladies we must not seek to cure, because they alone protect us from others that are more serious.'[12]

When the body becomes our enemy, it turns us into panting, miserable beings struggling to survive. Illness reveals a being that we never knew we had, especially when it occurs in childhood; it is then the stranger within that emerges from deep in our organs and expels us from ourselves. We 'catch' an illness that the body has secreted of its own accord, and we make this pathology our thing, our possession. It is a master imposing his own schedule on us, giving us a reason for being, since, as Canguilhem wrote, 'life ... admits of repairs which are really physiological innovations'.[13] Today's patients no longer remain in a fearful *tête-à-tête* with an all-powerful mandarin; they share their experiences to help each other, to act collectively. The 'good' disease is the one that torments you without destroying you; that you tame over the years and that haunts you at regular intervals. It is an unwelcome but faithful companion, who may well finish you off, but it will have given you a long reprieve. We sign temporary armistices with it and emerge from each crisis rejuvenated, happy for the respite.

There are people whose only identity is to be ill. In hospices and waiting rooms, these little bundles of misfortune recite their litanies to anyone who will listen. When existence is reduced to a list of troubles, it really is the antechamber of finality. And we wonder: when my turn comes, will I be that parrot, carrying on, or will I have the discretion to silently keep my ordeals to myself? Even as it makes progress, medicine remains, for serious pathologies, the site of verdicts and torments. Tragedy can be postponed but not abolished. The 'good end' for illnesses is to relegate them to the later stages of life. Otherwise, we have to endure the monotonous parade of their attacks, like a diabolical genius reducing us to a field of ruins, until the void itself arrives.

CHAPTER 3

Suffering produces laws

I suffer, it must be somebody's fault.

Friedrich Nietzsche

How did we pass from the heroic figure of Rosa Parks fighting discrimination in America to that of Greta Thunberg weeping over the fate of the planet? That's the story of the past half-century. In 1982, the French Minister of Justice, Robert Badinter, introduced a law in favour of victims, the 'masses the courts have forgotten', and in 1986, the French State created a guarantee fund for the targets of acts of terrorism.[1] This new concern coincided with a major event: in the mid-1980s the immense shadow of the Shoah propelled the deportee into the paradigm of martyrdom. Erected as a universal totem, the deportee became the prototype and the obstacle, as much coveted as hated. Add to this the collapse of Communism, making people less likely to be convinced that the future could be forged by political will alone. In the absence of collective salvation, we are thus destined to individual salvation under the dual guidance of the law and grievances.

In the meantime, suffering acquires a new sacred allure. Once a common feature of the human condition, it is now a passport that people flaunt to intimidate their contemporaries. It transforms one into an exceptional being who can show off on the public stage at little cost. Grief no longer wants to hide in the secrecy of the heart; it wants to expose itself. It is declarative and performative; all one has to do is say one is afflicted to be believed by others and consecrated as such.

The market for afflictions

For the last fifty years, what has made us free in Europe has been the combination of material prosperity, social redistribution, peace and scientific progress. It was in the shelter of these four walls that we were able to live with complete peace of mind. Should these supports falter, should climate hazards cast a shadow over the future, should war and terrorism threaten us, should precarious living conditions return to our cities, then we are affected to our very core. If the middle classes are becoming Robert Reich's 'anxious classes', if so many people are feeling helpless, it's because the traditional trade-offs and shock absorbers have lost their power, leaving everyone to face ever greater problems. From one end of the continuum to the other, the spectre of decline is threatening.

But we have kept the habits and thought patterns of prosperity. Our anxiety stems from the success that has numbed us. We have barely emerged from the delightful cocoon of the 'Trente Glorieuses' (1945–75) and we are approaching turbulent times with a mindset inherited from an era of opulence. We are experiencing the tragedy of satiated cultures, unfit to face adversity. Add to this a major change: everyday life has become litigious, at the same time as there is a market for afflictions. Over the last half-century, the law has become, alongside politics, a means of regulating conflicts. The weakening of political parties and trade unions, the exhaustion of the intermediary bodies that in France were the Catholic Church and the Communist Party, and the growing indistinguishability of right and left, have all accelerated this development.

It was a fundamental revolution in the law which, at the beginning of the nineteenth century, replaced Christian *redemption* with *reparation*. In 1804, article 1382 of the Civil Code no longer considered suffering as an accident but as a scandal that the law had a duty to remedy.[2] 'Any act whatsoever by man which causes damage to another person obliges the person through whose fault it occurred to make reparation for it.' These few lines would have a ripple effect. A movement unfolded that initially focused on industrial disasters: railway collisions, mine collapses and boiler explosions left witnesses stunned. The tools created by humans enslaved them to their violence and turned it against them.[3] The complaint must therefore include a new factor: chance. Until this point, individuals were accountable for their mistakes and could only blame themselves. But the multiplication of risks and accidents in the workplace would put personal failings into perspective and lead to the emergence of insurance and changes in legislation. All damage would have to be paid for.

From then on, it was up to judges to define the norm and the unacceptable. Through their procedures, the concept of prejudice was developed. As a result of technological and therapeutic hazards, which generate serious accidents, and natural disasters occurring on an unknown scale, we are moving from a system of liability based on fault to a system of compensation based on risk, where the overriding concern is to compensate victims and recalibrate any imbalances (this is no-fault liability).

The principle of solidarity means finding solvent legal entities, however remote their involvement in the dispute. Civil law was already familiar with the notion of 'liability without fault' (in François Ewald's phrase, *responsable sans responsabilité*). All that is required is to be insured, i.e. covered in the event of an accident or water damage, with a bonus/malus system. And the State is the ultimate guarantor in the event of a national disaster. Today, in the name of consumer protection, judges keep on having to trace the chain of people involved until they find one or more capable of paying: it's a hunt for 'deep pockets', those with enough cash to compensate the victims. And since every life inevitably encounters accidents, illness and injustice, it is the legislator and the courts that are entrusted with the task of mitigating the fragility of human affairs.

The notion of lost opportunity [*chance perdue*],[4] in the event, for example, of a botched surgery, has established the right to a cure as a fundamental demand of patients. Practitioners now protect themselves against possible runaway litigations by having patients sign waivers before surgery. Therapeutic risk masks an obligation to get results for patients, which are demanded, or at least implied: we are owed a good outcome and, if possible, a return to the prior status quo. In France, we could look at the law of 5 July 1985 (article 29) on road accidents, which rightly attributes the blame to the motorist, regardless of the carelessness of the pedestrian, described as a 'weak vehicle', out of all proportion to the size of a car. Only 'inexcusable fault' on the part of the pedestrian, voluntarily throwing themselves under the wheels of a vehicle, for example, would exonerate a driver. The issue has become more complicated in recent years with the proliferation of bicycles, scooters and two-wheelers in towns and cities. They are themselves the victims of numerous accidents, but they nonetheless cause serious injuries to pedestrians because many believe they are exempt from the highway code. Not to stop at a red light is an absolute taboo in town, otherwise no pedestrian could cross a street without fear for his or her life. Many cyclists and motorcyclists ignore this obligation. What can the law say in these circumstances? A bicycle is fragile in relation to a bus, but dangerous for those on foot. The result is a cacophony of precedence, all the more so as cyclists and scooters, in Paris at least, flout the ordinary rules, cross at red lights, go down one-way streets in the wrong direction, climb pavements, refuse to slow down, and risk their lives as much as those of the pedestrians taken by surprise. This is the result of the privileged status accorded to cyclists because of their compliance with the imperatives of climate change. Heroes of the transition, they discourteously crash into the human herd or each other, caught up in the same vertigo of speed as hit-and-run drivers. If the public authorities do not legislate on 'soft mobility', walking in towns and cities will remain a dangerous sport, for children as well as the disabled and elderly.

A compassionate Republic?

When it comes to politicians, any heads of state who fail to visit the scene of a disaster discredit themselves. People will remember George W. Bush flying over the scene of Hurricane Katrina in Louisiana in 2005 without setting foot there. Kanye West accused him of indifference towards African-Americans and the press was vocal about his lack of empathy. Not only do we need to leap to the assistance of those injured in fires, earthquakes and floods, but compassion has become an essential part of political life. Danish-style empathy classes are being promoted in classrooms; minutes of silence are being held after every tragedy; and crime is being fought with teddy bears, tears and flowers. We have entered the Republic of the news story under the dual sign of indignation and emotion: for the media, news boils down to listing the dead and the murdered. The right stresses the lack of security in our towns and countryside, the left the public apathy in the face of the number of migrants lost at sea over the last ten years or so.[5] Some denounce it as a political fact, others as a diversion. In our societies, watching the news is a painful experience, making us nostalgic for some vague earlier times we thought were over. In the first place, it means that the government no longer has control over sensitive areas or neighbourhoods. Its protective ambitions have been dealt a stinging blow. Gang rapes, fatal assaults, femicide, attacks, settling of scores – these are the revelations of a state of savagery that is no longer contained by the thin veneer of civilization, and they are leading the media, religious, psychiatric and police institutions to go through a painful examination of their consciences.

In all cases, commiseration is an integral part of citizenship and life in society. Governments, whether democratic or not, provide emotional and moral support; the role of the first lady and the president is one of consolation. As Hannah Arendt said of Greek tragedy, Man can always protect himself against the evil blows of fate with grand words. But great words and noble phrases must be matched by great deeds. These days, there is no room for error or improvisation on the part of the executive, where forecasting is extremely fragile and can fail in two ways: by underestimating the threats or overestimating them (as was the case in 2009 with the H1N1 flu virus). The fact remains that in times of drought, heatwave or flood, you have to be prepared for the worst in order to avoid it. Anticipate to adapt better. The aim of emergency management policies in the event of cyclones, massive forest fires, floods or earthquakes is to offer a range of rapid responses so that we are not caught unprepared. There is no such thing as a history of averted disasters, said Raymond Aron. But there is an art to making disasters avoidable: to prepare for something that cannot be predicted and is a matter of uncertainty – that is the greatness and fragility of politics. It is better for governments to err on the side of excessive mistrust than to be blinded by credulity. The aim is not just to reduce the surface area exposed to random events, but to offer a science of disasters; scientific responses to disproportionate cataclysms. But when recurring disasters such as the Pas-de-Calais floods bring the economy to its knees, when the insurance companies themselves desert certain regions subject to too many climatic hazards – coastal Florida, for example – what are the inhabitants left with but to put up with hurricanes and cyclones at the risk of having to rebuild their homes every three years, or move house? The great challenge is to collectively increase our tenacity rather than helplessly suffer the blows of fate.

THE DEMOCRATIZATION OF MARTYRDOM

In the past, poets, artists and painters were sometimes thunderstruck by a divine or beauteous inspiration, like Paul Claudel, who was converted to God on 25 December 1886 in Notre-Dame Cathedral in Paris at the age of eighteen: 'In an instant my heart was touched, and I believed.'[6] In the same way, today's citizens can wake up one morning and exclaim, as if struck with a revelation: I too am a victim. Who are my executioners? Capitalism, my family, the bourgeoisie, patriarchy, the system? The scapegoats are legion, and they can change and accumulate. Some volunteer to act as lightning rods for the anxieties of their contemporaries. Because life's promises are deceptive, I am never rewarded or gratified enough: 'We all demand', says Freud, 'reparation for early wounds to our narcissism, our self-love. Why did not Nature give us ... the lofty brow of genius or the noble profile of aristocracy? Why were we born in a middle-class home instead of in a royal palace?'[7] I was destined for a brilliant future, promised the highest office. My career is stagnating, my loves are lying fallow. I don't get the recognition I deserve. I owe my successes only to myself, my failures only to others.

Me too! With a certain kind of feminism, the ego is only accepted if it forms part of the wider circle of a suffering collective, and its expression involves the whole female gender in the great suffering adventure. If a woman dared to say, 'Me neither', she would exclude herself from the magic circle. This is what happened to Élisabeth Badinter, a feminist and fighter from the start, who had always denounced victimization.[8] A reprobate status can promote a woman into the ranks of a certain elite, turning stigma into glory. As long as testimonials remain rare, they are precious. If they are mass-produced, they become insipid and routine. If there are too many humiliated, the humiliated are killed off. Even titled millionaires are getting in on the act. Prince Harry's recent memoir is a torrent of maudlin poshness that has produced a worldwide bestseller.[9] The little prince and his wife Meghan were playing Cosette from *Les Misérables*! Their fortune and jet-setting lifestyle were pretty hard going.

Israeli novelist Zeruya Shalev recounts how, as a former social worker in the Israeli army, she suffered from 'lachrymosis', an identification malady. She could not hear soldiers' confessions without crying.[10] If the novel were one day to be reduced to the triumph of self-pity and philosophy to personal development, both would disappear. Revealing our little worries, rewriting the daddy/mummy scenario over and over again, broadcasting 'feel-good' messages would take the place of literature and reflection. Writing would become therapy, and writers and thinkers would become life coaches.

CHAPTER 4

The one-upmanship of martyrdom

<blockquote>
It seems that people are envious of the misfortunes that befall us.

Christine Villemin
</blockquote>

Christianity proposed *redemption* through suffering; modern law opposed it with *reparation*. Now it is *resurrection* that is promised to those who can qualify for contemporary martyrology. The Romantics had invented the melancholy snob to counter bourgeois satisfaction. 'The most beautiful songs are the most desperate ones', said the poet Musset. Since the bourgeois is the contented being *par excellence*, then being demonstrably out of sorts would count as an act of rebellion from the fringes of a society one finds insufferable. Only a beautiful heartbreak could inspire major works. Woe betide anyone who did not suffer from love or illness, for they would never produce anything great. Today, we are far removed from this dandyism of strutting one's suffering. If we open our wounds in public, it is to reap symbolic as well as material benefits.

The new 'offensology'

In the classical morality of the seventeenth century, we had to triumph over our passions. Nowadays, it's recommended that we empathize with ourselves, that we 'listen to ourselves'. Today, we are all *oversensitive*, lashing out at the slightest shock, the slightest remark. Likewise with the concept of micro-aggressions, accompanying any kind of blackmail, or remarks experienced as derogatory that torture us like a dripping tap. Asking someone, for example, how to pronounce their name or where they come from – experiences we all have on a daily basis – would be such an affront. 'Once is no big deal, but a million times is unbearable!' exclaimed ex-National Education Minister Pap Ndiaye.[1] The former Secretary of State for Foreign Affairs and Human Rights under Nicolas Sarkozy from 2007 to 2009, Rama Yade, suddenly discovered in 2021 that walking past the statue of Colbert, the author of the 'Code Noir' which governed relations between masters and slaves under the Ancien Régime, constituted a 'micro-aggression'. On New York University student cards, under the heading micro-aggressions, there is a telephone number that can be used to call anonymously and trigger an investigation into a particular professor.[2]

In 2015, President Obama, alarmed by the overcautious mentality of some young people, reminded us that universities are not day-care centres where students are pampered. A new meteorological concept, 'feels like ...', has entered the official discourse, all the more irrefutable because it is subjective and enshrines the pre-eminence of the affective.[3] The 'experts in offensology', in the words of Philippe Zard,[4] are demanding that the classics be rewritten so as not to offend our cherubs or infiltrate our malleable minds with sexist or racist ideas. Bad books, bad films, bad paintings need to be purged or sterilized to suit the tastes of the majority.

The war of consciences, so dear to Hegel ('each conscience seeks the death of the Other'), has been succeeded by the war of miseries that clash on the public or private stage. If everything that suffers opens up the right to rights, then how can we prevent misfortune from becoming the measure of all things, *a new conformity to despair*? Once they are recognized as such, categories of victimhood unfold, each with its own banner, its own stories, its own demand to protest if they feel mocked or misrepresented. In some Anglo-Saxon universities, for example, it is recommended that people stop applauding, which is a source of anxiety, and instead wave their hands. This would lessen discrimination towards the deaf and autistic. In the 1990s, 'Dieters United', associations for the protection of the obese, organized protest pickets outside cinemas in San Francisco showing Walt Disney's *Fantasia*. The reason being that the dance of the hippopotamuses in tutus ridiculed corpulent people. At the end of the last century, the French butchers' union protested against Slobodan Milošević's being called the 'butcher of the Balkans', seeing it as a touch of opprobrium against their profession. The categorical imperative of any publication, proclamation or public demonstration is to offend no one.

Take the headache of toilet signage. It wants to eliminate prejudice and fears that it has overlooked a group or sub-group that feels discriminated against. Micturition has become a political issue; men are being told, as they were in the 1970s, to pee sitting down.[5] The differences between the sexes need to be erased, and the signage needs to be cleaned up, while remaining legible for everyone. Skirts or trousers, vulva or penis, blue or pink. Not to mention enlarging the toilet area in the name of 'urinary parity'. The fear of spreading prejudice and endorsing a 'patriarchal' society overshadows the user's main concern: hygiene and, above all, cleanliness. But never mind this bourgeois problem, we have to satisfy every minority, however tiny, because of the fear of forgetting someone. And what about non-white people, frizzy hair, veiled women and people who are overweight?[6] The challenge is immense, vertiginous. In our thin-skinned society, any group or community can rise up and defend its image against any pejorative allusion.

Every case, no matter how far-fetched, becomes arguable, and the legal universe degenerates into a vast litigation fair, where lawyers, often with the backing of some class action, hustle online or in the courts to swell their client portfolios, stoking their anger and frustration. A premonition of harm becomes harm itself. In October 2006, passengers on a Djerba–Paris flight who had to turn back because of a technical problem that caused their oxygen masks to fall down set up a class action to compensate them for their 'anxiety damage'.[7] In 2019, a little American girl suffered second-degree burns to her leg in a car in Florida when she knocked over a box of nuggets that were 'unreasonably and dangerously hot'. Four years later, McDonald's was ordered to pay her $800,000. The family was seeking $15 million in damages.[8] This case is reminiscent of another. In 1994, juries had already ordered McDonald's to pay $2.86 million dollars (2 million euros) in damages to a resident of Albuquerque, in the state of New Mexico, who had scalded herself with a cup of coffee. In the end, the two parties reached an out-of-court settlement, as permitted by law.

Taking it to the limit

Misfortune has ceased to be obscene; it takes centre stage and as soon as it appears, it closes mouths and commands respect. For those who can claim it, the rules of ordinary ethics no longer apply; it is haloed in virtue. That's why the stock market price of the underprivileged fluctuates with the times and current events. Winning the entitlement and, above all, keeping it, is quite a challenge. Whatever we do, it will always be to the detriment of other oppressed people who do not benefit from the public spotlight. Tell me who your favourite victims are and I'll tell you who you are: for the Vatican, it's migrants, much more than Eastern Christians; for ecologists, it's the planet. Michel Serres once said that 'the Earth is moved', and activists in the same guise say that the Earth is rising up. For yet others, it is animals, (who were the 'that other of all others' for Lévi-Strauss), hunted by hounds, tortured in slaughterhouses, put to death in bullfights. On 21 January 2021, Karima Delli, an ecologist MEP, and Julien Bayou laid a wreath for the 'unknown stag' at Chantilly station, after a deer had been chased onto the tracks by a pack of hunting hounds. For others, the pariahs of the day are the Ukrainians confronting Russian imperialism, or the Kurds or the Yezidis. The Palestinians have made a remarkable comeback since the war in Gaza in autumn 2023. But this comeback is likely to be short-lived if their cause remains associated with terrorism. We can join the great tribe of the stigmatized by contagion, by contiguity, by solidarity with the oppressed who have been duly labelled: for example, the Poler Bears association, pole-dancers at Brown University, have co-signed a manifesto for Palestine, as have LGBT people and feminists, as inter-sectionality obliges one to.[9] If the genuinely crucified are flocking with the fakes, it's because of the innumerable candidates jockeying for status.

In Europe, as in the United States, we have a political class that, at the slightest suspicion of corruption or incompetence, cries 'innocence denied' (which is not always untrue, since some 'witch-hunting' magistrates are suspected of politicizing their enquiries). In the United States, former President Donald Trump, threatened with indictment by the judiciary, called the New York prosecutor a 'Gestapo agent', while his supporters likened Trump to the Messiah. Silvio Berlusconi, who has been prosecuted for various crimes, also had no hesitation in likening himself to Christ at an election rally in Ancona in February 2006: 'I am the Jesus Christ of politics, a patient victim who endures everything, who sacrifices himself for everyone.'

In France we have trade unions, workers' organizations, farmers' organizations, environmentalists, violent NGOs or factions of agitators who take the liberty of leading popular insurrections, burning down public buildings. But they refuse to be judged. In 2018 we saw the *Gilets jaunes*, or Yellow Vests, in the name of the holy anger of the 'People', destroy monuments, ransack the Arc de Triomphe, threaten the President of the Republic with death, savagely beat up the forces of law and order (who also blinded and injured a number of them) without being bothered unduly, or having to reimburse for the damage caused. The right to demonstrate and express one's righteous rage is sacred, especially when the nobility of the cause (the planet in danger, a martyred people) exonerates the brutality of the means used.

In France, where violence is a thousand-year-old tradition, rioting still has a positive connotation, in memory of the Great Revolution, the days of 1830, 1848 and the Paris Commune (1870). Global warming, the crisis in the rural and working-class world, the difficulties faced by truck drivers and farmers, and the 'disadvantaged' suburbs, all justify the depredations committed. The mob, 'that collective soul independent of the individuals who make it up' for Sigmund Freud, is always innocent and bankrupt, the enraged plebs are an indomitable deity, and woe betide anyone who dares to call them to account, especially in a court of law. Insurgent categories are beyond the reach of common law.

Reversing the first sentence of Tolstoy's *Anna Karenina*, we could say: 'All misfortunes are alike in their own way, only happiness is unique.' When it comes to misery, extremists on both the left and the right, in Europe and the United States, follow a similar pattern. They all take up the defensive discourse of the slave, the colonized who fights for their survival: thus the clumsy concept of 'francocide' put forward by Éric Zemmour in connection with the brutal murder of a twelve-year-old girl by a young Algerian woman. An atrocious news item has to be transformed into a symptom of a civilizational war. The tendency is to take reasoning to extremes in order to appease the public. As far back as 1993 in Dijon, Jean-Marie Le Pen, while a war was going on in Bosnia, thought the French were suffering from ethnic cleansing, and two years earlier he had used the word 'cultural genocide' when the left was governing because it was 'imposing a socialist or conformist art worthy of Doctor Goebbels'.[10] You have to capture the voter's attention, and the bigger the message, the more seductive (or repellent) it is. Today, as in the past, it is the Nazi referent that is relentlessly used, and the vocabulary of the Second World War is recycled *ad nauseam* on every subject. The same thing is happening on the left with so-called 'anti-fa' groups, who are fascists in reverse, content to lash out at anything they don't like, including Christmas nativity scenes.[11] It's hard to tell the possible from the probable, the virtual from the real. Didn't Mathilde Panot, a member of the *La France Insoumise* party, suggest that Emmanuel Macron was a Petainist?[12] Then, in March 2023, she compared him to Caligula!

The process is an old one, and one that is repeated with admirable constancy: victim imposture flourishes everywhere. Remember Céline, a relentless anti-Semite and active collaborator who, in 1957, lamented his condition, labelled himself an outcast, and regarded the ordeals of the Jews as trifles compared with what he endured, thanks to which he could continue to despise them in all good conscience. If he didn't win the Nobel Prize, it's because he's a real Frenchman, not one of those wops who have invaded everything: 'Maybe if my name had been Vlazine … Vlazine Progrogrof. … If I'd been born in Tamopol on the Don … but in Courbevoie, Seine. … Born in Tamopol on the Don they'd have given me the Nobel Prize years ago … but coming from right here, not even a Sephardim!'[13]

These days it was a real Nobel Prize winner, Annie Ernaux, who took advantage of her distinction to set herself up as an exemplary victim. Recalling that she writes to 'avenge her race and sex'[14] – in other words, her working-class origins – and to 'make amends for the social injustice of her birth' and her status as a woman, she pointed out that nothing can erase the bullying she suffered since childhood. Conceding that her prize was a collective victory for all those who suffer, she saw herself as a 'class defector', an 'immigrant from the inside' who had broken with the fine writing of the dominant classes. What's surprising in her case is that success, far from extinguishing her anger, rekindled it. Rage is her compass: honours plus tears, fortune plus resentment. Absolute privilege, the Nobel Prize, staggering sales in the millions, cast her into servitude. One has to admire this astonishing art of transforming privilege into a curse! A victim who succeeds remains a victim who bears the stigma of her condition to the end. Despite her undeniable talent – she has written some excellent books – she has given in to that disease of our age called bitterness. It's hard not to think of Marcus Aurelius' beautiful phrase: 'The best way to take revenge on an enemy is not to be like him.'

In *Le Monde*, a handful of academics, including François Héran and Éric Fassin, claim to be victims of threats from the ultra-right and fear that they are the new Samuel Paty of the French education system.[15] We would laugh at this false equivalence if it weren't obscene and if one of the signatories, François Héran, hadn't taken it upon himself in the media to sully the memory of Samuel Paty.[16] In a curious twist, the fortunate and the powerful also want to belong to the aristocracy of the margins, to form new disenfranchised castes. To be really distinguished these days you have to pose as a dissident; to be a real master you call for the masters to be trampled underfoot. Why do we desperately want to look like we're exploited when we've got everything? To top off the ease of opulence with the sulphurous prestige of the damned, to bring down upon oneself the splendid light of torment, to give the monotony of one's life the beauty of an epic.

Nazi, my sweet Nazi

What kind of complaint is acceptable? A story about an obvious offence that stays within the bounds of credibility. Everyone must feel the outrage of the crime. Hence the temptation, in order to win hearts, to exaggerate the harm suffered. Generally speaking, for a cause to gain public support, you have to present a miserable view of yourself, which is the only way to win sympathy. When Covid happened, the high-minded wanted to take the politicians to court for their lack of prevention and responsiveness. All you had to do was file a complaint online using a downloadable form to generate a mass effect of several thousand complainants and trigger legal action. In 2021, a delegation of far-left activists travelled to The Hague to sue Emmanuel Macron for 'crimes against humanity' and 'human rights violations' as a result of the measures taken during the lockdown. In France, when the epidemic broke out, former Health Minister Olivier Véran and former Prime Minister Jean Castex were targeted for failure to assist a person in danger, manslaughter and unintentional injury. The former Health Minister, Agnès Buzyn, was brought before the Court of Justice of the Republic in 2021 for 'endangering the lives of others'. According to their detractors, all these officials should have put in place the appropriate measures from day one and planned the response, as if they had all the information they needed to combat this unknown virus. Despite many management errors, ministers cannot be blamed for ignoring scientific evidence that became clear one or two years later. But the cohort of outraged people were determined to lash out at a few key figures, when they were not accusing them of having knowingly triggered the epidemic in order to enrich Big Pharma, sell vaccines and thereby better control the population through a system of injected microchips.

How can we forget the outrageous things said in mainland France and the Antilles by opponents of vaccination during the Covid crisis, in an alliance that stretches from Florian Philippot to Marine Le Pen, Nicolas Dupont-Aignan and Jean-Luc Mélenchon, like the famous red-brown pact? They spoke out successively in favour of hydroxy-chloroquine, then against the vaccine and finally against the health pass. On *La Chaîne Info*, Florian Philippot criticized 'this completely crazy society where we are enslaved, domesticated as a people. ... Our freedoms are being taken away. What are they going to take away from us tomorrow? Cash? Our own home?'[17] A number of associations called for a day of tribute for those who died as a result of Covid-19. In Poland, a slogan brandished by far-right demonstrators, 'Vaccines make you free', echoing the inscription on the pediment of the Auschwitz camp, 'Work makes you free', provoked an outcry.[18] On Mont-Valérien near Paris, the main site for paying tribute to the Resistance, an inscription reading 'AntipaSS' was spray-painted with the SS letters.

In Toulon, another poster showed Emmanuel Macron dressed as Adolf Hitler with the text 'Obey, get vaccinated'. Unfortunately, the cherry on the cake came from a revisionist philosopher, Giorgio Agamben, who sees Nazism everywhere but in Nazism: in the migrant detention camps and in the confinement imposed during Covid, 'this supposed epidemic', this 'sort of flu'[19] that justified the totalitarian state of exception. These are just some of the examples that allow many protesters to pass the Godwin point unhindered. If your opponent is a Nazi, that makes you a perfect deportee, a poor unfortunate taken to the next level. There is no a priori direct relationship between the various examples set out above, between the fury of a certain category of citizens or workers and the diatribes of this or that representative, except that from the top to the bottom of the social ladder, from the distinguished to the marginal, everyone fights to occupy 'the most desirable place, the place of the victim'.[20] So, in France as in Europe, such customs and predispositions are indeed what are pushing us down into the depths of universal complaint.

Indulgence credits!

Since the Enlightenment, modernity has enjoyed seeing the great adventure of the downtrodden coming onto the public stage – women, children, Jews, blacks, slaves, colonized peoples, homosexuals – so everyone is able to access all the privileges of ordinary citizenship. But if we assume that certain previously disadvantaged groups should benefit from a structural advantage, they will be tempted to create professional lobby groups of oppressed people whose status is automatically transmitted from parents to children, like a title of nobility. In the United States, for example, if one is to believe Critical Race Theory,[21] being born white (or Jewish or Asian) makes you a lifelong dominator, whatever your opinions, and being born non-white makes you a dominated person, whatever your income. Suffering is an evil, but it is also an income that can grow, with interest.

Because, historically, certain communities or peoples have been enslaved, imprisoned or exterminated, the individuals who make them up, even centuries later, enjoy an indulgence credit for eternity and are born with a portfolio of grievances to build on. To claim to be a victim is to acquire the dual power of incrimination and complaint. Each of us could go back up our family tree and find a slave, a serf or a hanged man to explain our present misery. The principle of democracy is that fault and injury end with the person who committed or suffered them: the son of a gangster is not a gangster, the son of a deportee is not a deportee, even if the memory of the trauma remains alive. No child is born guilty or victimized by the actions of his or her forebears. Humanity begins anew with each of us, and I do not carry within me the stigma of my ancestors. I have a family history, but I am not that history, it is in my power to take it elsewhere. How do you reconcile a concern for freedom with an awareness of heritage? The ethnic obsession with origins, among some on the left and the right, is revealing in this respect: each individual would be the sum of his or her ancestors, nothing more, nothing less. No one escapes their social or pigmentary determinisms. Take the white activists in the United States who knelt down to wash the feet of black activists after the death of George Floyd in the spring of 2020. They wanted to atone for the sins of their forebears even though they themselves had played no part in slavery or segregation. Political struggle has one radical aspect in that it takes the score back to zero: it creates free and equal men and women who are proud of the rights they have won and the achievements they have made.

It's worth noting that the motto of Joseph Pulitzer in his will in 1904 – founder of the prize of the same name, which was supposed to reward excellence in the fields of journalism, fiction and music – 'Comfort the *afflicted*, afflict the comfortable' has more to do with resentment than justice. Once the powerful have been demoralized and humiliated, how can the people left behind be any better off?

Privilege in reverse

Victimization is the sorrowful version of privilege, allowing us to rebuild our genealogy on the basis of real or imagined oppression. It suggests that the law applies to everyone but me, that I am entitled to subtract myself from all the networks of obligations and reciprocity that make up social life. Like the French *de* particle in a name, it is a distinction that is passed down from father to son, mother to daughter, the new blue blood that inducts you into one of the only two nobilities recognized by democracies, that of merit and that of injury. For example, you can become a 'descendant of a slave'[22] in the same way as one becomes a woman in Simone de Beauvoir's work, with a reconstructed ancestry that emphasizes the struggle of the 'maroons', those captives who rebelled against their masters. Victim entrepreneurs are first and foremost memory entrepreneurs who revive a painful past in order to take advantage of it and rally together. It is an aristocracy of the sorrowful that sketches out a reverse caste system where the fact of having suffered a prejudice replaces the advantages of birth. So many of our intellectuals and politicians take pride in their humble birth, their modest extraction.[23] You have to prove that you belong to the people simply by virtue of your birth, that you come from this mystical body of modern republics and are therefore entitled to express yourself, unlike the privileged who have taken the spotlight.

In our society – affluent but grumpy – the choice of victimization always signals a political failure when it does not mask a structural dissatisfaction on the part of the privileged. Look at the category of people who are 'never happy' even when they win, such as the singer Yseult, winner of a *Victoire de la Musique* at the age of twenty-six, who on the occasion of accepting her trophy on TV moaned 'that they don't want to let us overweight Black people rise to the top'. This is the height of the culture of complaint,[24] of the whining individual who is distressed by everything, even their successes. Preferential policies in favour of minorities 'send us the message that there is more power in our past sufferings than in our present achievements', as the African-American essayist Shelby Steele puts it.[25] This would make it pointless to seek fulfilment today, as the trauma of trafficking and segregation would weigh too heavily to be overcome. If the United States is thinking of reducing or eliminating positive discrimination, it is because this temporary correction of inequalities, which penalizes Asians above all, was only meant to be temporary before all citizens were placed under the same law. It was mainly African-American intellectuals, such as the linguist John McWhorter, the economist Glenn Loury and the writer Thomas Chatterton Williams, who protested against the pity shown to their black compatriots by the white liberal elites, seeing it as a form of reinforced contempt and discrimination.[26]

The damned of the earth could become a hereditary profession: dynasties of the dishonoured and outraged would cross the ages flanked by their prerogatives and their progeny. At the risk of seeing the victim's position degenerate into posturing or even imposture, the clever have become masters in the art of smuggling such conditions. Then the law as protection of the weakest would disappear behind that trickery as promotion of the most cunning, leaving the unfortunate with the sad privilege of answering for their actions and being judged accordingly.

COMPLAINT AND PRAYER

The ancients considered it beneath a man to lament, to cry out and moan, to be overcome by pain.[27] Our modern democracies, on the other hand, are characterized by the omnipresence of complaint, of which the ledgers of complaints [*cahiers de doléances*] of the French Revolution remain the template. The age-old cry about existential misfortune spans the centuries. Complaining means throwing your infirmities in the face of others as if they were responsible for them by the mere fact of hearing them; no one can escape it, and it's an excellent way of not changing your lifestyle. Our grumbling, moaning and railing at the world proliferate like weeds. The big difference between the English and the French is that the former have the fortitude to take adversity in their stride. For a long time, they were the only bulwark against Nazism in Europe, even if, with Brexit, they succumbed to a populist wave.

To pray, on the other hand, is to rise, to seek a source of light, to reflect while chanting. There are mechanical prayers and inspired prayers. The former are mumbled like an automatic flow, but the latter can be a source of firm resolution. Prayer can be a strategy of pride, with the certainty that God must be interested in our little worries. As if he had nothing better to do with his nine billion people than to listen to us in particular. The Lord's strength is his silence. It is to an Absent One that we deliver our endless monologues. That is, unless we imagine a 'God stricken with Alzheimer's' as Guéorgui Gospodinov put it, who instantly erases the murmurs and reproaches addressed to him by his creatures.

Freud noted a legal dimension to complaining. To complain is to lodge a complaint against others, the world, fate. There is even a 'sorority of complaints' when several people reinforce the legitimacy of their struggle by pooling their grievances. Prayer may be silent, but recrimination is always talkative. The major problem with our Western democracies is that we have partly lost our immune defences. We can neither rejoice nor put up with it. We remain in this mediocre register of perpetual complaint. Don't overwhelm your loved ones with your whining. Enliven them with your plans and your joys.

We also pray collectively, it's a communion with an upward movement, an expression that improves things, summoning up higher forces. For the fervent, everything becomes adoration, a ceaseless admiration. The mystery of prayer: it serves no purpose, yet it is essential. It is thanksgiving for existing, exalting the beauty of the world, praising the Most High, unlike a lament, which is the cry of ill-bred creatures. 'I go every morning to pray', said Matisse in 1947, 'pencil in hand, in front of a flowering pomegranate tree.'

PART TWO

Victimist Competition[1]

CHAPTER 5

The thieves of suffering

> We demand that slavery and colonialism be recognised as a double holocaust and a crime against humanity, and we demand reparations from the West for the plundering of raw materials, the forced displacement of populations, the inhuman treatment and the current poverty of Africa, the fruit of this history of crimes and plundering.
>
> ALIOUNE TINE, SPOKESMAN FOR AFRICAN NGOs IN DURBAN, 2000

In 1943, two Jewish lawyers, Raphael Lemkin and Hersch Lauterpacht, one of whom had taken refuge in London and the other in the United States, urged the Allies to give a precise description of the type of barbarism being perpetrated by Nazi Germany in the form of the extermination of entire populations on the basis of race, creed or ethnicity. Lemkin coined the term *genocide*, Lauterpacht that of *crimes against humanity*. At Nuremberg in 1947, it was the first, more powerful term that triumphed. Lauterpacht already feared that this momentum would lead to a battle between the victims, with crimes against humanity appearing to be the lesser evil.[1] And rightly so. For some, 'to be labelled a victim of genocide has become "an essential component of national identity"', explains Franco-British jurist Philippe Sands.[2] Since 1947, the use of this word has snowballed exponentially, and it has been appropriated indiscriminately by all peoples and minorities who suffer persecution. There is one condition for being inducted as a target of genocide: the scarcity of candidates. As soon as they proliferate, they find their best enemies in their peers. In this competition, the person to be eliminated is no longer the oppressor but the one whose suffering offends yours. In this respect, UN assemblies resemble a vast agora where aggrieved peoples want to make their voices heard, even if it means overplaying their misfortunes to eclipse those of their neighbours.

The Shoah, it's me, it's us, it's not you

In San Francisco, in 2021, Black Lives Matter activists put up a sign in front of their stand: 'From 1619 to 1861, more than 15 million Africans were sold into slavery and more than 35 million were killed by slave traders, making the slave trade the greatest holocaust the world has ever known.' Thirty-five million, who can beat that? The Jews can kiss their six million Shoah goodbye. As the African-American neo-Nazi Luis Farrakhan once explained: 'The Black Holocaust was a hundred times worse than the Jewish Holocaust.' But in this competition, the world champions remain the Russians. In 2017, a Duma commission re-evaluated the number of casualties between 1941 and 1945 and arbitrarily increased the official figure of 27 million, endorsed by historians, to 42 million (23 million civilians and 19 million soldiers). Unverifiable and therefore dubious, these figures for the Russian ordeal are intended to impose on the whole world 'and in particular on the West, a kind of political and moral superiority for Russia'.[3] Escalating the numbers is a method of intimidation to secure the global prize for the Most Damned. In a planet saturated by overpopulation and awash with mass crimes, no one will be moved by anything less than a few million. We set the bar so high that a crime below that threshold leaves us cold. We disqualify it for not measuring up. Here, mathematical extravagance serves a barely concealed will to power. As the Russian poet Maria Stepanova wrote, 'the past is a secular cult that feeds on human sacrifice'. But the enormity of the Shoah continues to overshadow the other struggles. Was it not Mahmoud Abbas, current President of the Palestinian Authority on the West Bank, who, in front of Chancellor Scholz, accused Israel of having committed fifty holocausts against the Palestinians, remarks that he later withdrew (17 August 2021), perhaps judging them to be excessive? However, he repeated them to US Secretary of State Anthony Blinken on 5 November 2023, during a visit to the West Bank, in reference to the Israeli bombardments of Gaza. Produced on an assembly line like this, the term ends up losing all meaning.

'They expect the worst – they do not expect the unthinkable',[4] said Charlotte Delbo, a former member of the Resistance who was sent to Auschwitz and Ravensbrück (where she exchanged a ration of bread for Molière's *Le Misanthrope*, which she learnt by heart to sustain herself). After 1945, the revelation of the camps was experienced as a black hole in the mind, an abyss in which both hope and reason were sunk. Now, we have reversed the point of view, we see the worst as always certain; the first atrocity leads to an escalation of extremes. The only thing that can happen is Auschwitz, the same horror, repeated over and over again, whatever its contingent incarnations. Even the economic system is a form of genocide, if we are to believe the sociologist Monique Pinçon-Charlot: 'The conscious and determined objective (of capitalists) is to exterminate the poorest half of humanity with the terrible weapon of climate change.'[5] The overuse of the word empties it of meaning.

Since the Second World War, Jewish suffering has become the benchmark and the Shoah the founding event on the basis of which to think about crimes against humanity: 'The victims of Auschwitz', Paul Ricoeur has rightly said, 'are, *par excellence,* the representatives in our memory of all history's victims.'[6] But the Jews have not earned this title, and many groups and minorities do not want to hear about delegation. They want to be the new holders of the yellow star and see genocide not as the height of barbarity but as an opportunity to be misfortune's new elect. The nightmare of Nazism has become the dream of many peoples; this is no longer cultural appropriation but memorial appropriation. Claiming to be the object of a new holocaust allows them to shine the most powerful spotlight on themselves. But it's hard to claim ownership when there are so many people vying to be on the list. The Jew then becomes the rival to be slaughtered, usurping a place that should rightfully belong to Blacks, Palestinians, Muslims, Salafists, women, indigenous peoples, First Nations, etc.

For a long time, attempts have been made to maintain firm boundaries among the various types of killing, but to no avail. Yet failing to distinguish offences is in itself an offence against the spirit and upsets the intelligibility of human violence. We have to learn to distinguish between a misdemeanour and a felony, between manslaughter and premeditated murder, between genocide and a crime against humanity, between a war crime and an ethnocide, between face-to-face carnage and carnage at a distance, between ecocide and urbicide – these are all categories of offence that are not subject to the same logic or the same punishment.[7] Some researchers, such as Jacques Sémelin, classify them under the general umbrella of massacres carried out to terrorize and subjugate.[8] This kind of classification is intolerable for the victims, but essential for investigators, politicians, historians and judges wishing to establish a scale of penalties.

From this point of view, the Shoah becomes a screen crime that must be stolen from those who claim it. Two attitudes are possible: identification or expulsion. There is a risk that the Holocaust will be perceived as the Jews' only misfortune, so singular that it becomes incommunicable and concerns only a minority of the human race.[9] Wrenched out of its time, the event merely confirms the cursed status of Moses' people, 'a glorious chapter in our eternal history', as Elie Wiesel wrote.[10] It is a timeless disaster that dismisses the rest of humanity. So how can we learn anything from this episode if it is absolutely incomparable with the present? The past can no longer teach us anything about the future.[11] But genocide is so prominently situated that everyone dreams of settling there if they want to. And how can the first occupants be dislodged? Either by elevating their own misfortune to the status of a major crime, or by minimizing the scale of the Judeocide. So when Pope John Paul II, in Poland in 1991, likened abortion to the Nazi genocide (the Polish Diet had just voted to decriminalize abortion) and spoke of a 'cemetery of the victims of human cruelty in our century [being] extended to include yet another vast cemetery, that of the unborn' and of a 'legal extermination', he was straying into an outrageous comparison. However, he cannot be suspected of anti-Semitism, since, in an address to the Great Synagogue of Rome on 13 April 1986, he declared: 'You are our dearly beloved brothers and in a certain way … our elder brothers' and, after John XXIII, would be the architect of Jewish–Christian reconciliation. He just got lost in what has been dubbed the 'controlled designation of origin' quarrel.

But for most people, the Shoah is a stockpile of symbols that should not be left to the Jews alone. It's a place we can put all of the tortured, the Amerindians, the slaves, the Africans, the Palestinians from Gaza, the gays, and so on. We are not trivializing genocide; on the contrary, we remain fascinated by how this absolute evil can benefit other, more deserving groups. In this respect, Robert Faurisson's Holocaust denial, or that of the Turkish government, is a kind of symbolic barter: they deny the existence of the gas chambers (or the annihilation of the Armenians) the better to condemn those who are laying claim to it. The Jews hide their crimes in the Middle East behind the cloak of the Holocaust; the Armenians hide their complicity with Turkey's enemies in 1915. The stakes are high. Perhaps we need to change the way we teach about mass crimes and go into this history not by feeling sorry for the victims but, like Iannis Roder, by studying their executioners.[12] Misfortune has the huge advantage over good fortune in that it provides us with a destiny. It alone inducts us into a new aristocracy. But in this mental registry, places come at a premium: it's a very private club from which we have to keep out indelicate members, plagiarist pretenders or imitations. Victimism is a ruthless Darwinism.

Hitler as the truth of the West

Everything is happening as if Hitler had preceded himself by several centuries and would continue into the future, the one and only devil figure until the end of time. The Third Reich is not the regime that came to power through the ballot box in 1933 and then disappeared under the strikes of the Red Army and the Allies in the rubble of Berlin in May 1945; it is the matrix of European history, or to put it another way, its true face. This is why historians claim that Africans, Arabs and South Americans have the privilege of anteriority. Hitler was already with Cortes, Pizarro, General Bugeaud, Savorgnan de Brazza, Livingstone and Stanley. 'There is a dynamic relationship between the destruction of the indigenous peoples of America, the annihilation of Black people and the policy of extermination introduced in Europe by the Nazis in the first half of the twentieth century', argues Rosa Amelia Plumelle-Uribe, a Colombian lawyer based in France.[13]

The reasoning dates back to Aimé Césaire's 1950 *Discourse on Colonialism*, where the Martiniquais poet warned that one should:

> reveal to the very distinguished, very humanistic, very Christian bourgeois of the twentieth century that without his being aware of it, he has a Hitler inside him, that Hitler *inhabits* him, that Hitler is his *demon*, that if he rails against him, he is being inconsistent and that, at bottom, what he cannot forgive Hitler for is not *the crime* in itself, *the crime against man*, it is not *the humiliation of man as such*, it is the crime against the white man, the humiliation of the white man, and the fact that he applied to Europe colonialist procedures which until then had been reserved exclusively for the Arabs of Algeria, the 'coolies' of India, and the 'niggers' of Africa.[14]

This is a strong statement, which was preceded by 'they tolerated that Nazism before it was inflicted on them, ... they absolved it, shut their eyes to it, legitimized it, because, until then, it had been applied only to non-European peoples; that they have cultivated that Nazism, that they are responsible for it, and that before engulfing the whole edifice of Western, Christian civilization in its reddened waters, it oozes, seeps, and trickles from every crack'.[15] Aimé Césaire may have been carried away by the rhetoric here. Colonialism and transatlantic slavery, with their undeniable crimes, are not of the same nature as the programmed extermination of a people. In the twentieth century alone, the Ottoman Empire committed two genocides, that of the Armenians in 1915 and that of the Assyro-Chaldeans in 1915–18; in Cambodia, the self-purging of the Khmer Rouge (1975–9); in 1994, the Rwandan genocide committed by the Hutus against the Tutsis, not forgetting the cultural ethnocide of the Uighurs by the Chinese authorities and that of the Rohingyas in Burma. All mass crimes perpetrated by non-Westerners. The obsession with the colour white is the congenital weakness of the decolonial movement, which was content to turn the imperialist discourse on its head, the better to accuse the European powers.[16] All peoples, all empires, are capable of the same ignominy, such is the terrible truth that we have been facing since the turn to independence. The West's only fault is to admit its crimes when others hide them. Since Aimé Césaire, many have wanted to hitch the wagons of colonization (in Algeria, Africa or Asia) to the great train of the Shoah, in order to take on board its vocabulary, atmosphere and spirit.

The American political scientist Samuel Huntington once said 'The West versus the Rest', but this is an offensive oversimplification. Not all the oppressed have the same interests. Out of hostility to Iran, which wants to annihilate it, Israel is giving massive aid to the Azeri dictatorship, which is attacking Armenia and wants to steal its territory. Armenia is allied to Iran, which has its eye on part of Azerbaijan. The Kurds, persecuted in Iraq, Iran, Turkey and Syria, have clashed in terrible civil wars, between the Barzani and Talabani clans in Iraqi Kurdistan in the 1990s, resulting in thousands of deaths. Not to mention the hostility that prevails between the Kurds of Syria in Rojava, who pledge allegiance to the PKK, a terrorist party in Turkey, and those of Kurdistan. In the Middle East, the PLO and Hamas have been in violent conflict for twenty years over the ownership of a state that remains virtual for the time being. Every political commitment is a cacophony, a tearing apart: we support causes that have internal divisions.

The demonization of Israel

Ramón Grosfoguel, a theoretician of Puerto Rican origin and professor at Berkeley, organized a conference in Paris on 13 January 2012 with the *Parti des Indigènes de la République* (PIR) on the theme: 'Towards a decolonial reading of the Shoah'. The aim was simple: to do double duty by delegitimizing the State of Israel in its struggle against the Palestinian people and inserting the Holocaust episode, so as to play it down, into the long history of the slave trade and Western imperialism.[17] Unlike Hannah Arendt, for whom Nazism and Stalinism, two totalitarian regimes, are absolute historical innovations, particularly in their use of terror (even if they have resonances in Europe's past), the decolonial movement puts the Shoah on the same level as other events in the history of colonialism. It was the lawyer Jacques Vergès at the Barbie trial who never stopped repeating like a mantra – it was his life's struggle – that Nazism is just the other face of colonialism,[18] an epiphenomenon in the absolute abomination that was Western imperialism.

A minor figure in the decolonial movement, Houria Bouteldja, who is close to Alain Soral and Jean-Luc Mélenchon, has written countless books explaining that Jews are the 'darlings' of the Republic. In her view, the Shoah is not a 'detail', as it might have been for Jean-Marie Le Pen, 'it's not even visible in the rear-view mirror'. 'The Shoah? The colonial subject has known tens of them. Exterminations? Any number.'[19] Never mind the figures or the nuances. What must be stolen from the Jews is their deportation uniform, which has become another enlightenment costume. 'The world will never forgive the Jews for Auschwitz', was the insight of the Israeli psychologist Zvi Rex. In 2001, the Durban conference in South Africa marked the height of anti-Jewish hatred under the guise of denouncing European colonialism and slavery.

Joëlle Fiss wrote in her *Durban Diary*:

> Wherever you turn, Israel is compared to Nazi Germany. Posters associate Israel with the former South African regime and its apartheid policies. Everywhere, there are images of suffering Palestinian children. Arab women display photos of their 'martyred' husbands, killed during the Second Intifada. The stand of the Arab Lawyers Union is selling *The Protocols of the Elders of Zion*. Caricatures are hung up. One of them depicts a rabbi with *The Protocols of the Elders of Zion* under his arm and an Israeli army cap on his head. Another poster describes how the Jews make their bread: with the blood of Muslims.[20]

Once again, it was the Cameroonian philosopher Achille Mbembe, an opponent of apartheid and colonialism, who called on Jews to disavow the State of Israel, failing which they would have no one to blame but themselves for the hatred they arouse. Accused of anti-Semitism in Germany, he replied that he was being attacked because he was Black and African. For this supporter of the right of Africans to move anywhere in the Old World because of the 'colonial debt', Israeli apartheid is 'far more lethal' than that of the former Republic of South Africa, because the occupation of Palestine 'is the biggest moral scandal of our times'.[21] For him, Israel is an example of the former victim becoming the executioner, and its birth was a catastrophe for the Palestinians, the Nakba, a mimetic double of the Shoah. Both words mean 'catastrophe' in their respective languages.[22] In the Middle East, a global struggle is being waged between the former holders of the title of pariah (the Jews) and the new champions of absolute martyrdom (the Palestinians).[23] We should therefore be campaigning for a 'global isolation' of the Jewish state and doing everything possible to destroy this racist entity. In 2016, in his article 'The Society of Enmity', Achille Mbembe condemned the 'fanatical policy of destruction aimed at transforming the life of Palestinians into a heap of ruins or a pile of garbage destined for cleansing'.[24]

Whatever the Hebrews do, they are wrong. Even if a Palestinian state were established between the West Bank and Gaza, Israel would remain illegitimate. All anti-Zionists, left and right, repeat it over and over again: the Jews have no right to a national home. Right up until 7 October 2023, Netanyahu's government, with its determination to trample on the Supreme Court, to impose a Mosaic theocracy and the rapid colonization of the West Bank, seemed to confirm the judgement of the Hebrew State's most bitter enemies. In a terrible twist, the annihilation of Israeli democracy would come not from its enemies but from within society itself. Hamas's savage aggression restored unity to the country and increased hatred of Israel tenfold in the Arab-Muslim world and on certain North American and European campuses. After Durban, it was the biggest explosion of unabashed anti-Semitism in the Western world. The cry of 'Death to the Jews' rang out in many cities of the Old World, where people of that confession had to keep a low profile to avoid being attacked. In Paris, Jews have even been banned from taking taxis.[25] In France, anti-Semitic acts have skyrocketed, from 436 in 2022 to 1,676 in 2023.

With the 7 October war, the wolves started circling. It was the most massive coming out of Judeophobes in recent years, especially from the far left. The most astonishing thing was the *insurrection of the delicate*: didn't we see the very sensitive Greta Thunberg side with Gaza without a word for the victims of the 7 October pogrom and retweet about genocide in this narrow strip of land? So her defence of the climate was aimed at freeing the planet from the Zionist octopus! (She seems to have regretted her post afterwards.) And the distinguished Mona Chollet, a Swiss anti-patriarchal activist, declared the fusing of anti-Zionism and anti-Semitism[26] to be 'criminal', flew off the handle because *Libération* had put photos of Israeli families fleeing Hamas[27] on its front page, and described Zionism as a 'morbid and delusional colonial project'.[28] Judeophobia has thus shifted to the repulsive figure of the 'settler': exported anti-Semitism. Many feminists, so fussy about relations between men and women, did not bat an eyelid at the rapes and mass killings committed by Hamas on 7 October: they were 'white' Israeli women who did not deserve their sympathy. 'Zionism, criminal DNA of humanity', was the cry in the streets of Paris during a protest march against the war in Lebanon on 30 July 2006. In a terrible misunderstanding, Israel's enemies are not expressing their love of the Palestinian cause but their hatred of the Jews in the Middle East. To quote Bernard Lewis: 'The Arabs are really nothing more than a stick with which to beat Jews.'[29] Their rage erupts with intensity every ten years, a symbolic *kristallnacht* that smoulders quietly for the rest of the time.

The Western world is criticized for valuing the lives of Israelis more than those of Palestinians. Our dead against yours: but our dead only have value if they are killed by yours, in this case the Israelis. It really is a double standard. The war in Yemen launched in 2014 by Saudi Arabia, which has killed 370,000 people, 220,000 of them from indirect causes, has never raised the slightest protest. Nor the 400,000 victims of Bashar El Assad, nor the tens of thousands killed in the war against ISIS (Daesh). When Arabs kill each other, nobody flinches. When Israelis clash with Palestinians, there is instant talk of 'genocide': remember that the Palestinian population has tripled in fifty years (from 1,340,000 in 1948 to nearly 5 million today). And since the Jews no sooner liberated from the camps than went on to found a new colonial state in Palestine that reproduced the defects of the old empires, some have even spoken of a second Shoah committed by the Germans: 'Because of how closely linked the aftermath of the Nazi genocide is to the occupation of Palestine, Germans would also do well to reflect on their implication in that ongoing injustice', said Michael Rothberg.[30]

Others are calling for 'the liberation of Palestine from German guilt'. Petitions have even been launched in France to boycott German cultural activities. Like the anti-Semitism of which it is the offshoot, the dislike of Israel is a passion that nothing can appease and everything can nourish. The most extreme will rehabilitate Hitler, make Zionism into a carbon copy of Nazism, mixing the descendants of the victims and the descendants of the executioners into the same excoriation. As the Chilean writer Luis Sepúlveda put it in 2005: 'Today, as in the past, we hate the Nazis for what they did to the Jews, the Gypsies, the homosexuals, and to their opponents. Today, tomorrow, the Jews will be hated because of what a warrior caste, led by Sharon, is doing to the Palestinians. In Auschwitz and Mauthausen, in Sabra, Chatila and Gaza, Zionism and Nazism join hands.'[31] Instant reversal: if the Jews oppress, it must be in the way of the blonde thug. We believe in the reversibility of victim and executioner: a raped child will become a rapist parent; a beaten boy will beat his offspring. Once the targets of genocide in Europe, the Jews in Israel, whenever they commit crimes – and they do, like all states – can only perpetrate genocide. Judaizing the Palestinians immediately Nazifies the Israelis[32] and deposes those Jews who do not publicly repent about Israel, 'that usurping entity'. Any mention of them and the National Socialist referent is brought out: they were persecuted by the Nazis and they became Nazis.[33] It's as simple as that. When South Africa lodged a complaint against Israel for genocide in Gaza in The Hague in January 2024, it killed three birds with one stone: it toppled the Jewish State from its pedestal as the nation that inherited the Shoah; it minimized the Shoah in world history; and, above all, it set up an innocent global South against a North that has always been guilty of colonialism.

It is not from oblivion that Auschwitz has to be rescued, but from being kidnapped by memory pirates. Today's anti-Semite begins by denouncing anti-Semitism, only to restore it to its rightful place under the name of anti-Zionism: you have to admire the plasticity of an abhorrence that can be endlessly recycled without getting tired. In a certain progressive mythology, the Palestinian is our last good savage, innocent even when he kills and slits throats. He is the great Christ-like icon whose beatification process has been going on for fifty years. But we are doing this cause a great disservice by subjugating it to radical Islam: even if the plight of the civilian population of Gaza is atrocious, even if we want a two-state political solution, Islamist terrorism risks tamping down solidarity for a long time to come. Paris saw it with the Bataclan theatre. Hearing members of Hamas, Islamic Jihad and their supporters screaming 'Allahu Akbar' and proposing to eradicate Jews, Christians and infidels around the world is bloodcurdling. One day, the curse of mutual enmity will have to be broken. It will be up to the Israeli extremists to abandon their dream of a Greater Israel and up to the Palestinians to detoxify their political project of all the false friends who want to feed off it, starting with the Muslim Brotherhood and the ultra-leftists of the West. The way in which a liberation movement conducts itself during its struggles foreshadows the society it wants to establish afterwards. The establishment of a caliphate to the east and south of Israel is simply inconceivable.

Is there a lesson to be learned from mass crime?

In all the pages that were written after the liberation of the death camps in 1945, there were several interpretations in succession: Auschwitz was largely ignored by the French until the early 1980s, in favour of the Resistance movement. The traumatized nation only wanted to know about heroes, and the Gaullist rhetoric of a France united against the occupying forces soothed the wounded pride of a country that had been defeated in the space of a few weeks during the 'phoney war'. Racial crimes were downplayed, and only the *maquisards* and political deportees were given the red carpet. The historian François Azouvi has dispelled this preconceived notion, demonstrating that, from 1945 onwards, public opinion was aware of the tragedy of the Jews but forgot about it.[34] There was no repression but what was already known was rediscovered; memory was reorganized. We have moved, according to Henry Rousso, from a political to a moral perspective on the event. Since then, the equation has been reversed. Auschwitz is suffocating under its own success, while disputes rage about the 'unique uniqueness' of the Shoah. After Claude Lanzmann's 1985 film of that name it became a veritable 'civil religion' of the West, its primordial scene. As the Hungarian Nobel Prize winner for literature and camp survivor Imre Kertész (1929–2016) put it in his book *The Holocaust as Culture*, kitsch took over Auschwitz and killed it.[35] The event rose above the century like a sidereal star, parallel to Nazism itself, detached from its context, becoming a kind of satanic excrescence that could be moved along the centuries like a cursor, forwards or backwards. From that moment on, the victim was hoisted up on the gallows in front of their executioner. We have stayed frozen in this tête-à-tête. Not only can the Jews be sacrificed once again on the altar of this cult of which they are the transitory idols, but the qualifier 'Nazi' can be applied to any figure or people over the centuries, yesterday Napoleon, today Zelensky, tomorrow the European Union, depending on the mood of the public prosecutor.

It is no exaggeration to say that Auschwitz, like any 'monster event', is maddening, the product of both law and delirium. It has become the yardstick of human suffering, the 'new Golgotha' (John Paul II), as if Christ had died there a second time. Above all, it has encouraged a perverse metaphysics of the victim. But the Holocaust is not only the quintessentially desirable horror that each of us would like a part of, it also opens us up to understanding mass crimes. The history of Europe is that of a slow process of civilization: it is the slave trade plus abolition (announced in Portugal for the first time in history in 1761);[36] it is colonialism plus its slow disintegration under the impact of independence struggles; it is Auschwitz plus Nuremberg and the European Convention on Human Rights after the destruction of the Third Reich; it is the abomination in action and its outlawing by law and its enforcement; and it is, finally, the last miracle, the reconciliation of eternal enemies. Genocide is not a closed concept reserved for one people, nor a safe whose guardians keep the key for their sole use, but an experience accessible to all of us, a model of intelligibility for understanding the present.

It was a unique event, like any mass slaughter, but it has been fruitful to chronicle: it has enabled the most sinister episodes of the past to be reinterpreted from a new angle. If the entire history of humanity is in a sense the history of crime against humanity, it is also the history of a growing number of people being averse to its spontaneous ferocity. The abhorrence of slavery since the Enlightenment and Condorcet, first in Europe and then in the rest of the world, linked to the revolts of the captives themselves, the extension of the right to warfare, the birth of humanitarian law from the battle of Solferino in 1859 with Henry Dunant, public opinion being sick to death of the atrocities of conflict, the growing rejection of colonialism and empires – with the notable exceptions of Russia, Iran, China and Turkey – all reflect what the German philosopher and critic Gotthold Ephraim Lessing (1729–81) would have called the collective education of the human race. It has already taken decades to put the death camps and the Gulag in symmetry rather than equivalence, two expressions of totalitarianism, of the age-old ingenuity with which humans torture and trample on each other. Communism and Nazism achieved the feat of re-establishing slavery in Europe, against all historical progress, one in 1917, the other in 1933. The range of inhumanity is endless, from the Uighur camps in China, to the Rohingya camps in Burma, to the camps in North Korea, to the disciplinary camps in Russia, or even the undignified prisons and detention centres in democracies. Barbarity is plural, and our understanding of its mechanisms limited. We want to condemn evil without seeking to discriminate among its various facets. Making distinctions among crimes seems to us to be a matter of self-satisfaction.

Since Nuremberg, the exterminations of the Amerindians of the North and South, the Australian Aborigines, the Hereros in Namibia, the Armenians and the Assyro-Chaldeans have been viewed in a different light, and the Second World War sounded the death knell for the great Western empires. This process was not just a manifestation of the victors' justice: it was a creative act, as Karl Jaspers had already seen in 1946. It laid the foundations for a new criminal order. Without Nuremberg, there would be no International Criminal Tribunal for Rwanda in 1994, or for the former Yugoslavia in 1995, and no special body to judge the crimes of ISIS and Hamas, those of Putin, or the militias in north-eastern Congo.

If Auschwitz means infinitely more than Auschwitz, it is because no event has ever been interpreted so broadly as to be claimed by forces so inimical to each other. It is one thing to say that the Jewish catastrophe makes it possible to think about human abjectness in all its diversity; it is quite another to assert that it obscures our misery and must be eliminated. For Holocaust deniers, it manifests an a priori preference for the suffering of a single people. They wish to 'dejudaize' the catastrophe the better to shoah-ize their own misfortunes. But the Holocaust remains a legal reference capable of accommodating all the reprobates, all the martyrs. Ethnic chauvinism on the one hand, universal hospitality on the other: we are not yet out of this dilemma, which is a time bomb in itself.

CANNON FODDER

There are regimes, such as Russia, and terrorist groups, such as Hamas, that use their populations to protect their weapons and, conversely, there are states that protect their population and their soldiers with their weapons. For the former, people are merely a random variable, an inexhaustible asset that can die in large numbers. The United States and Europe, which have abolished conscription and have professional armies, may experience moments of great solidarity and patriotic outbursts, but they are not in any shape to be in a state of permanent war, since the message of democracies is love of life and self-fulfilment. We no longer want to pay for belonging to a homeland with our blood, unlike Putin's Russia, which regards its children as future corpses: 'Today our brave soldiers are doing their duty in Ukraine. One day it will be up to them to pay their debts to their country. Yes, it's painful to sacrifice your children. But a boy is born to be a defender of his country. A girl is born to be the guardian of her home', in the words of Olga Zakhran, a youth instructor in Putin's army).[37] In Ukraine, Russian soldiers, doped up on captagon or alcohol, are dying by the tens of thousands, in waves, their bodies randomly abandoned and left to decay. It's true that in Russia, death in combat is also a business: when a soldier is killed at the front, their family receives 120,000 euros, the average salary being 300 euros a month. Parents who see their son go off to war can hope to buy themselves a nice house and a car as soon as the youngster is mown down by the enemy. The thanato-business is flourishing.

For half a century, our intellectual, political and media elites have shown unbelievable tolerance towards Palestinian terrorism: attacks and explosions are condemned but paid lip service to, or even justified as 'an act of desperation', the legitimate repayment for the savageries committed by Israel. Never mind the culture of death spread among the youth of the West Bank and Gaza. The chic left on American and European campuses does not wonder whether this encouragement is not primarily suicidal for the Palestinians themselves and does not stifle their desire for peace and decency, since there are times 'when people aspire to be able to raise their children in places other than cemeteries', as Jean Daniel supposedly said. Our fascination with bloodbaths, mass executions and the redemptive martyrdom of Hamas or Islamic jihad is not just on-screen pornography, like Jean Baudrillard's jubilation at the collapse of the New York towers. More than that, it shows our contempt for a people whose women, children and elderly have been reduced to human shields. Even Amnesty International refuses to describe Hamas as terrorists: they are fighters. The Palestinian cause will always be about human bombs. We prefer the aesthetics of crime to the ethics of compromise. At risk is this stub of a state, already divided between two governments, with no future other than terror, racketeering and corruption.

CHAPTER 6

Putin, or the petty civil servant of crime

Suffering is our capital, our natural resource. Not oil or gas
– but suffering. It is the only thing we are able to produce
consistently. I'm always looking for the answer: why doesn't
our suffering convert into freedom? Is it truly all in vain?

LECTURE BY SVETLANA ALEXIEVITCH,
WINNER OF THE 2015 NOBEL PRIZE FOR LITERATURE

When you take Putin's career and put it in parallel with
Hitler's, it's a bit frightening … Putin is a rabid little
civil servant.

PRINCE OTTO VON HABSBURG, KTO TV, 1 JULY 2008[1]

There was a dress rehearsal for Russia's war against
Ukraine in the former Yugoslavia, with Belgrade fighting
against the Union between 1991 and 2000. This is why
Moscow supported Milošević, condemned NATO's armed
intervention against Serbia in 1999 and above all the
recognition of Kosovo's independence in 2008. Russia

is attached to Serbia by ethnic, emotional and religious ties; it is the mother of pan-Slavism and the guardian of the Orthodox Church. It casts a long shadow and its glorious past gives Serbs the feeling that they are not alone. For those in Moscow, in the ruins of the Soviet Empire, who dream of taking revenge on the West, the Moscow–Belgrade connection remains essential. And current Serbian President Aleksandar Vučić is, whatever he may say, a pawn of the Kremlin in the Balkans. It was the 'Yugoslav laboratory', in the words of French politician Roland Dumas, that opened the Pandora's box of forced border changes, and this was the taboo that the Russian army broke in Ukraine in February 2022.

The Yugoslav precedent

If one thing has characterized the fierce confrontation among Serbs, Croats, Bosnians, Montenegrins and Kosovars, it is the massive and shameless use of victim rhetoric by the authorities in Belgrade. It was the novelist Dobrica Ćosić, the main inspiration behind Serbian nationalism, who wrote: 'Serbia is the new Jew of the late twentieth century, the victim of the same injustices, if not the same persecutions: the new martyred people.'[2] But, speaking of the Croatian extermination policy carried out by the Zagreb Ustashis, he added that the Serbs were more Jewish than the Jews because they were 'victims of a genocide surpassing the Nazi genocides in its methods and bestiality'.[3] Almost a year after the outbreak of hostilities in Ukraine and seeing the Western camp coalesce against Moscow, Foreign Minister Sergei Lavrov used the same metaphor on 18 January 2023, comparing Western actions against Russia to Hitler's 'final solution' against the Jews: 'Just as Hitler wanted to solve the Jewish question, now

Western leaders ... are saying in no uncertain terms that Russia must suffer a strategic defeat.'[4]

Vladimir Putin justified his offensive in Ukraine by starting to Nazify the Ukrainians and pointing out that some of them, in particular the Banderites named after the nationalist Stepan Bandera (1909–59), had actively collaborated with the Third Reich, which is true. Bandera, who is still honoured today in western Ukraine, created the Ukrainian Legion under the direction of the Wehrmacht before being arrested by the Germans and interned in the Sachsenhausen camp. He was murdered by the Soviets. Many Ukrainian nationalists took part in the elimination of Jews, notably at Babi Yar, a ravine near Kiev where in 1941 33,000 Jews were executed in two days by the *Einsatzgruppen*. Nearly 60,000 people – Jews, Gypsies, Poles and Ukrainian partisans – were subsequently killed in the same place. Similarly, Bogdan Khmelnitski (1595–1657), the Ukrainian Cossack leader who committed incredibly cruel pogroms against the Jews, is still celebrated as a hero. Like all the countries that suffered under Russian colonialism and Soviet dominance, Ukraine welcomed the Wehrmacht as liberators, especially in the West, at the price, for some of its members, of collaborating with the Nazi authorities, and the anti-Semitic persecutions and massacres were shocking.[5] But the new government in Kiev wants to put an end to the ambiguities of this period and President Zelensky, himself Jewish, took part in the Babi Yar commemoration ceremony on 29 September 2021 to exorcise this tragic episode. Historians will certainly have their work cut out to untangle the threads of this complex and painful past.[6]

The Ukrainians want to join Europe to escape a double curse: the residues of Sovietism visible everywhere in the former Eastern Bloc countries and, above all, the Russification of the world, that mixture of violence, corruption and lies that has characterized the world of Moscow for centuries. Russian spirituality, said the great writer Vassilli Grossman in the 1960s, is a veil concealing a profound taste for servitude, with its two iconic characters, the muzhik and the serf.[7] In his view, all Russian prophets have fought, in the name of spirituality, for slavery and the barbed wire of the Gulag.[8] Unfortunately, nothing to date has disproved this assertion.

In Putin's ideology, the qualities of executioner and victim are passed on. Fascism is a contagious disease; its genes pass from one generation to the next. It is an immutable property attached to a people, especially if they are hostile to the Kremlin's policy. Like Milošević before it, Moscow alternates victim rhetoric and planetary threats. The whole world is ganging up on Russia, including degenerate Europe, deceitful America and all the spiteful satellites of the former USSR. The Serbian nationalists had also been afflicted by grand delusions, certain that the whole world was bent on destroying Holy Serbia: 'If the whole world goes to war with Serbia, then a world cataclysm, a flood will drown the whole world, except for little Greater Serbia.'[9] Perpetual paranoid delusions go hand in hand with megalomania and allow one's country to be inflated to the scale of the planet. Putin's Russia is certainly a huge country with an impressive nuclear arsenal. But the Muscovite empire, considerably amputated after the collapse of the USSR, is orphaned from its former grandeur and from the dialogue of equals with America, as in the days of the Cold War. Barack Obama's perceptive remark at the Nuclear Summit in The Hague on 25 March 2014, 'Russia is a regional power that is threatening some of its immediate neighbours, not out of strength but out of weakness', really upset the Russian elites and made them determined for revenge. Because Putin wants to be seen as a world leader, every restraint is an affront to him.

This huge civilization remains a mystery. It is European, and even global, in its culture, but it is resistant to the message of the Enlightenment and always prone to fall back into the ruts of autocracy and the Gulag. To understand this phenomenon, we need to go back to another text, Alexander Solzhenitsyn's 'A World Split Apart' speech given at Harvard in 1978. This speech caused a scandal, because, far from thanking the United States for harbouring him as a dissident, Solzhenitsyn delivered a violent indictment of the West, as guilty of materialism and the loss of religious sentiment. He explained that the violence suffered by the peoples of Greater Russia had forged exceptional characters that were no longer to be found in the West. We readily believe him, since he himself was an example of what he was talking about, a man nearly destroyed who grew into a giant. But is it necessary to plunge an entire society into savagery in order to forge a few great souls? Solzhenitsyn was convinced that once Communism disappeared, Russia would once again live up to the Slavophile doctrine, the spiritual guide of Christianity, the Christ of nations. In other words, the true West, whereas the West that prevails in Europe and the United States has wallowed in the pursuit of well-being and the cult of LGBT minorities that infuriates the Moscow chiefs. It would be an understatement to say that this hope has been dashed. All the evils that Solzhenitsyn attributed to the West can now be attributed to Russia, with the addition of the brutality and messianic nihilism theorized by Turgenev and Dostoyevsky in the nineteenth century. What characterizes Slavophiles is their propensity to preach. Putin, ensconced in his armchair, takes it upon himself to lecture us and hold up his failure as an example! Russia wants to save the world, but a large part of the world only wants to save itself from Russia.

The Great Patriotic War

Since the Second World War, in the Communist bloc, anti-fascist rhetoric has always enabled the various powers to discredit their opponents. To deny glorious socialism was to declare oneself an enemy of humanity. But Kremlin rhetoric cannot be the same as Milošević's in Serbia, because of differences of rank and prestige. Russia remains an empire of 150 million people, but Serbia has just 7 million today. Russia dominated the world via the USSR, which, as de Gaulle clearly saw, was the springboard for Great Russian nationalism. Serbia ruled the Balkans and the eastern flank of southern Europe, but lost the war to the Croats. Finally, Russia is a nuclear power that no longer seems to respect the rules of deterrence and threatens to nuke anyone who opposes its plans. The Kremlin is therefore going to balance victimhood with nuclear blackmail, invoking pride rather than fear. The Kremlin talks about Ukrainian 'Nazis' in the same way that the Nazis talked about Jews, Gypsies and Slavs, as vermin to be eliminated. Starting with the elites in every town. Dmitri Medvedev, a moderate President from 2008 to 2012, who became an extremist, describes Westerners and Ukrainians as 'degenerates', a wink in the direction of the National Socialist propaganda that banished degenerate art, modernists, cubists and expressionists. On 7 June 2022, he repeated the same epithets about the Ukrainians, while advertising his clear desire for extermination: 'They are bastards, degenerates; they want us dead, they want Russia dead. And as long as I am alive, I will do everything I can to make them disappear.'[10] The more the Kremlin team castigates Nazism, the closer they come to it in strange slips of the tongue. Ukraine never existed, so it can disappear by absorption, its language must be banned; ethnocide by inclusion.

Barbarity wraps itself in the saccharine rhetoric of peace and friendship among peoples; the executioner hiding behind soft assurances. It is never attacking; only defending. To this end, the Russians have a major historical asset at their disposal: the Great Patriotic War, a propaganda motif introduced in 1965 by Leonid Brezhnev at a time when the prestige of the USSR was beginning to decline in the face of Maoist China and the revelation of the horrors of Stalinism. The total war that pitted Nazi Germany against the USSR, initially allies in the German–Soviet pact of September 1939 and then enemies from June 1941 to May 1945, claimed between 20 and 27 million lives depending on the estimate, and was replete with crimes against humanity on both sides. There was the German extermination of Jews, Gypsies and Slavs; deportation of Crimean Tatars and Volga Germans by Stalin; mass rape of German women by Red Army soldiers condoned and even encouraged by the general staff; mass murder of dissidents, officers, teachers and clergy in the invaded countries (Czechoslovakia, Poland with Katyn, Bulgaria, etc.). We can never say enough about how lucky we were in the West to have been liberated by the Allies and not by the Soviets! But this war won by Stalin, through the unprecedented sacrifice of millions of men sent like pieces of meat to the enemy lines, was financed and armed by the Americans thanks to a lend-lease from Roosevelt and massive deliveries of weapons without which the peoples of the USSR could not have held out. It is possible, moreover, that the warrior spirit has been broken in Russia today and that the bellicose tornado of state propaganda will one day die out, as the relative failures of the former Red Army prove, yesterday in Afghanistan and today in Ukraine.

No matter: by arrogating to itself the title of victor over the Third Reich, by disguising Stalin's deep complicity with Hitler for more than a year, the Kremlin is conveying the following idea: we are owed everything because of the hardships we endured; we cannot be denied anything. We are the ones who defeated the demon from Germany; the world is in debt to us. The Russian extremist Vladimir Zhirinovsky (1946–2022), notorious xenophobe and anti-Semite, supporter of the return of Alaska and Finland to the Federation, extravagant clown, great friend of Jean-Marie Le Pen whom he met through the fascist writer Édouard Limonov and who was best man at his wedding, wrote in 1993:

> In the past, Russia saved the world from the Ottoman Empire by sending its armies south. ... Seven centuries ago we stopped the Mongols. ... Thanks to the Russians, Europe was freed from fascism ... that's why other peoples must be grateful to the Russians.[11]

Note that Vladimir Zhirinovsky was also in favour of using nuclear weapons against Moscow's enemies and wanted to install giant fans to blow radioactive waste back to the Baltic states. The Serbian nationalists had already taken macabre burlesque to an unprecedented level during the war in former Yugoslavia. The Russians have surpassed them in the art of staging their crimes by attributing them to others. In the process, they have confected a new kind of kitsch dripping with blood.

Respect your enemy

It was the insignificance of Putin – who started out in Leipzig as a small-time KGB civil servant traumatized by the fall of the Wall in 1989 – that fooled the world. With close links to the St Petersburg underworld, whose customs and language he adopted,[12] the 'thieves within the law'[13] who plunder the country's assets,[14] he came to power with a single obsession: to punish Europe for having caused the collapse of the USSR. A skilful dissembler, he bamboozled a number of diplomats and intellectuals by giving them the speeches they wanted to hear, going so far as to quote Immanuel Kant and human rights to a few pushovers! The idea held dear by some diplomats that Putin is a monster created by us and above all by the United States is seductive, but doesn't hold water.[15] It repeats the eternal refrain of Western guilt for all the ills that plague the world. The *mea culpa* was never a good tool for realpolitik. Putin's attitude changed radically after the intervention in Kosovo and the colour revolutions in Georgia and Ukraine, which he saw as an encirclement and even a Western plot. It was then that he vowed to stifle the slender artistic and political freedoms granted by Gorbachev's perestroika (Giuliano da Empoli framed his excellent novel, *The Wizard of the Kremlin*[16] around this). All the ills that Russia suffers from are due not to the dual despotic heritage of Tsarism and Communism, but to corrupting Europe and satanic NATO. What the Kremlin boss fears from the West, the symbol of freedom and critical thinking, is mostly the spread of democracy, the export of a new Maidan uprising to Russia, and even the outbreak of civil war.

What he learned from his time in the KGB is a founding principle of Sovietism: the salami strategy, which allows you to slice up the countries you want to take over before swallowing them: Ossetia and Abkhazia in Georgia, Crimea and the Donbass region in Ukraine in 2014, Transnistria in Moldova, and perhaps tomorrow, if we let him, the Suwalki corridor linking Belarus and the Russian Kaliningrad enclave on the border with Poland and Lithuania. All in the name of the well-known adage: 'What's mine is mine, what's yours is always negotiable.' His belligerence explains the demands for NATO membership from all the countries on his periphery. None of them can live in security on the borders of present-day Russia unless they lie down. Even the very pacifist Finland and Sweden have applied to join NATO, and the former has even built a wall on the Russian border to sever all ties! The skill with which Putin has divided many EU countries, financed or bought ruling parties, enticed or fascinated intellectuals and politicians, proves that his aim is indeed to do away with the 1989 insult, the fall of the Berlin Wall. The fact that Emmanuel Macron invited him to Brégançon in the summer of 2019 to discuss 'the architecture of European security', like inviting the wolf among the sheep, is further proof of Western blindness, even if the French President, offended and double-crossed, later made up for it in his support for Ukraine. 'Russia's borders end nowhere', Putin quipped on 24 November 2016. Without needing to declare war on us, he has helped to eject France from its African bases (Central African Republic, Mali, Niger, Burkina Faso) via the Wagner group, intervened in the American and French elections, and launched multiple cyberattacks. On 29 August 2014 in Brussels, he confided to José Manuel Barroso, then President of the European Commission, who then leaked the information: 'If I want, I can be in Kiev in a fortnight.' Everything had been said and announced a long time ago.

A great avenger, Putin has long enjoyed astonishing popularity in France. Referring to his small stature, the former President of Georgia, Mikheïl Saakashvili, called him 'Lily Putin'. He has a black belt in judo, and his authoritarianism fascinates the weak. He likes to parade bare-chested on horseback, play with weapons, fly a bomber and play all kinds of sports. This hypervirility, now somewhat softened, explains the cult enjoyed by this Muscovite Rambo on both the far right and the far left (including Éric Zemmour, Marine Le Pen and Jean-Luc

Mélenchon) as well as among African juntas, who prostrate themselves before this alpha male. But he is completely paranoid, surrounding himself with a Praetorian Guard and living in sanitary isolation, fearing the slightest germ or microbe. The entry into the Ukraine war of the murderous President Kadyrov's Chechen militias, heading off into battle to cries of 'Allahu Akbar', and the practice of beheading their enemies, places the Russians in ISIS and Hamas fields of action, whom they know how to support from time to time. Putin, like Erdogan, uses jihadism as an instrument of power; it was in Grozny in January 2015 that Kadyrov organized a huge demonstration of 1 million people to condemn the *Charlie Hebdo* cartoonists who had just been murdered in Paris. And in October 2021, the father of Samuel Paty's murderer, a Chechen, congratulated himself 'that his son had died defending the honour of all Chechens and all Muslims in the world'.[17] Putin is not so much mad as fanatical, convinced of the messianic nature of the Russian nation. The regime has become brutalized, with the physical removal of opponents, including Anna Politkovskaya and Boris Nemtsov and former friends such as Prigozhin, which goes hand in hand with a moralizing message that claims to rehabilitate traditional values, faith, children, the Christian family and especially the banning of homosexuality. He has a phobia about 'Gayropa', a contraction of gay and Europa. Vitali Milonov, a member of parliament close to the government and a 'pederast' hunter, said: 'As a former demon-hunter, I have a nose for gays. You can usually smell them. Naturally, they smell of sulphur.'[18] Putin is a mass murderer disguised as an evangelist. He destroys lovingly. Devoid of oratorical talent, he is neither Peter the Great, nor Hitler, nor Stalin, but a synthesis of the three. From Orthodoxy he borrows his unctuousness and bling; from Tsarism his obsession with lost greatness; and from Communism and Nazism their totalitarian rituals and mass murders. Hitler the hysterical monster, Stalin the debonair ogre, Putin the laborious torturer.

In any confrontation, you have to distinguish between the main enemy and the secondary enemy. Putin is just as dangerous for Europe today as Tehran or Erdogan. Turkey's position is interesting. It is an ally of Moscow in Libya; obsessed with the Rojava Kurds it wants to eliminate; linked to the Azerbaijani despot Aliev who would like to wipe out Armenia; dogged by hatred of Greeks and Christians in general, it supplies arms to ISIS and jihadist militias in sub-Saharan Africa, Syria and Libya, yet it has condemned the annexation of Crimea, delivers drones to Kiev and closes the Bosphorus Strait to Russian ships. It has fought hard to obtain a role as mediator between Moscow and Kiev. But above all, it shares Putin's hatred of Europe that contributed to the dismantling of the Sublime Porte by the Treaty of Lausanne in 1923. Erdogan still dreams of reconstituting the Ottoman Empire, retaining northern Cyprus and re-establishing the Caliphate over the Sunni world.

Our first duty towards enemies is respect. They say what they will do and they will do what they say. Alexander Solzhenitsyn once stated a simple principle about Communist propaganda: 'They lie. We know they are lying. They know that we know that they are lying. They continue to lie nonetheless.' To decipher this rhetoric means first of all getting into the habit of understanding everything in reverse. So when Moscow accuses Ukraine of wanting to commit genocide in the separatist republics of Donbass, it is because it is itself plotting the annihilation of Ukrainian resistance. In 2015, in order to prevent a 'genocide' in Crimea, Russian troops invaded the territory and seized the entire fleet in Sebastopol. Russia did not attack Ukraine on 24 February 2022, but was forced to launch a pre-emptive strike, because only six hours later Ukraine would have attacked first. What's more, Kiev was in the process of developing an atomic bomb. The lie no longer even needs to be plausible; it floats in a pervasive hallucinatory ether. For the Russians, every accusation is a confession or an anticipation of the next crime.

'Europe is condemned to death'[19]

But perhaps Putin has read too many decadent Europeans with their mournful homilies about the end of the West, and he has fatally misread our cultures. He has embraced the theses of European decline, certain that we would collapse as he begins his tilt for power. He saw us as degenerate sodomites and paedophiles, lost in consumerism. In 2013, he formulated his thoughts radically: 'In the West, they are pursuing policies that put large families and same-sex families on an equal footing, faith in God and faith in Satan ...'. Satan! The word is out, and this is where Putin joins the jihadist vision of the world: the Occident is evil and must be destroyed or re-educated. Putin mixes his imperialist doctrine with a religious eschatology linked to Orthodoxy and Islam (let's not forget that Russia has 6 million Muslims). Didn't he say in Sochi in 2018, like a jihadist leader, that he was ready to die in a nuclear confrontation: 'We will go to heaven as martyrs'? The Kremlin's propagandists, including Vladimir Soloviev,[20] now speak of Ukraine and the Western world in demonic terms, echoing Khomeini's propaganda. We Europeans and Americans are once again Satanic, great and small, plunged into the abyss of Sodom and Gomorrah. When it comes to demonization, there has never been anything better than the old Christian Satan taken up by Islam.

In the great Stalinist tradition, the more monstrous the crime being planned, the more monstrous the future victim must appear. The crimes the victim is suspected of are in fact programmatic, foreshadowing those that are going to be perpetrated against it. Thus the March 2022 images of the tortured bodies in Bucha in the suburbs of Kiev were denounced by Russian propaganda as a film montage performed by actors taking a cigarette break between two scenes, or as crimes perpetrated by the Ukrainians against their own citizens. With Putin, as in the past with Hitler, we have to interpret every sentence backwards from its obvious meaning, and get used to the fact that violence speaks the language of peace, fanaticism the language of reason, aggression the language of self-defence, colonialism the language of the protection of minorities, and crimes against humanity the language of prevention. Nothing sums up the conduct of the men in the Kremlin better than that of the Serbian nationalists, as George Steiner once said to Hitler in one of his books: 'You will adopt my methods while disowning me.'[21]

What is Nazism in Putin's propaganda? Not a major event of the twentieth century, but an ahistorical block that has stood the test of time, and which stands for everything that is bad for Moscow. Since the French Revolution, we have been mentally incapable of thinking about evil. We persist in reciting our catechism, repeating Bertolt Brecht's line that 'the belly is still fertile from which the foul beast sprang', as if the regimes of Benito Mussolini and Chancellor Hitler would endure beyond their destruction. We forget to see that what is new about contemporary 'fascism' is that it is anti-fascist in its utterance, just as racism is anti-racist in its formulation. The fact remains that the 'nazification' of Ukrainians by Russian propaganda did not take hold in Europe, unlike with the war in the former Yugoslavia, where European governments, François Mitterrand in France at the time, united with Milošević, allowed themselves to be fooled by the delirious accusation that the Croats and Bosnians were Ustasha. Moscow's Nazi slur against Kiev deflated as soon as it was uttered. It even turned against Russia. The way the designated enemy's language contaminates is all the more powerful because it is unconscious and we believe we have exorcized it. Vassili Grossman illustrated this magnificently in a dialogue between a Nazi officer, a prisoner of the Soviets at Stalingrad, and a Bolshevik militant: 'if you should conquer, then we shall perish only to live in your victory'.[22] The vanquished are resurrected in the skin of their victors and ventriloquize them in spite of themselves.

In the spring of 2022, Sergei Lavrov again explained that Hitler was a bit Jewish and Vladimir Putin had forbidden Russian Jews to emigrate to Israel, on pain of sanctions. The same Lavrov added in May 2022: 'History unfortunately knows of tragic examples of cooperation between Jews and Nazis.' In an interview on 5 September 2023, Putin himself repeated an old cliché of anti-Semitism, explaining that Zelensky, an 'ethnic Jew', was at the head of a Nazi nation. The equivalence between Judaism and Nazism is thus validated. Judeophobia is an integral part of Russian history, and after 1905 the Black Hundred made a name for themselves with bloody pogroms, including that in Bialystok. Bolshevism remained faithful to this tradition, especially Stalin, who, after the Second World War, launched a vast campaign of arrests against Jews, especially doctors. This was the famous 'white coats' conspiracy which broke out in 1953, where doctors were accused of wanting to assassinate Soviet leaders, including Jdanov, the presumed successor to the supreme leader. Stalin declared that 'every Jew is a potential enemy in the pay of the United States' and at the end of his life seemed to want to prepare public opinion for a Russian version of the 'final solution', discreetly masked under the name 'anti-cosmopolitan campaign'. The mere fact of being Jewish made one a potential criminal. Only his death, in March 1953, prevented Stalin from sowing terror one last time against that sector of the population. The authorities then admitted that the accusations were false. Today, the last Russian Jews think only of leaving the drunken boat that is the Russian Federation as quickly as possible, where their lives are once again under threat.

Nihilism and Russian degeneration

In 1960, Grossman, cited above, submitted the manuscript of his masterpiece *Life and Fate* to *Znamia* magazine. The editor-in-chief, Vadim Kojevnikov, was appalled by what he read and passed it on to the KGB. The book was immediately confiscated, virtually kidnapped, because the lesson of this very large book, 1,200 pages long, was unbearable for those in power. Grossman explains that Nazism and Communism are two enemy brothers who clash all the more because they are basically the same. Their rivalry is mimetic, and today we know the fascination that Hitler exerted on Stalin, his admired and abhorred double, before Stalin in turn fascinated the Führer as the Red Army pushed back the Wehrmacht. Fanaticism over race was just as good as class fanaticism, both being purveyors of mass murder. As Grossman pointed out in his last novel, *Everything Flows* (1954), those who thought they were enemies were twins, but the crushing of the Third Reich by the USSR and above all the Allies concealed this terrible truth for a long time. Another illusion was born, that Russia would follow the Western path and that time would iron out the differences born of the monstrous Communist parenthesis. But the wars in

Chechnya and Syria, the culture of Putin's satrapy, which stifles all dissent, muzzles the press, rehabilitates Stalin and has its opponents murdered, all reveal the farce of 'Russian democracy'. It only lasted about fifteen years at best, and then only under the rule of a consummate drunkard, Boris Yeltsin, who, in spite of himself, equated it with anarchy and misery, under the domination of corrupt oligarchs who settled their disputes with kalashnikovs. Along with gas and oil, violence, prostitution, alcohol and poisoning have been the Russian Federation's main exports since the turn of the century.

Again, Vassili Grossman tells us that while the history of the West is the story of a gradual expansion of freedoms, Russian history tells the opposite story, a gradual expansion of servitude: 'Russian progress and Russian slavery were shackled together by a thousand-year-old chain. Every move forward toward the light only deepened the black pit of serfdom.' As far back as 1839, the Marquis de Custine, who is to Russia what Alexandre de Tocqueville is to the United States, wrote, going against the tide of a Russophilia that had blinded Voltaire and Diderot: Russians ... 'great and small' are 'drunk with slavery'.[23] The USSR never examined its conscience as the Germans did after the war. The Soviet mentality of submission to the powers-that-be persisted in so-called 'democratic' Russia.

But in France we love a romantic Russia, infused with nostalgia and passion for Rachmaninov, Tolstoy and Pushkin, set against a backdrop of landscapes sparkling with snow. This fiction acted as a screen between the French elite and the reality of this continent. Not forgetting all those in the anti-American camp looking to Moscow for a counterweight to Washington. Now, after more than twenty years of autocratic power, Vladimir Putin and his team of oligarchs, leading lights and lackeys, all thirsting for revenge against Europe and the West, launched the war in

Ukraine, certain of crushing the power of Zelensky and his clique of 'Nazis', or rather 'Ukronazis' (not forgetting the 'LGBT Nazis'), in a matter of days. The military setbacks suffered by his troops and the revival of NATO are further proof that despotism only has a future when democracies are asleep. We have overestimated the power of the former Red Army and underestimated the deep state of submission in which 'eternal Russia' lives, despite the courage of some exceptional dissidents, including Alexei Navalny.

A geostrategic challenge

We now know that the long period of calm that followed the Second World War was an exception, not the norm. Dialogue, goodwill and gentle commerce have never succeeded in disarming tyrants. You don't choose your enemies; it's they who vindictively single you out and decide that your mere existence offends them. No matter what we do to prove our goodwill, they will never stop trying to diminish or enslave us. Not only has Ukraine woken Europe up, it has also brought the United States out of its humiliation, after twenty years of lost wars and the debacle in Kabul in August–September 2021. After a few weeks of prevarication, the Biden administration realized the benefits it could draw from Ukraine's first victories. America, strengthened by its military and technological advantage, is majestically back on the scene without losing a single patriotic son. Although deeply divided, it is once again Madeleine Albright's 'indispensable nation', leader of the free world in its support for oppressed peoples, until perhaps a new President decides otherwise. Europe, alas, remains a political and military dwarf, of its own volition, cowering under the NATO umbrella. America is deploying its new weapons on the ground and sending an unambiguous signal to the Chinese: if you touch Taiwan, you will pay a high price.

The real challenge for Ukraine will not only be military, it will be cultural. How can they escape the Russian magnetic effect, whereby the immense wealth of literature, music and film that was partly stolen from Kiev the whole world, rightly or wrongly, continues to attribute to Russia? Gogol, for instance, may have been born in the heart of today's Ukraine, and may have begun his career with Ukrainian stories, but in our eyes he will always be a Russian writer. Can this surgical divorce, sealed by rivers of blood, take the torch of the Slavic world from their great neighbour and eclipse it? Ukraine is also teaching us a lesson in courage and realpolitik. We moan about a few degrees more or less in temperature, while the Ukrainians are resisting in the dark, the mud and the cold. We see ourselves as collective victims; they are reviving the figure of the ordinary hero, fighting for the most sacred cause of all, freedom. They are dying for a future where brutes and barbarians will no longer have the right to dominate and enslave people. Europe has loved peace too much, but so has Israel, despite its warlike reputation. The worst enemy of peace is peace itself, by providing a false sense of calm and invincibility.

A delicate reckoning for the Allies: Ukraine must not collapse, but neither must Russia, lest its 6,000 nuclear warheads fall into the wrong hands. The Union, plagued by the risk of civil war, must hold out at all costs. This explains the Western palinode, with its drip-feed delivery of weapons, tanks, cannons and aircraft to Kiev, which is prolonging the war and the suffering of civilians.

As the Marquis de Custine said as long ago as 1839: Russia is a vast prison in which the Tsar is only the most decorated inmate. Who will free the Russian people from their chains? Who will rescue them from poverty, sadness, arbitrariness and apathy?[24] Both Moscow and Tehran are betting, perhaps rightly so, on Europe and the United States tiring of the situation. 'Victory goes to he who holds out for the last quarter hour', as Clausewitz famously put it. If the fortunes of battle turn against the Ukrainians, if the Russian steamroller ends up rolling over them, they will be found wanting. Already the professors of resignation, in the name of realism, are urging them to negotiate at any price with a Putin who is far from defeated. If, by some misfortune, Ukraine were to fall, NATO would in turn collapse and Europe would be threatened to its very foundations, at the mercy of the Moscow ogre. It would become a luxury sanatorium, ready to be torn apart piece by piece by any predator. Any unreasonable accommodation with the current Kremlin would be paid for a hundredfold by our children and grandchildren. As for the 'global South', to use that rubbery term, it will follow the winner. If Russia, the bridgehead of the international federation of thugs, wins, predators of all kinds will be rubbing their hands. Looting, killing and violence will be exonerated by the example of big brother in Moscow. On the other hand, if Putin's army is held in check, despots on every continent and terrorist groups will think twice. This is an opportunity for democracies to seize this historic moment and strive for a new 9 November 1989, bringing down the wall of all tyrannies, from Beijing to Moscow, from Tehran to Baku, not forgetting Ankara, Caracas, Algiers, Havana and a few others. It's a fragile glimmer of hope in the darkness of barbarism.

FORGERS AND IMPOSTORS

In 1995, a certain Binjamin Wilkomirski, a Swiss musician and instrument maker, published a book in German entitled *Fragments: Memories of a Wartime*

Childhood, in which he recounts his youth during the Nazi occupation of Poland and his internment in Majdanek and Auschwitz. The book was enthusiastically received and translated into thirteen languages, with glowing reviews in *Le Monde*, *The New York Times* and *The Guardian*. He received invitations from Jewish associations all over the world. But the Swiss press began to question inconsistencies in the story, and an investigation revealed that Wilkomirski was not born in Latvia but in Switzerland to a certain Yvonne Grosjean, who placed him in an orphanage, after which he was adopted by the Dössekker family. If he experienced the German extermination camps, it was as a simple tourist. His book was withdrawn from sale. And the sad truth emerged that the author of the hoax simply wanted a bit more tragedy in his life.

Enric Marco (1921–2022) was a Catalan mechanic who for a quarter of a century was the spokesperson for the Spanish deportees. He claimed to have been interned in the Flossenbürg camp in Bavaria. His outspokenness and energy carried his listeners along, and he even brought the Cortes parliamentarians to tears as he told of the dogs and beatings by the SS.[25] At the age of eighty-four, unmasked by an historian, Marco half-heartedly admitted his deception. In 1941 he was a civilian volunteer in an assembly plant in Kiel, in northern Germany, where he claims to have been imprisoned and tortured by the Nazis. The novelist Javier Cercas devoted a novel to this brilliant dissembler, who continued to lie and trick his interlocutors, even after he had been caught out.[26]

But the fabulists are multiplying and spreading their fictions. In July 2004, a young woman of twenty-three told the police that she had been the victim of an anti-Semitic attack on a suburban train. Young people of immigrant origins had allegedly slashed her face and drawn a swastika on her stomach with a felt-tip pen. An investigation revealed that the attack was all made up, and the young woman was given a four-month suspended prison sentence. Other incidents of the same type followed. In 2014, an ex-Femen woman claimed to have been attacked by Salafists in Place Clichy. Between 2014 and 2015, bus drivers claimed to have been attacked with box cutters by young people from the suburbs, and a teacher at a Jewish school in Marseille claimed to have been stabbed by three men allegedly members of the Islamic State. These incidents take place against a backdrop of real violence and attacks that are, unfortunately, not imaginary. The simulacra could not have happened without the probability factor rendering them plausible. At the same time, before or after, citizens of the Jewish faith were killed by Islamists, bus drivers assaulted and a secondary school teacher beheaded. The false victims multiply as the cries of the real victims echo down through history. A context of verisimilitude is needed to make the fakes possible. Imitators want to take advantage of public compassion to usurp a status. But forgeries do not erase the originals.

Victimization is the appropriation of a title that one does not deserve. One can call oneself a victim by hearsay, by ricochet, by contiguity. The Bataclan theatre on 13 November 2015 had its share of charlatans, a few dozen, driven by the lure of gain or the need for notoriety. The most famous is Florence M, alias Flo Kitty, who invented a false friend at the

Bataclan and forged a perfectly meticulous story. A professional mythomaniac, she infiltrated the Life for Paris survivors' organization, making herself indispensable, organizing concerts and parties and in turn exposing the liars who passed themselves off as survivors. One can envy the happiness of others, but even more so their misfortune, which provides one with a beautiful story, offers the warmth among survivors, and an active community. This symbolic decoration gives us every right; it makes us more interesting; it takes us out of the anonymous mass. We exist, at last, in the full light of day.

CHAPTER 7

Towards a generalized 'gynocide'?

How should we think about relations between men and women? Only through crimes against humanity, says a certain North American feminism. As early as the 1980s, the activist Andrea Dworkin (1946–2005) saw the porn industry as 'an instrument of genocide' or, to put it another way, 'Dachau brought into the bedroom and celebrated.'[1] The common thread linking the Third Reich to *Playboy* and even more to *Penthouse* (soft-porn magazines of the late twentieth century) is pornography, which some liberals insist on defending even though it is 'worse than Hitler', if we are to believe the jurist Catharine MacKinnon: 'Even Hitler didn't know how to turn killing into sex the way the pornographic industry does.'[2] There has apparently been a war between men and women since prehistoric times.[3] According to Marilyn French (1929–2009), making love to a man is almost always synonymous with brutality and murder: 'American culture – movies, books, songs, television – teaches men to see themselves as killers, to identify the act of murder with sex, and the sex act with violent conquest. This is why so many men find it difficult to distinguish between rape and lovemaking.'[4]

From prehistoric times to the present day, it seems, rape has played a particular function: 'a conscious process of intimidation by which all men keep all women in a state of fear'.[5]

Comparison is folly

Forty years ago, these activists who placed the relationship between the sexes under the aegis of the Shoah set an example. To take a recent case, after lodging a complaint against director Christophe Ruggia, who was accused of sexually assaulting her when she was twelve, the actor Adèle Haenel was described as a successor to Primo Levi. According to Frédérik Detue, an academic and 'specialist in mass crime',[6] there is a real overlap between the young actress who was the victim of the assault and the Auschwitz deportee. Both were in compliance with the principle of sobriety in order to prepare the ground for the judges without resorting to 'the pathos of the victim or the vehemence of the avenger'. The actor, who admits her admiration for Louis-Ferdinand Céline and, along with French director Céline Sciamma, in March 2023 called for the release of Palestinian terrorist Georges Ibrahim Abdallah, who is being held in France with the support of Hezbollah and Iran, did not deny this comparison. Note that Primo Levi wrote *If This Is a Man* in 1947 to prevent his experience as a deportee from being forgotten, as the atrocities of life in a concentration camp made it hard to believe for the general public. The names of Robert Antelme, another Buchenwald deportee, and Walter Benjamin, the anti-Nazi German philosopher who committed suicide in Portbou (Spain) on 26 September 1940, are also shamelessly brought forward to evoke the 'survivor' Adèle Haenel.

The parallel is not only surprising, it is inappropriate. There is no Richter scale of suffering, but couldn't we envisage a gradation that would allow us to evaluate the different crimes? Do we have to go all the way back to Nazism to think about sexual aggression, thereby trivializing the vocabulary of crimes against humanity? Confusing intimate wounds with extreme situations sheds no light on either. Why should anyone who has been the victim of an attempted rape be equated with the men and women tortured during the Shoah? This *reductio ad Hitlerum* marks the desire to make rape a crime worse than murder and its victims the representatives of modern genocide. It was after the war that psychiatrist Leo Eitinger (1912–96), a Norwegian from Moravia and a former deportee to Auschwitz and Buchenwald, identified the 'survivor syndrome' and paved the way for the concept of post-traumatic stress disorder for camp survivors.

There are countries where an actual war on women has been declared: Afghanistan and Iran. In Afghanistan, women are locked up, banned from school and university, confined to the home, reduced to the role of breeders and housewives, and forced to wear the burqa. In Iran, thousands of young girls are being poisoned in dozens of schools for rebelling against the mullahs' orders and wanting to take off their headscarves. In both cases there is repression, torture, death by hanging or beating: 'Young girls are being excluded from their own epoch and prevented from living in today's world. It's a blow to any little girl's curiosity; it murders the wonderful idea of childhood', Véronique Nahoum-Grappe and Marie Ladier-Fouladi rightly say.[7] 'Genocide against one of the sexes is impossible for the human race. But the Taliban can dream of it.'

In this specific case alone, the notion of 'gynocide' (coined by the feminist activist Antoinette Fouque[8]), including the selective abortion of female foetuses in India and China, as well as infanticide, could be brandished by an international court to indict the powers concerned. In short, Afghanistan, Iran, Pakistan under the thumb of Islamists, sub-Saharan Africa where the practice of clitoridectomy and infibulation dominates, and the Great Lakes region where mass rape has been taking place for twenty years, as denounced by the gynaecologist and Nobel Peace Prize winner Denis Mukwege, are all areas where a real war against women is in full swing.

While women have for too long remained without rights – citizenship, the right to control their own bodies, economic rights – the consolidation of legal equality has been a long road, almost completed today, at least in most liberal democracies. In a strange twist, a whole section of the feminist movement prefers to make a general accusation against men rather than incriminating this or that culture for fear of being suspected of racism. It is on the issue of the Islamic veil that the debate has stumbled. The philosopher Judith Butler urged Afghan women not to remove their headscarves after the fall of the Taliban so as not to collaborate with American imperialism. They had to 'understand the important cultural meanings of the burqa, an exercise in modesty and pride, a protection against shame, a veil behind which feminine agency can and does operate'.[9] One has every right to hate the United States, but recommending that Afghan women remain under lock and key sounds strangely like colonial condescension on the part of a woman who enjoys every freedom. To refuse to distinguish between liberal regimes that grant rights to their citizens and dictatorships that flout them is only to show how indifferent Ms Butler is to the situation of women in Afghanistan. A certain kind of feminism is caught between its militant convictions and its hatred of men (especially if they are white and heterosexual). The craze for the veil does a poor job of masking the Orwellian reversal that presents servitude as liberation, or the headscarf as an instrument of deliverance. As the ecologist senator Esther Benbassa declared: 'The veil is no more alienating than the miniskirt.'[10] So let's hail the apartheid of women in Islamic lands as a dawn of freedom!

Violence against women

If there is a genocide against women, we should be seeing a decline in the world's female population. In France, on 1 January 2019, women represented 51.6% of the population, 2.2 million more than men. In the European Union, which has 447 million inhabitants, 51% of the population is female. Worldwide, there are 102 men for every 100 women, and it is in the United Arab Emirates that the percentage of men exceeds that of women, with a ratio of 221 to 100 (due to the presence of a large number of immigrant workers. This is the highest ratio in the world, apart from the Vatican!). The term *gynocide* is therefore imprecise if it is not geographically and politically localized.

What remains is the absolute outrage of what is now called 'feminicide' (even if the word has not entered the Penal Code, which in 1994 also abolished parricide, matricide and infanticide[11]) to replace the old term 'crime of passion', since we fortunately no longer accept the idea of husbands going mad and killing. How, then, are we to describe the murder of a wife's lover by her lawful husband, or the premeditated murder of her husband by a jealous or exasperated wife? What's to say that love isn't closely linked to hatred in certain cases? But there is a gulf between hatred and acting it out, a gulf called civilization, or restraint.

Violence, as we know, is mostly masculine, which does not make all men brutes, the nuance being significant. Feminicide combines two scandals: savagery – killing a woman because she leaves you[12] – and the negligence of the authorities ignoring calls for help. What could have been avoided came to pass. In 41% of cases, the victims had warned the police of the risks they were running.[13] Like the murder of children, feminicide comes at the end of the long fight for the rights of the weakest members of society that began several centuries ago and was wrongly thought to have been won. This collective desire to put an end to infamy is relatively recent. In France, the fight against domestic violence has been a national cause since 2019. Filing complaints has been made easier; police officers and judges have been trained. There were 122 women killed by their partners in 2021; 102 in 2022; 94 in 2023; 208,000 have suffered domestic violence according to a census by the Ministry of the Interior and every political party is involved in the fight. Progress has been made; the 'grave danger' telephone number can be used to alert the authorities; bracelets restricting dangerous partners have been fitted; and the law of 28 February 2023 created universal emergency assistance for victims of domestic violence in the form of a loan. Yet the murders continue, atrocious murders, and everyone wants to find a way out of the abjection this macabre accounting puts us in.

But 'to kill one's wife is not to kill a woman'.[14] Feminicide has two meanings: the murder of a woman by chance or intention, and the murder of a wife or partner out of revenge. The Argentinian-Brazilian anthropologist Rita Laura Segato explains that a war is being waged on women as women. A merciless war, adds the Italian Silvia Federici,[15] and this violence against the weakest of the weak is said to be the breeding ground for all the brutalities that have appeared on earth. We know of these 'masculinist' groups who meet in the forest to rediscover their lost male strength, or who organize men-only seminars. Anglo-Saxons have coined an interesting neologism, *Incels* (*involuntary celibates*), to describe heterosexual bachelors who, because of their lack of romantic success, resent women in general (and attractive men). They take revenge through misogyny, resentment and even mass murder.[16] If the first condition of any amorous education is consent, an intangible dogma, the second is the possibility of rebuff. If I like someone, it doesn't mean they like me, and my desire is no contract of indebtedness for others to pay back. Seduction is also a market in which each of us has a value that varies according to our physical appearance, age, knowledge, people skills and wealth; the fortunate have a procession of suitors chasing them, the unlucky a host of fiascos. The terrible thing about a snub in our society is that it can't be blamed on society or the State. So, no matter how much I plead with the other, it's my very being that leaves them cold. The sentence is as clear-cut as in a court of law: no thanks, not you. But making all women pay for the failures suffered by a few is a pathology. If all those rejected by love had to react by killing, our streets would be littered with corpses.

A new grammar of love?

The past half-century has seen sexuality removed from the realm of mere hedonism to become a huge domain of error; a kind of ironic reversal of the old Puritanism, which has found its ultimate triumph in this metamorphosis, in the name of protecting women. The penis, in turn, has sunk into the age of suspicion.

The great success of #MeToo, apart from the conviction of famous rapists, is that it has rewritten the grammar of love from the criminal point of view. All the stages of seduction, from consent to the carnal act, have been reconsidered, not in the name of enjoyment but with the possible violation of a person's integrity in mind. The movement has been in the pipeline since the 1980s, at least in the United States, but #MeToo is successfully seeking to rewrite the Criminal Code to supersede the old one.[17] Investigative journalists in every profession (publishing, theatre, film, opera, sports, politics) are conducting surveys to determine the percentage of sex offenders and pillory them, the American 'name and shame' movement. If we believe feminist activist Caroline De Haas's theorem ('One man in two or three is an aggressor') that women are the victims and men the offenders *par excellence*, all seductive acts are subject to mistrust. A light-hearted proposal or a gaze that is too intense is tantamount to an assault or an attack. Erotic relations must be viewed from the perspective of the worst crime. This is the meaning of the famous notion of continuum, which assumes a logical correspondence between boys' mini-assaults on girls, lecherous glances, inappropriate smiles and, worst of all, forced sex, assault and murder. The main effect of extending the definition of rape to include trivial gestures is to drown this crime in the indistinct sea of microscopic offences and exonerate the aggressors. It's all the same; the main thing is not so much to punish the outrage as to straighten out the behaviour of boys, from childhood to adulthood.

By suggesting that violence will be perpetuated according to the old principle of 'he who takes an inch will take a mile', we are evacuating an idea that is at the very foundation of justice: the proportionality between crime and punishment. As in Spielberg's 2002 film *Minority Report*, we need to strike at the heart of masculinity and detect wrongdoing before it even happens, using a whole system of prevention. This is called 'zero tolerance', as in some American states, including California, where breaking a window results in immediate imprisonment. And three jail terms mean life imprisonment. This is the principle behind the alarming 'three strikes' law, which punishes repeat offenders, even for minor offences, and abandons any idea of rehabilitation. So there is no need to distinguish different kinds of actions, running the risk of a return to the worst judicial practices of the nineteenth century, which saw the petty thief's delinquency as the seed of a future crime boss. In England, until the end of the nineteenth century, children were hanged for stealing a piece of fruit. An invisible thread links a saucy remark, inappropriate gestures and forced sex in an irrepressible spiral. What they are calling for is a radical overhaul of the whole world of amorous relationships to build what Irène Théry calls a 'new sexual civility'.

A *new name for passion?*

In this way, being in love can be renamed 'having a hold over' [*emprise*] and the courts have sought to recharacterize it in legal terms.[18] If I love someone, whether I like it or not, I give that person full power over me and the ability to put me on a pedestal or throw me into the gutter. There is an element of subjugation in this feeling, an excessive control that is abused by would-be despots. But you can't love someone without alienating all or part of their freedom. Even in the throes of passion, you can become possessed by the other person. The only way out of love is from a mixture of enchantment and servitude, or rather an enchanted servitude. If you want to remain master of yourself and the universe, and not allow yourself to be taken over by the other person, then you are not in love, or you are confusing a sentimental relationship with a contract. All passions bring joy and unhappiness, indiscriminately, for women and men alike.

As for consent, American jurist Catharine MacKinnon and others have argued that it too is deceptive and needs to be deconstructed from a legal point of view, since it brings two people of unequal status and strength face to face.[19] How could a woman freely desire her tormentor? The MeToo hashtag not only frees speech and denounces sexist violence, it also makes male desire suspect.[20] What used to be called seduction is in reality a form of control. The gaze, for example, is not neutral; it is a sometimes unwarranted taking of possession that can turn into 'eye rape'. In the United States, an insistent stare in a public place can justify calling the police. Speech itself is a double-edged sword: it can embellish, trapping the other person in misleading compliments and nonsense, but it can also offend when it objectifies the body and reduces it to a number of parts. It would be sexist to comment on women's dress, even to admire it. Such an attitude is a form of discrimination, lookism, the pathological attachment to appearance. It is well known, of course, that women never judge a man on his looks, only on his 'inner beauty'. So chatting up or flirting is predation, pure and simple. It's worth noting that historian Ivan Jablonka has attempted to define a form of 'nice guy' seduction based on 'gender justice' which would get rid of the condescendingly sexist kind of flattery.[21] He fell right into it. Feminists, furious to see a male encroaching on their field of expertise, put him in his place. Camille Froidevaux-Metterie was 'outraged' to read Jablonka's book. It had no right to ascribe a pioneering role to itself, by playing down the work of women who have been thinking about male domination for ages.[22] A man can never be feminist enough for feminists because he is forever guilty of being a man.

Fairy tales and rape culture?

Nothing should be said about women any more; that some are frivolous, flirtatious or narcissistic, intelligent or silly, ugly or pretty, fat or thin. The mere use of a qualifier, whether laudatory or not – because a compliment is also an affront – is sexist. Women have become untouchable, barely describable beings, like God in negative theology. The day after the death of the French-Czech writer Milan Kundera, in July 2023, *The New York Times* pointed out, after the usual tributes, that his novels were riddled with weak or ridiculous female characters (the male characters are too). A crime of *lèse-majesté* that deprived him of the Nobel Prize! According to some feminists, women alone escape all definition, standing beyond all categories, in a kind of idealism outside language. For Judith Butler, there is no such thing as female sexuality, which would be tantamount to fixing women in a biological destiny constructed by and within male discourse.[23] Since women have always lived under a patriarchal regime, they have only ever been represented through the male gaze, which was true until the post-war period. But women today are painters as well as painted, novelists as well as novels' heroines, directors as well as actors.

But should we reject all the female characters in past paintings, literature and theatre? 'Children's stories are also the primary testing ground for rape culture',[24] as *France Culture* put it in 2017; a British mother had taken offence at the fact that the kiss given to Sleeping Beauty was not consensual, and for good reason, since she was asleep. Snow White herself was woken by a prince who kissed her without asking. The kiss, which had accompanied the liberation of morals after 1945, once again became a source of turbulence and prohibition, as it was under the Ancien Régime.[25] Molière's *Les Précieuses*

Ridicules, a shameful mockery of the second sex's desire to learn, and Proust's Mme Verdurin, the consummate snob, are also deconstructed as examples of blatant misogyny.[26] And let's not forget the female characters in paintings, such as Picasso's, the epitome of the macho rapist and predator described by an Icelandic artist, Olafur Eliasson, as 'the Harvey Weinstein of his time'.[27] We can no longer even say the word woman, according to Judith Butler, which presupposes an identity and a subject produced by a dated social system,[28] a function of an historical context.[29]

Women are therefore advised to be wary of those they love. A romance would be nothing more than 'rape embellished with meaningful looks', according to Andrea Dworkin,[30] a relationship of domination in disguise; and for Susan Faludi, women become reconciled to living with the men in their lives.[31] These propositions are perfectly reversible. Do we not know that heartbreak also affects men and drives some of them to suicide? But it is absolutely essential that women are the symbol of the exploited and the embodiment of the most abysmal suffering. She can only exist in a state of collapse, never a strong subject, sure of her rights and determined to build her own life. A certain neo-feminism doesn't so much want to liberate women as to *dictate* to them, to make them ashamed to continue to associate with men. It wants them to be broken so that it can control them better. Victimizing all women means infantilizing them, denying them all freedom and responsibility.

Justice on trial

In France, the judicial system looks like a tanker paralysed by its massive size and lack of funding. Many citizens give up on filing a complaint, discouraged in advance by the inertia of this enormous machine, capable of crushing any individual. Its frosty pomposity is enough to frighten the layperson, with its language as abstruse as ecclesiastical Latin. Let's imagine the ordeal for a rape victim, the humiliation of having to explain every stage of a forced penetration to officials who tend to be sceptical. This is why police officers responsible for dealing with abused or battered women and children need even better training. The crisis in the justice system is twofold; on the side of the complainants, who feel forgotten, and on the side of the accused, who want to clear their name. It is rare for a verdict to satisfy all parties. The convicted person groans at the intransigence of the judgement, the victims deplore the laxity. Like democracy, justice by its very nature disappoints in the quest for an impossible balance between crime and punishment. A trial can be carried out perfectly but be unsatisfactory in its decision. The more the institution ignores complaints and mistreatment, the more it reinforces the suspicion that it is biased. The desire for trial by social media then triumphs, favouring a parallel justice system, electronic or street justice, which settles in alongside the other. Digital mobs are not 'sentimental mobs' but hellish mobs. Every accusation is a conviction, regardless of the evidence. The ancient practice of lynching in the name of virtue is thus rehabilitated. How many neo-feminists would like to rewrite the Penal Code, institute special courts for rapists or supposed rapists, and suspend all the constitutional guarantees attached to each and every one of us?

To take up an oft-misquoted figure, it is not 1% of people accused of rape who are convicted but 14.7%, according to statistics from the Ministry of Justice.[32] The percentage may be deemed insufficient, but we cannot dictate the sentence for the judges and ignore the founding principle of 'reasonable doubt' protecting the accused. Our system is based on evidence, which is always difficult to adduce in cases of rape. There is a risk that the number of cases dismissed will skyrocket because of a lack of tangible facts, if we are content to simply let people talk without educating them. The challenge is to fight crime while preserving the presumption of innocence. Back in 2020, women criminal lawyers were already expressing alarm at the fact that 'the presumption of guilt is too often invoked in cases of sexual offences'.[33] The petitioners continued:

> We take great pains to point this out, but no accusation is ever proof of anything: it would otherwise be enough to assert the truth alone to prove and condemn ... to presume the good faith of any woman who claims to be a victim of sexual violence would be tantamount to arbitrarily sanctifying her word, and in no way to 'liberating' it.[34]

Taking victims at their word runs the risk of confusing a justified complaint with a slanderous denunciation. Why bother with an investigation and why not throw the accused straight into prison, without a trial? Why not reintroduce the law of suspects? Justice is not a literary 'story' but the most accurate possible way to establish the facts ascribed, once they have been heard. Judicial truth is conformity with events, and deliberation must be based on evidence, without which there can be no fair sentence. Judges' detachment, far removed from human passions, is also what enables them to weigh up the pros and cons, at equal distance from the cases put by the prosecution and the defence. Judges are constantly faced with two voids: letting a wrong go unpunished, and punishing the innocent. But the fact that there are miscarriages of justice and that certain offences go unpunished does not mean that we should disdain justice as merely an offshoot of the powers that be. If it is legitimate to criticize it relentlessly, it is in order to improve it, not to discredit it because of its imperfections. Otherwise it is 'kidnapped by its victims' and paralysed in its exercise.[35] We must patiently follow the long process of the law, or return to barbarism.

Since 10 April 2018, the statute of limitations for rape of a minor has been set longer than for war crimes or terrorist crime, since in the former case the thirty-year period begins when the victim reaches the age of majority.[36] Some even argue that rape should be punishable by life imprisonment with no statute of limitations, like crimes against humanity.[37] So where is the penalty scale? Should rape be punished like murder? It's a truism that you can survive rape, but never murder. The #MeToo theology is merciless: forgiveness no longer exists; sinners cannot be redeemed even if they serve their sentences. They are thrown alive into the cauldron of the damned. There is an intransigence with our new (feminist) investigators that makes them strangers to two essential dimensions of human affairs: redemption and proportionality.

Shared savagery

Finally, in what universe are women better than men? The fact that they have been oppressed or relegated for centuries in most societies does not mean that they have all the virtues. Rape might be overwhelmingly male, but barbarity belongs to both sexes. We have confused a provisional inability to do evil with ontological candour. Whenever women have been in positions of power, in Nazi concentration camps or in ISIS, they have behaved with the same savagery as men. Margarete Buber-Neumann, deported to Ravensbrück after having been in Siberia under Stalin, recounts the incredible sadism of the female SS guards and kapos towards the women inmates.[38] These 'grey wolves', with their terrifying uniforms, were fascinated by Hitler and eager to correct the 'recalcitrant elements' of Nazi society.[39] Spacious, comfortable accommodation, good salaries, access to positions of responsibility that were usually closed to them, they had female prisoners at their beck and call: servants, sex slaves and guinea pigs who could be tortured and killed at will. They were guaranteed an idyllic life where there was no shortage of distractions, sports, cinema, outings and casinos.[40] There were female executioners throughout the concentration camp system (Irma Grese, Maria Mandl, Hermine Braunsteiner, among others), some of whom were hanged after the war for crimes against humanity. Lina Haag, a survivor of the Lichtenburg camp, has testified as follows: 'They are fantastic, frightening creatures, reminiscent of dark fairy stories. They have no pity; they are probably more dangerous than the SS executioners because they are women.'[41]

As for the Islamic State's black widows, the *muhâjirât*, they have occupied a fairly high position in the organization's hierarchy. As propagandists, recruiters, bloggers and killers, their cruelty and sadism terrify all those who have the misfortune to fall into their hands. Thousands of teenage girls from the West and the Middle East – barbarism always recruits from among the young – have gone to Syria to take part in the jihad. Here too, as in the case of the Nazi kapos, joining ISIS 'is the primary factor of attraction for European and Western women, who are given quite different roles and positions from those they had in their countries of origin'.[42] Some have risen very high in the narrow circle of ISIS ideologues, occupying various positions in the ministries and displaying a total lack of pity, justifying beheadings, attacks, the killing of infidels and other miscreants as well as the enslavement of Christian, Yazidi and Kurdish women, etc. Female 'returnees' are now systematically indicted to stand trial on an equal footing with men, despite persistent clichés about maternal compassion.[43] A thirty-year-old German woman who left to join ISIS was sentenced to ten years' imprisonment for leaving her five-year-old Yazidi slave to die of thirst in the sun. Knowing that these radicalized women have returned to France, and can therefore be released in a few years' time, is not at all reassuring. But, in the name of the saccharine image of motherhood, these mothers or wives are deemed worthy of immediate repatriation.

Cruelty increases when ordinary people are given the power of life and death over others. Germaine Tillion, who was deported to Ravensbrück, calculated that it took between four and twenty days to brutalize the very young female supervisors in the Nazi camps. Novices, who were almost apologetic to the prisoners at first, by the end of a week would beat them to a pulp, sometimes to death. Female fanaticism keeps up with its male equivalent. It was the uniform plus the boots and the headgear that turned them into bloodthirsty killers, just as the abaya and the veil metamorphose a little Breton girl or the schoolgirl from Berlin or Madrid into a fury ready to slaughter for Allah once they get to the land of Sham (Syria). Have we forgotten that at Abu Ghraib, the American detention centre in Iraq at the turn of the century, women also administered torture and beatings to the prisoners? The photo of Lynndie England, aged twenty-two, holding an Iraqi prisoner on a leash went around the world.[44] Even more recently, did we not see a female footballer, Kheira Hamraoui, a midfielder for Paris Saint-Germain, beaten with an iron bar on the orders of her teammate, who was mad with jealousy and wanted to break her legs?[45]

If the problem of our societies is men's violence against women, women are also aggressors, even if this truth is difficult to hear. As long ago as 2000, John Archer, a specialist in human aggression, noted, based on numerous studies of family conflicts, that female violence was a neglected problem. This is borne out by the figures for altercations, assaults and injuries in LGBT couples, with a prevalence among lesbians and bisexual women. Women are just as violent with each other as men are with women, and the same is true of bisexual and trans women.[46] There are also abusive mothers who make their children ill (Munchhausen syndrome by proxy), incestuous mothers (in small numbers) and mothers who are complicit in the rape of their offspring. Wherever women have taken power, in business, academia or politics, they have generally behaved like men. Neither worse nor better, just human, terribly human, capable like everyone else of the most generous initiatives as well as the most awful acts.

Towards creative discord?

The hatred of men expressed by some feminists is all the more strange given that almost everyone agrees on rape, incest, paedophilia and harassment. That's the problem: the more global the consensus, the more conflict needs to be re-created. Need we be reminded that men are not just enemies to be destroyed, but also lovers, partners, brothers, fathers, friends and husbands? The insurgency often waged jointly by both sexes, as in Iran today, should never exclude the possibility of reconciliation. Futile obsession over this confrontation erases the formidable gains made by the feminist movement over the last century. We also forget the powerful force of attraction that, despite everything, the two sexes exert on each other, the multilayered poetry of carnal pleasure that only pious women or the stubborn seem to want to crush. Nothing does more harm to neo-feminism than the army of its advocates, bogged down in their pointless quarrels between rival sects, with their anathemas and their overblown rhetoric. The desire to make all women, whoever they may be, into the victim class *par excellence* (whether society dame, princess or proletarian, regardless of age, social class or gender) is a clear contradiction in terms.

It's a way of stealing the problems of the oppressed instead of coming to their rescue. Syrian human rights activist Omar Youssef Souleimane, a naturalized French citizen, bitterly denounces woke agitators as spoilt children from rich countries, when so many men and women in the Arab-Muslim world are fighting 'against a truly patriarchal and oppressive dictatorship'.[47] Let's be honest, wokeism also affects conservatives on the American right, such as Ben Shapiro and Charlie Kirk, who are outraged by the *Barbie* blockbuster movie and see it as 'propaganda for the transgender mafia'. That such a flash in the pan should scandalize people says a lot about the porosity between the American left and right.[48] Not to mention the works of Shakespeare banned from certain schools in Ron DeSantis's Florida because they were deemed too sexual.[49] In the United States, political correctness and cancel culture transcend party lines and draw on the common ground of McCarthyism, itself a product of Protestant puritanism.

We often, quite rightly, talk about the glass ceiling facing the second sex; we forget the mud floor: the dirty jobs that men have to do – garbage collectors, bicycle delivery guys, construction workers, sewage workers, soldiers, and so on. Neo-feminist victimization is not the result of regression but of undeniable progress in the status of women, even if the gains made are never irreversible. The criminalization of abortion by the Supreme Court in the United States, a concession made to the most conservative Christians, led to the Republicans losing in the mid-term elections in 2022 and prompted Ohio to enshrine the right to abortion in its Constitution in November 2023. Women are forced to arbitrate among their professional, family and amorous obligations, and have to reinvent themselves, uncertainly, through trial and error. While discrimination and violence remain undeniable, it is in everyone's interest that they be corrected or punished. As we have known since de Tocqueville, it is when the principle of equality is achieved for all that the remaining inequalities become intolerable. If everything has (almost) already been won, the last bastions to be taken give rise to robust irritation. As one law succeeds another, the closer the men's and women's situations become, the animosity between them increases exponentially.

In just three generations, the lives of women in the West have changed radically. Control over fertility with smaller families, economic control with entry into working life, sexual control with the freedom to choose partners and conceive children without a father, financial independence. The transformation is so profound that it is difficult to assess. While women are storming the public arena and taking over the most senior professional sectors, men are embracing the domestic sphere – bringing up children, cooking, housework – without feeling they are falling behind, and are happy to have their paternity leave. This interchange of skills is without doubt the most interesting phenomenon of the last half-century.

A spectre is haunting neo-feminism: a possible victory after the decisive struggles of the last sixty years. Yet every victory is a disappointment. Not only has the autonomy won by women not removed the burdens associated with their condition, but it has also resulted in the heart-breaking feeling of everyone for themselves. It is the burden of the contemporary individual to have to plead every day for the weightiest cause of all, oneself, at the risk of being misunderstood. If you can hang your doubts or failures on an external cause or a grandiose structure, like patriarchy, then you are absolved of all responsibility. This is the curse of freedom, which by its very nature is disenchanting, since we can only blame ourselves for our failings. *Freedom is to liberation as prose is to poetry*. It's tempting to make a big deal out of minor events to avoid seeing that women, in the West as a whole, are winning, that the old patriarchy is on its last legs. We can play around with semantic gimmicks, switching from 'patrimoine' [heritage] to 'matrimoine', from 'hommage' [praise] to 'femmage', saying 'j'esmère' instead of 'j'espère',[50] advocating inclusive writing whose main characteristic is above all to exclude those who do not possess the codes. This grammatical tinkering does not put the masculine on an equal footing with the feminine, it draws a line between the progressivist elite and the backward plebs. This means that the hardest part has been done, and that we're now fiddling with the details so we can look like warriors without spending a penny. A strange alliance of intransigence and frivolity.

Clearly, what part of the feminist movement was aiming for was not so much equality as what Owen M. Fiss of Yale Law School has called 'preferential treatment',[51] independence described in terms of oppression, the most delightful position of all, offering the advantages of autonomy without the burdens it entails. We are free, but we continue to wrap ourselves in the toga of the insurgent to push responsibility as far away as possible. In this way, we benefit from the dual position of the victor and the vanquished, and we continue to fight in good conscience for freedom, equality and immaturity. Is demeaning men the only way to promote the emancipation of women? Liberation will either be joint, as in Iran, or it will be bogged down in silent bitterness. There is no point in dreaming of perfect harmony between the sexes. The division of labour and anatomical inevitability (for example, the ability to give birth, differences in enjoyment) hinder the dream of idyllic harmony. Each sex remains unfathomable to its opposite, neither as close nor as far away as it thinks, and always mysterious. The essential thing is that between them there remains a world of shared pleasures, of happy cohabitation where what brings them together is stronger than what divides, and avoids the fanatics of both sides, always ready to raise the banner of martyrdom, point an accusing finger, or indulge in outbursts of hostility. For a long time to come, we will oscillate between armed peace, passionate belligerence and secession, like two tribes camped on opposite sides of a river that is sometimes called the Enigma, sometimes the Attraction or the Grief.

IS FRANCE ITS OWN EXECUTIONER?

There is a very unhappy country in the centre of Europe, whose population is enduring torments worthy of the Inquisition, and it is France. This country was recently subjected to an iniquitous law that forces the French to work until the age of sixty-four, like all other members of the European Union (in Belgium and Germany, the retirement age is sixty-seven). 'They've already robbed us of two years of our lives with Covid', a trade union leader lamented on television. For four months, France was the scene of demonstrations, strikes and destruction. The fight against this law brought together two mythologies: the Bolshevik revolution of 1917 and the Resistance. All railway workers, including TGV drivers who retire at fifty-three, mobilized to the tune of the Battle of the Railways that had been sung between 1940 and 1944, when they were resistance saboteurs. In the media, union representatives, intellectuals and politicians came out to denounce the injustice of the plan. President Macron was called a 'hired killer', Caligula and Hitler. High school and university students marched heroically for their pensions alongside the workers. Protesting against a poorly thought-out project, against standards that strangle you, like European and French farmers during the winter of 2024, is perfectly legitimate; but why, over a simple adjustment measure, this collective hysteria that looks more like an exorcism than a revolt?

Our compatriots are caught in an aporia. They are traditionally hostile to money because of their Catholic and egalitarian culture, they would like to benefit from all the advantages of a developed economy – fast transport, free and efficient healthcare, cheap education, guaranteed income – without conceding to the market economy. Wealth-creating capitalism, sure, but if possible without labour, capital and its ugly bosses. 'Suffering in France' was how the psychologist Christophe Dejours entitled his 1998 book, comparing factory and office conditions to concentration camps. Our nation has a fatal addiction to moaning. Unable to rejoice at the slightest piece of good news, the French nonetheless take off on good days. They riot during the week but take their cars to the sea or the countryside on Fridays, and scrupulously respect long weekends and public holidays. The psyche of our compatriots is divided between two sacreds: the right to strike and holidays. With the arrival of spring in May, there are fewer work stoppages, trains run, petrol flows at the pumps, and the mass migration to beach and leisure activities begins. The Bolshevik revolution can be taken up again in September. This shift from insurrectionary fury to the pleasures of life is our guilty pleasure. Who could convince this people, who were capable of sudden outbursts, that they are not living in hell? Who will give the French back their *joie de vivre*? Perhaps the tens of millions of tourists who visit this land of plenty, populated by 67 million raging depressives.

The Stoics already knew. There are countless ways in which people work towards their own downfall. In France, the situation is tense, the debt has risen to 3,000 billion euros, the country is getting poorer, labour productivity is collapsing, but the unions and political parties, because of the simple proposal to raise the retirement age by two years, have found nothing better than to go on a general strike to 'bring the economy to its knees' (the CGT union). A bad economy? Let's find a way to make it even worse. A big country in trouble puts all its energy into falling even further, in a nihilistic spiral. Let's make anthropological notes on this change. In Ukraine, since 2014 and especially since 24 February 2022, young people have been fighting and dying for their freedom. In France, in 2023 as in 2010, young people were marching in the streets for their pensions ... singing the Internationale!

CHAPTER 8

Decolonize the decolonizers?

What is a cinematic remake? Usually an updated version of a classic or a re-creation based on a similar plot. Should the copy be seen as another version or as a genuine innovation based on past forms? For anyone who lived through the 1970s, 80s or 90s, what's happening today looks like a strange rehash of the past. Feminism, anti-colonialism, anti-imperialism, anti-racism, radical ecology – it all seems to be recycled *ad nauseam*, like the 1993 *Groundhog Day* film applied to our own time. When history breaks down, we can always gaze back through the rear window and plunder past achievements. The younger generations think they're inventing things, but they're rehashing them as they blame their elders. Faced with this army of replicants who seem to have come straight out of a series of franchises, with their endless declensions of prequel, sequel, spin-off and reboot applied to Frantz Fanon, Sartre, Edward Said, etc., it feels a broken record playing the same music with different voices.

But weren't we the same at their age? Wasn't May '68 itself a parody of 1917, 1936, Fidel Castro and Che Guevara? The children of the bourgeoisie played at

Bolshevism by throwing paving stones at the police. When an era looks at itself through the eyes of its predecessors, can we speak of generational plagiarism? And what's more, arrogant plagiarism: the copy seeking to shame the original for its shortcomings. Perhaps it's an age-old illusion. The heirs wanting to erase their parents while their elders denounce their ingratitude. Behind the remake, a new story is trying to emerge. Are we witnessing invention or farcical repetition?

Ah, the good old days in the colony!

The more the Western world declines, the more it puffs itself up and claims responsibility for all the horrors that are coming, global warming included. Postcolonial guilt is a symptom of our loss of influence, the latest attempt by the former dominators to believe they still matter. With each historical upheaval, we carry on repeating that it's our fault, our big bad fault. Just as one section of the left still can't get over the Bolshevik revolution, another camp is still reeling from the end of the Western empires. If Western Europe was wise enough to have given up its colonies, whether willingly or not, many of its citizens are still nostalgic for them, and not just on the right. It's as if we're back in the 1980s, last century, when the newly independent nations of Africa were accusing the former colonial power of blocking the emancipation of their peoples. It's a kind of telescoping of time and space, a superimposition of continents and eras where everything blends together. Everyone can, according to their inclinations, inhabit the virtual land of slavery, colonialism and patriarchy, which have become blurred concepts, temporary habitats that people use to highlight their anger, disgust or dismay. It is always difficult to come to terms with the times we live in. To make them easier to understand, people are strongly tempted to apply yesterday's frameworks to the present in the hope that they will make sense.

In *Le Monde* on 26 January 2023, General Bruno Clément-Bollée, former commander of the French forces in the Ivory Coast, explained that once-dominated Africa wants to cede to a sovereign Africa, and that we are living through a new phase of decolonization summed up by the slogan 'Africa for Africans'.[1] Africans will no longer put up with the arrogance of the former occupiers, who continue to reign despite simulated withdrawals, even though many of these countries' budgets are funded by Western aid. On closer inspection, this anti-French and anti-European anger seems above all to betray the desire of the Sahelian elites to do away with democratic regimes, the free press and parliamentary rule and return to autocracy, coups d'état, corruption and nepotism. Many African states, plagued by insurrections, are not so much seeking a new independence as a new sponsor, and are cheering the Russians on, the better to free themselves, just like them, from all the rules of decency and democracy. The same military juntas in Mali, Burkina Faso, the Central African Republic and Niger that want to oust the French and UN troops are delivering themselves hand and foot to the Russian Wagner criminal organization, which thrives on pillage and murder. They are less interested in regaining their independence than in changing protectors and continuing to plunder their countries with new partners. When Julius Malema, leader of a radical left-wing party in South Africa that calls for the killing of the Boers, i.e. the whites, exclaimed at a rally in July 2023: 'I support Putin, I love Putin, I am Putin', he was simply telling a truth that is inaudible to our delicate ears: I too want to be a beast like the head of the Kremlin; I want to be able to kill, murder and steal as I please. As we have seen, there is a fascination for the hammed-up virility of the Kremlin boss. But some people in Africa and Asia might be shocked by Emmanuel Macron's see-sawing ambiguity, which can appear very 'gender-fluid', more of a charmer than a leader, always ready to embrace his visitors and partners.

France's weakness makes it an ideal target: despised for no longer being tough. It has become the country people love to hate, an object of lasting resentment, according to El Hadj Souleymane Gassama.[2] That said, France has made so many mistakes in Africa – mistakes of tact, vision, arrogance and thinly disguised paternalism – that it failed to see the epidemic of coups d'état coming. You have to know when to leave when you are no longer wanted. In 2017, Macron should have abolished the CFA (African) franc and deployed French troops to English-speaking Africa and Eastern Europe. Instead, he palavered and procrastinated. But to act as if the West were still the only global player when China, India, Brazil and Russia are challenging its hegemonic role is to be tragically out of step with the times. Just as for the last seventy years we have been fed a diet of 'resistance fighters' who dream of washing away the stigma of collaboration by fighting 'fascism', so we are seeing the resurgence of a generation of 'Third Worldists' who, more than half a century after the independence of the countries of the South, are taking up the liberation struggle again, feverishly mumbling their anti-colonial catechism. Decolonization is never over, and it will continue for another fifty or a hundred years.[3] The global South myth is trotted out like a bogeyman with every analysis; this hidden jurisdiction to which we should be accountable. We are told in all seriousness that the colonial past is the 'last taboo' in French history, yet not a day goes by without an article, a book or a film on the subject! You can't see the wood for the trees.[4]

Everything has to be 'decolonized' these days – sport, cooking, philosophy, opera, music, mathematics, bodies, especially women's bodies[5] – and above all sweep away the cursed white patriarchy that generates 'androcentrism', the heart of Western tradition. What does this mean in concrete terms, what kinds of acts and projects does it involve? It's a mystery; no sooner spoken than it's done. We go back fifty or a hundred years as if nothing had happened in the meantime. All these theories bring to mind those Japanese soldiers scattered across the Pacific islands almost thirty years after the surrender of Tokyo, who still didn't know that the Second World War was over. It's a vocation to be a hero once the big battles are over, it gives you a maverick gloss without exposing yourself to the slightest risk. Serious historians of colonialism cannot let ideology or political considerations dictate their profession without reducing their discipline to the level of mere propaganda. The principle of all research is not to prejudge the results, even if they contradict the original postulates. However, in postcolonial studies – an 'academic carnival' for Jean-François Bayart – all you have to do is concur.[6] One knows in advance what one is going to find. As the manifesto of the *Parti des Indigènes de la République* put it in 2005: 'France was a colonial state ... France remains a colonial state.' It is likely to remain so until the end of time, like an indelible original sin. This is essentialist immobility; decolonialism or postcolonialism could thus last two or three times longer than the period of colonial occupation itself, or even for centuries. In truth, the trial of colonialism is being reopened not because it has been ignored or repressed, but because it provides clarity for all those who are nostalgic for the old divisions. It serves as a substitute Marxism for an entire left faction that is losing its understanding of the world.

Europe, the eternal whipping boy

But what are all these African or North African thinkers looking for when they drag old Europe into the pillory? They come to collect their compassionate dividends: the status of intellectual from the South who explores the nooks and crannies of the Western guilty conscience functions as an excellent niche. The relationship is fixed between two roles: inquisitors who apostrophize and the guilty who flagellate themselves. It is difficult to deny the history of colonialism shared by a few European nations, eight out of the twenty-seven that make up the Union today (the others, especially in the East, were for the most part colonized and enslaved by the Russians or the Ottomans, not forgetting Spain, colonized for seven centuries by the Arabs, and Languedoc from the seventh to the tenth century). Nor can we erase the history of the slave trade – but why put the burden of it solely on Westerners and exonerate the Orientals and Africans themselves? It is dubious to think that Europe owes everything to Africa and that no compensation could amortize this incalculable debt. Decolonial intellectuals present themselves as moral tax collectors, often subsidized by universities or state bodies in the Old World or the United States. Invite me in so I can curse you! In the truest sense of the word, they are rebels funded by our subsidies, just like so many others in the world of art and culture.[7]

They challenge the West using concepts developed by Westerners.[8] These moral tax collectors may claim to have decolonized philosophy and to no longer owe allegiance to Plato, Spinoza, Hegel and Marx, but they are still in thrall to these ideas. If all these brilliant minds alienated from the West were coherent, rather than emigrating to our metropolises to denounce us, they would be working in Africa to rebuild their societies. The Franco-Senegalese novelist Fatou Diome has said it with a certain virulence: 'The colonization and slavery refrain has become a trade commodity.'[9] In 1950, the Martinique poet Aimé Césaire wrote: '"Europe" is morally, spiritually indefensible.'[10] And yet Césaire, who invented the concept of negritude with Léopold Sédar Senghor and was mayor of Fort-de-France until 2001, never wanted to leave France, even though he argued successively for independence, autonomy and assimilation. Europe is a good mother; she can be insulted and trampled on, but she acquiesces gravely, admits her fundamental guilt, castigates herself and beats her chest. She may have behaved very badly in the past, but leaving her shores comes at a price that many brave pen pushers are unwilling to pay. So we understand the refrain about the mounting financial reparations that we keep dispensing, while it is explained that it won't be enough. 'Ours is ... not so much the age of reparation as that of an incessant demand for reparation that is never really fulfilled or satisfied, against the backdrop of an unprecedented rationale of victimhood', writes Johann Michel.[11] Nothing will ever fulfil expectations.

French neurosis about Algeria

In 1992, the historian Daniel Rivet welcomed the fact that, with the era of the colonies and decolonization behind us, 'passions are inexorably cooling. ... Whether neo-colonial, anti-colonial or postcolonial, today's historians no longer have to atone or defend themselves, accuse or apologize. Our colonial past is sufficiently distant for us to finally establish a relationship with it that is free of the arrogance complex or the guilt reflex.'[12] Unfortunately, the opposite has come about. The more time passes, the more an imaginary colonialism comes back into discourse as an instrument for understanding the world. Not only does it make a comeback, but it imposes itself majestically as the key to explaining the contemporary world. Take the case of the Algerian regime. Here the stakes are high: to transpose the war of independence, which was also a civil war, into a fight against the Third Reich. In this way, France and the French can be Nazified at the drop of a hat. It was President Bouteflika (1937–2021) who, in 2005, took advantage of the commemoration of the repression at Sétif on 8 May 1945, with its thousands of dead, to accuse Paris of genocide during the war of independence, referring to 'ovens similar to Nazi crematoria where hundreds of fellaghas were burnt'. In this way, Bouteflika gave himself an unlimited claim on the French government and glossed over the atrocities committed by the Algerians themselves during their struggle for liberation. Firstly, against Messali Hadj's Algerian national movement, a competitor of the FLN. Their confrontation resulted in several thousand deaths in both mainland France and Algeria. Finally, he ruled out the use of terrorism in the name of Allah. Jean Birnbaum has reminded us of the FLN's links with radical Islam and the use of attacks on civilians as a political argument.[13] Without forgetting how the mujahidins' abominable massacre of the 'traitorous' harkis and the brutal expulsion of the pieds-noirs on the principle of 'suitcase or coffin'. Also forgotten is the corruption of the dictatorial FLN state from 1962 onwards, the repression of the Kabyle movement and more recently of the Hirak between 2019 and 2021, not to mention the atrocious civil war (1991–2002) which left at least 150,000 people dead, even though this war saved us from the establishment of an Islamic republic an hour's flight from Marseille. All these evils have been denounced by Algerian dissidents such as Kamel Daoud, Boualem Sansal and political leader Saïd Sadi. Bouteflika pointed the finger of vengeance at France and spoke of a 'genocide of Algerian identity' [*sic*] to spare his homeland from examining its conscience and reflecting on the endemic violence that afflicts it.

In Algiers, the reference to the French as enemy only serves to revive the unquenchable debt that Paris owes to its former department. All the more surprising to see this discourse taken up by Macron during his political candidature as early as 2017 during a visit to Algiers, when the future President spoke of French colonization as 'a crime against humanity'. Copying Jacques Chirac, he confessed that he wanted to do for Algeria what his predecessor at the Élysée had done with Vichy in 1995. The comparison is enormous, but justified by the fact that the Algerian War is the 'unthought-of aspect of our remembrance policy'. Unthought of? Really? Very talkative for something unthought; prolix for a silent history; there are countless thousands of books, hundreds of documentaries and dozens of films devoted to this episode. While there was a period of silence and even forgetfulness, today we are a long way from repression; in fact we are in the throes of massive disinhibition. Algiers cannot seem to exist without demonizing France, the eternal and indispensable adversary. In the very long interview with Kamel Daoud in January 2023,[14] the French President first of all rejected any request for forgiveness. That would be too easy. It would settle scores because 'the word would sever all ties'. Really? But then he gives the impression of not knowing what to think about this conflict, so overwhelmed is he by the subject. To a very pertinent question from Daoud, 'What are we guilty of, what are we innocent of? Are we victims of victimhood on both sides?', Macron replied that we carry our past with us, whether we like it or not. Apart from this truism, one thing is clear: Macron does not want to divorce us from the Algerian War. Perhaps unwittingly, he continues to speak the religious language of contrition to avoid committing Paris and Algiers to a relationship of peaceful partnership. He is Atlas, carrying this eternal burden that he is entrusting to posterity. In spite of himself, he established a dubious link between colonization and the Holocaust. The wound must continue to fester, but why?

If we have to look our history in the face, we must also look at the reality. It is in France that Algerian dissidents take refuge, and it is to France, the stepmother as much hated as desired, that Algerian youth turn, greedy for visas. Algeria wants to remain France's victim so that it can hold it to account and reiterate the 'wages of memory' [*rente memorielle*] that Macron so aptly denounced in October 2021 before retracting, as if frightened of his own audacity. The French President can sometimes drop an uncomfortable truth that embarrasses his interlocutors. This is the nature of the cliché of his 'having it both ways' [*en même temps*]: he angers everyone, including Morocco on the issue of the Western Sahara, without satisfying anyone. No matter. The President wants to keep up the pathos as long as divorce can be put off. He was right to condemn the crimes of colonialism, such as that of the young mathematician Maurice Audin killed by paratroopers in 1957, and to condemn the torture carried out by the military during the Battle of Algiers in 1957. He was right in his role when he recalled the shootings in the Rue d'Isly – dozens of supporters of French Algeria were killed by the army on 26 March 1962 – or the racial attacks of 5 July 1962 when a mob of Algerians, fed on hatred, massacred hundreds of Europeans in Oran. He pardoned only the harkis who had been abandoned by France, when he could have cut the Gordian knot with Algiers and opened up a dispassionate future for the two countries.

In philosophical terms, we could say that he prefers remorse to repentance. The latter would have made it possible to acknowledge the atrocities of French colonialism in Algeria, the better to lighten the load and entrust the writing of it to a group of historians from both sides of the Mediterranean. It is this work alone that will one day make the difference. Repentance frees us from the weight of the past, which is all the more repressed because it is so little known. If we cannot change the past, we can lighten the burden it places on the memory of the living. 'What must be broken is the debt, not the memory', says the philosopher Olivier Abel.[15] Hence the importance of public apologies made by a government, an institution or a state to a nation or a minority that was once persecuted. When this is done, the verb becomes performative, it acts out an unprecedented situation, giving birth to the possibility of concord. All the more so since a pardon addressed to Algeria would have enabled the page to be turned and new relations to be initiated. In turn, it might have encouraged the country to look inward, to question its own mythologies, to shed light on the dark pages of its young history. After all, there isn't a nation in Europe with which we haven't had centuries of fighting, massacres and occupation, and yet we live in peace with our now mellowed pasts. The opposite of memory is not oblivion, it is history, and there is no shortage of competent specialists to carry out this task. Instead, in January 2021, the Élysée tried to outline a reparations policy. But the proposals put forward by historian Benjamin Stora, the official emissary of the Élysée, quickly turned into a laundry list. For example, building a stele in Amboise with Emir Abdelkader's portrait displayed, returning the skulls of Algerians killed in 1849, returning the Baba Merzoug cannon taken by the French in 1830 during the capture of Algiers, etc., without forgetting the 'follow-up commemorations'.[16] All these measures are supposed to hasten our reconciliation with the Algerian people, as if we were angry! How much longer are we going to pay for the faults of colonization, when Turkey, which occupied Algeria for three centuries, has no outstanding 'duty to remember'? Macron wants France and France alone to carry the burden.

It is a sign of lucidity for a democracy to admit its mistakes, provided it does not sink into systematic atonement. At a time when our relationship with Algiers needs to be clarified and transformed into a partnership of equals, Emmanuel Macron continues to wax lyrical. For example, the former French ambassador to Algiers, Xavier Driencourt, explained that Paris should repeal the 1968 preferential agreement on visas that governs the stay of Algerians in France, at the risk of creating a diplomatic crisis.[17] This agreement is seen as a debt owed to the Algerians for 132 years of colonization. Denouncing it would undoubtedly bring about a welcome upset, changing the balance of power and enabling us to rethink our relationship with Algiers on a different basis from that of accusations and the constant *mea culpa*. How can we fail to mention the statement by the Algerian President Abdelmadjid Tebboune, who on 26 June 2023 in Moscow described the invader of Ukraine as a 'friend of humanity' (Putin himself seemed embarrassed by this compliment), while the teaching of French is banned in private schools in Algeria? The same President Tebboune explained in an interview with *Le Figaro* in December 2022 that 'Algerians should have French visas lasting 132 years', the duration of French colonization. And this is the man with whom Paris would like to speak on equal terms? The Algerian government, backed by Russia, is raising the spectre of war against France. We must be aware of this and do everything we can to thwart these belligerent plans. It's time to drop the Algerian taboo!

Is the Muslim the new Jew?

There are several stages in the struggle to become the world's pariah. First affiliate with a people regarded as martyrs, then equal and, if possible, supplant them. In the Western world, in the eyes of radical Muslims, it is the Jews that one has to strip of their credentials in order to increase one's political and symbolic advantages. The first step is to counter the hostility towards Islam that has developed since the attacks of 11 September 2001, and to characterize it not for what it is – deep mistrust, legitimate or otherwise, for a proselytizing religion – but as a form of racism known as 'Islamophobia'. The word was coined at the beginning of the twentieth century by French colonial administrators in Dakar to remind Paris of the loyalty of Muslim subjects to the principle of the Empire,[18] unlike the more turbulent Christians and animists. The term disappeared from common usage but returned in the late 1980s in England and in the Iran of the mullahs at the time of the Salman Rushdie affair. It was then used to describe all those who dared to criticize the Quranic religion and its prophet and question a single article of faith, such as the headscarf for women. But 'Islamophobia' is a lazy and empty concept that includes all sorts of phenomena of unequal importance, scepticism, satire or indifference to God. While religious persecution is an offence in all democracies (but Christianity, Hinduism and Judaism are persecuted in a majority of Muslim countries), questioning dogma is an absolute right. But Islam wants to establish itself as an untouchable faith, protected by a semantic shield and immune to all attacks. Christianity, Judaism, Buddhism and Hinduism can all be condemned, but only Islam ought to escape scrutiny. No laughing at the Prophet, on pain of beheading. But a term, even an intimidating and hollow one like Islamophobia, is not enough; it needs an additional quality, and that is what the status of 'new Jew' brings to Muslims.

For example, in December 2021, at a meeting in Perpignan, the Mayor of Paris, Anne Hidalgo, said that the language of the 1930s, applied to Jews, was now being applied to Muslims. The then rector of the Grand Mosque of Paris, Dalil Boubakeur, expressed alarm at the same time at the fact that 'Islamophobia and Islamopsychosis are nowadays certainly comparable in seriousness to the French anti-Semitism of the 19th century'.[19] The journalist Edwy Plenel, viscerally hostile to Israel, who in 1973 in the Trotskyist newspaper *Rouge* rejoiced at the death of Israeli athletes at the Munich Olympics (he has since regretted it), cites the 2013 report of the National Consultative Commission on Human Rights in his 2016 book *For the Muslims*: 'If our epoch is compared with the pre-war period, it could be said that today the Muslim, closely followed by the North African, has replaced the Jew in the representations and construction of a scapegoat.'[20] Once again, on 3 November 2023, the Grand Mosque of Paris, through its rector Chems-Eddine Hafiz, denounced 'the gradual increase of racist and hateful speech against Muslims in France'.[21] On that date, if hate speech was unleashed, it was directed solely against Jews: synagogues were guarded by the police and army, as were churches, and people were shouting 'Death to the Jews' at all the demonstrations. Fortunately, no one shouted 'Death to the Arabs', and no mosques were attacked.[22] Victim capture never stops. When it is in the minority in a country, Islam claims to be oppressed. When it is in the majority, it keeps the other faiths under control, harassing or persecuting them – Hindus, Buddhists, Christians, Jews – with very rare exceptions such as Morocco, even if a welcome wind of reform, temporarily suspended by the war in Gaza, is blowing through the Middle East. As Claude Lévi-Strauss noted in *Tristes Tropiques*, Islam has a problem with alterity, 'this great religion … shows itself incapable of putting up with the existence of others as others'.[23]

It was the American-Palestinian professor and polemicist Edward Saïd who first established a link between Jews and Arabs, back in 1978, in his seminal book on decolonial studies, *Orientalism*.[24] Since both are Semites, Western opinions need only draw on the same sources when they shift from hatred of Jews to hatred of Arabs. All it takes is a cognitive shift that involves no change of scenery. Especially since, with the creation of the State of Israel, according to him, the Jew has gone from being persecuted to persecutor. The time has therefore come for the Muslim to take the place of the Jew. In 2000, Edward Saïd jokingly told the Israeli newspaper *Haaretz* that he was the last authentic Jewish intellectual in the region, the last disciple of Adorno: 'a Palestinian Jew'. It was also the historian Enzo Traverso who explained how 'for the new racism, Islamophobia today plays the role that anti-Semitism once played … it fits perfectly into what we might call the anti-Jewish archive … anti-Semitism has therefore transmigrated towards Islamophobia'.[25] This assertion is false. It assumes that anti-Semitism has disappeared in our times, which is inaccurate, as attested by the twelve French Jewish citizens killed because they were Jews by radical Islamists over the last twenty years[26] and the explosion of anti-Jewish hatred following the Hamas pogrom in Israel on 7 October 2023 and the Tzahal (IDF) response in Gaza. It was as if the killing of hundreds of Israeli men, women and children had unleashed an appetite for murder against Jews the world over, from San Francisco to Dagestan.

In November 2019, during a demonstration against 'Islamophobia' organized by associations that have since been dissolved, and supported by Jean-Luc Mélenchon, EELV (ecologist party) Senator Esther Benbassa posed in a photo surrounded by several demonstrators. Among them was a little girl wearing a sticker showing the yellow star associated with the crescent moon, the emblem of Islam. The photo caused a scandal. It implies that Muslims in France are experiencing hardship and insecurity comparable to that of Ashkenazim from Eastern Europe in the 1930s and 40s. This is the lazy theory of the Great Replacement, dreamt up by others in connection with immigration, but it's absolutely essential to feed the voracious anti-racism machine. As one Internet user put it in the free speech section of the Mediapart website: 'Jews are no longer pariahs ... but pariah peoples still exist. In the Middle East, they are the Palestinian people, and in France they are the Muslim men and women, whose headscarves and excessively long dresses are appallingly hounded ... fidelity to the tragic memory of the shtetl and Yiddishland means defending the Muslim women harassed by the warlike secularism of the Republic.' Never mind the indecency of the comparison between democratic laws passed by parliament and the actions of the SA or SS hordes against Jewish or Gypsy minorities. It is pretty clear that new blood is needed in the small, closed world of racism and that competition is fierce between its various sects. All the more so since wokeism, what Jean-François Braunstein calls an 'academic religion',[27] coming from the United States, has designated white men and women, Jews included, as born racists, whatever effort is made to free themselves from this fate. In the eyes of this doctrine, it is not only legitimate but recommended to be anti-Semitic.

This desire on the part of some Muslims to be more Jewish than the Jews, what Alvin H. Rosenfeld called the 'stealing of the Holocaust',[28] is contemporaneous with the rejection of the State of Israel in the Middle East since 1948, barely mitigated by the Abraham Accords, which are now being called into question.[29] Anti-Semitism remains vivid in many North African communities in Europe and among many Black Lives Matter activists in the United States, who are encouraged by the anti-Zionist ultra-left. 'Hatred of Israel is the most powerful aphrodisiac in the Arab world', said the late King Hassan II of Morocco. If Israel disappeared tomorrow, if all the Jews from the Jordan to Haifa were thrown into the sea, the Arab mob would sing and dance for months from Rabat to Baghdad, but so would the left in Europe and America. Then they would have to find an equally effective scapegoat. Anti-Semitism remains an unsurpassable horizon for our times.

For the Jews, the Shoah has become the equivalent of a shirt of Nessus; what was supposed to protect them burns them, an armour consuming them from within. Worst of all, it has reinforced anti-Semitism, as if it were another privilege, also taken away. It's clear that they've got it all to themselves! In short, the figure of the Jew combines the two main forms of racism, inferiority – they have traditionally been subhumans condemned to the ghetto, the dhimmi in the Muslim world subject to a special tax – and superiority, which makes them objects of jealousy. Trampled on in the one case, envied in the other. As in the National Socialist doctrine, they are said to be all-powerful, but in the disguise of weakness. They endure persecution only to maintain their rule. In Nazi propaganda, they were both the Bolshevik who wanted to destroy capitalism and the financier who promoted it; they appeared in humanity in the dual guise of revolutionary and banker, destroyer and corrupter. We can therefore hate them without compunction. What's more, they are absolute chameleons who hide in every race: white, but also black (Falashas, Ethiopians) and Arab, Indian, Chinese, everywhere hidden and scattered across the face of the earth and difficult to identify. When we have exhausted the round of scapegoats, Jews are always there, the ideal lightning rod, 'chosen for hatred' as Leo Strauss put it, destined to take upon themselves the rage of those who seek to oust them. The only new thing is that most of the hostility towards them comes from the ultra-left and especially from the 'anti-racist' left. Doesn't that sound like a Jewish joke?

GANG WARFARE LACED WITH TEARS

Any category of person can benefit from being anointed as a victim. Even the looters during the riots of June–July 2023 were redecorated, by the progressives, as victims of systemic racism. It's a good trick, but it didn't work on the majority of the population. What happened on those riotous nights? A perfectly coordinated drama in which the insurgents responded to a scenario that had already been written since at least 2005. The drug traffickers, taking advantage of the tragic death of young Nahel at the hands of the police, declared war on the French State by sending their henchmen into an attack on prefectures, town halls, schools, crèches, media libraries and so on. The ransacking was remarkably well organized and nothing withstood the onslaught. Anything that could improve people's lives had to be smashed to keep them under gang control. Police checks had been hampering the traffic from Morocco and Latin America. It was a business war rather than a religious one. The imams had all confessed their inability to catch up with the young men ready to do battle with the police, even if they were burning cars and shouting 'Allahu Akbar'. There is only one step from the local *caïdat* to the caliphate, but not everyone takes it. The gang bosses were able to benefit from the reserve army of kids, many from poor single-parent families, happy to take part in what looked like a big bust. What is a rioter? A consumer in a hurry who doesn't have time to go through the checkout. In exchange for their participation, the looters were rewarded with a host of consumer goods, some of them luxury items such as mobile phones and jewellery. The suburbs have not been abandoned; on the contrary: it's because the State had started very expensive building renovations that the mafias woke up.

In 2005, the insurgents, born in the era of television and supermarket, demanded, as one of them put it, 'cash and chicks'. They wanted the benefits of the commercial dream more than a proletarian revolution. Born French, but wanting to become French, they felt blocked by their skin colour and above all their social and suburban origins. Like today, they had no plans other than to burn down all the official buildings in a suicidal move that cut them off even further from the rest of the nation. It was an initiation ritual, a form of negative integration in which the fight against the police took the place of an impossible adolescent revolt against an absent or non-existent father. France ignores or despises them and their rage could be interpreted as a cry of disappointed love, a way of saying: we are here, we exist.

Ever since Mathieu Kassovitz's 1995 film *La Haine,* the savagery of the riffraff [*caillera*] has fascinated showbiz and many left-wing intellectuals. This lumpenproletariat, 'this dregs of corrupt individuals from all classes', as Engels put it in 1870, seduces sociologists, actors, film-makers and journalists. For them, as for Marx, violence is the great midwife of History. Any excuse is good enough to justify brutality, especially the alibi of 'systemic racism', even though the French State is constitutionally anti-racist and numerous studies have refuted the existence of structural xenophobia in the police force.[30] These popular outbursts are paradoxical in that they mainly penalize the people, by making their living conditions worse, and they increase the isolation of those communes cut off from the nation. Both the left and the right are making the same symmetrical mistake by reducing the demonstrators to their skin colour. Racists for some, ethnic barbarians for others. This overlooks the large number of French people of North African or African origin who are perfectly integrated and no longer visible, being present at all levels of society.[31]

What is a gang? It is a Hobbesian world where disobedience is punishable by death and torture, where rivalries are settled with kalashnikovs and where the only dialect is that of violence. Failing to see this reality, politicians wander between contrition and accusation, filling the void with old ways of reading things. This was the real novelty of the 2023 mutinies: the transposition to the main part of France of a situation already present in Marseille, Holland and Sweden: all-powerful narcos with their child soldiers and serial killers. It's not underprivileged suburbs versus a racist police state, but drug mafias against the Republic. And if the uprisings stopped after five days, it was because the godfathers had decided that business should resume. It was a warning.

Money is no solution for getting 'the Republic's lost territories' out of this situation.[32] There is no point in rebuilding buildings that will go up in flames the next time there is an uprising. It will take a combination of intransigence and generosity. Cracking down on the most hardened criminals, reaching out to others to rescue them from cycles of failure and certain death. There's not much in common among the Yellow Vests, the far-left thugs, the black blocs, zadists and eco-terrorists, the vandals of the suburbs, other than the indiscriminate use of violence and instantaneous extremism. The barbarians are circling like the Indians of Westerns around the wagon of the Republic, looking to finish it off. That's the worrying thing. The weaker the State, the more it is accused of being brutal because it is no longer the legitimate repository of force. It is naked, it no longer controls anything, and the President of the Republic appears helpless, pusillanimous, incapable of reassuring and bringing people together. We expected a lighthouse, or at least a rock, but what we got was a weather vane at best. Authoritarian because he lacks authority, verbose because he lacks eloquence. France has always had a tradition of violence, but that was violence contained by institutions and charismatic personalities. It's hard to say whether the current President has had some kind of curse put on him, or whether he is a catalyst for disaster. The fact remains that this chaos will always be associated with his name.

PART THREE

How Can We Live with Our Wounds?

CHAPTER 9

Barbarism as a cover-up?

'troubles overcome are good to tell' … it is good to sit
surrounded by warmth, before food and wine, and remind
oneself and others of the fatigue, the cold and hunger.

PRIMO LEVI[1]

In August 1994, in Sarajevo under siege, I was introduced
to an elderly man, Marek Edelman. I knew nothing about
him. I then learned that this renowned cardiologist, a
former member of the Bund, a Jewish socialist movement,
was one of the last survivors of the Warsaw ghetto, living
from 1919 to 2009. He took up arms with 220 resistance
fighters in 1943, miraculously survived, and took part in the
Warsaw uprising in 1944. After the war, he chose to remain
in Poland, despite the anti-Semitism of the Communist
regime. In his book, first published in 1945 in Warsaw,
Edelman described the denial mechanism admirably: while
the terror continued to increase in the ghetto after it
was set up in 1942, and every day the Germans, assisted
by their Ukrainian auxiliaries and the Jewish police,
deported or killed whole families, the inhabitants remained

convinced that they had to knuckle down if they wanted to survive.[2] The execution in the Lublin forest of an entire convoy of Jews who had arrived from Germany a year earlier was forgotten. It was a massacre too horrible to be true. Incredulity prevailed, even as the terrible news was pouring in: 'A normal human being with normal mental processes was simply unable to conceive that a difference in the colour of eyes or hair or a different racial origin might be sufficient causes for murder.'[3] The machine-gunning of entire buildings and the street executions of children and pregnant women did nothing to change this. The disavowal persisted. The diabolical intelligence of the Nazis consisted in encouraging the victims to collaborate in their own destruction via the Jewish Council: 'the Germans made the Jewish Council itself condemn over 300,000 Ghetto inhabitants to death'.[4] It wasn't until the population fell from 300,000 to 60,000 that people finally woke up and the Jewish Armed Resistance Organization took up arms against the Waffen SS, at the cost of almost being decimated (only forty escaped through the sewers). A few hundred men and women decided to fight, not to defeat the enemy, but to postpone their inevitable demise. All the fighters knew that there was a worse fate than evil: the dishonour of not having resisted it. 'There were only two hundred and twenty of us left in the Jewish Armed Resistance Organization. Wasn't it more a question of not letting them come and slit our throats? Basically, it was just a matter of choosing how to die.'[5]

Hide this genocide so I cannot see it

Camouflage was always a favoured rhetorical device for barbarians. In a major address to senior party officials in Posen on 6 October 1943, Heinrich Himmler famously said of the extermination of the Jews: 'This is a glorious page in our history that has never been written and never will be.'[6] Until then, the Nazis had used coded language in their documents, but the coding was simple enough to be understood by insiders. It was necessary to suggest the crime while hiding it. Even the regime's official press reported the massacres in the form of hearsay. If Himmler, in this speech, revealed the aims of the annihilation in a roundabout way, it was because he was on familiar ground in front of senior SS officials. But the Third Reich was no longer in a favourable military situation, so the use of circumlocutions had to be kept for the outside world.

On the other hand, in the Stalinist world, in the Solovki Islands, birthplace of the Siberian Gulag from 1917 onwards, seagulls were shot for carrying messages from prisoners, the Zeks. No one was supposed to know what was happening in the Far East. Nothing was allowed to filter out of the concentration camp system except to a small circle of informed people, in order to maintain the fiction of how great the socialist homeland was. Nazism and Communism have always had two different rhetorical styles. National Socialism defended a sovereign monstrosity that slaves and corrupters were trying to crush; Marxism took up the cause of the exploited. The former eliminated the weak and the subhuman for the survival of the superior race; the latter would carry out massacres for the good of the people and of humanity as a whole. Nazism, evil committed in the name of Evil; Communism, evil committed in the name of Goodness. But this distinction diminishes the similarities between the doctrines. Right up to the end, the Nazi regime spoke two languages: that of a Germany humiliated by the Treaty of Versailles and the Judeo-Masonic conspiracy, and that of triumphant Aryanism. Stalin's Russia itself was built on excusing force and terror, promising brutal death to anyone who got in the way of a triumphant socialism. The two systems, enemies though brothers, were faced with the same delicate problem, almost a cognitive enigma: how can one perform the mass slaughter of human beings for whom one has no hatred, as Vassili Grossman asked?[7] By turning women, children and the elderly into 'criminals who had not committed a crime'.[8] In the case of Nazism, it was necessary to instil hatred and repulsion for the Jews in the hearts of the people. In the case of the USSR, it was necessary to hate in the name of love for all humanity. The new world was to be built for the people who were the main obstacle to its construction.[9] Most dictatorial regimes combine a discourse of victimhood with the need for revenge in order to legally place themselves outside the law and present their appetite for conquest as a concern to protect their minorities. By invoking the persecuted of yesterday, they justify new persecutions that are built under the auspices of freedom and justice. As the Shakespearean saying goes: 'The devil can cite Scripture for his purpose.'

State lies and scandalous disclosures

Throughout history, the truth has often come out as a special revelation: Albert Londres telling the French about the reality of the Cayenne prisons, André Gide denouncing the misdeeds of the mining companies in the Congo and later the sordid reality of the USSR, Alexander Solzhenitsyn and Varlam Shalamov confirming the existence of the Gulag for the world to see, the Vietnamese exposing the atrocities of the Khmer Rouge genocide, all of which are conveyed in an almost instantaneous transition from darkness to light. The governments implicated were quick to deny it. Tyrannies are kingdoms of official lies. Living with the discrepancy between their declared doctrine and their actual practices, they have to conceal themselves from the eyes of the international press. Two telling examples from France: in 1932, Joseph Stalin launched the Holodomor in Ukraine, a policy of extermination by starvation to punish small farmers who opposed the State requisitions policy. The law of 7 August 1932, known as the 'ears of corn law', punished anyone who stole a few ears of corn or potatoes with death or deportation. Millions of Ukrainians (as well as small Russian peasants) starved to death, and cases of cannibalism were reported. In the summer of 1933, the Mayor of Lyon, Édouard Herriot, visited the USSR; he wanted to bring France closer to Moscow as a counterweight to Germany, which had just fallen into Hitler's hands. Having visited Ukraine in the company of officials who showed him nothing but Potemkin villages, he exclaimed: 'I have crossed Ukraine. Well, I assure you that I saw it as a garden in full yield.'[10]

In 1948, David Rousset, a former Buchenwald deportee, took advantage of his fame to denounce the camps in the USSR. In November 1949, in *Le Figaro*, he called for the creation of a commission of enquiry into the Soviet prisons, the centrepiece of the Stalinist system. The outcry on the left was unanimous: Jean-Paul Sartre and Maurice Merleau-Ponty wrote an article in *Les Temps Modernes* in which they acknowledged the existence of the camps but maintained that the USSR was on the right side of history. A Communist MP accused Rousset of being a 'well-known Hitler-supporting journalist'. More seriously, Pierre Daix, editor-in-chief of *Les Lettres Françaises*, a Communist weekly, suspected David Rousset of publishing false documents and concluded outrageously: 'The re-education camps of the Soviet Union are the culmination of the complete elimination of the exploitation of man by man.'[11] Rousset sued *Les Lettres Françaises* for defamation. After lengthy proceedings – in which Margarete Buber-Neumann, deported to Siberia in 1938, then handed over to the Germans by Stalin and sent to Ravensbrück until 1945, testified – *Les Lettres Françaises* was convicted. A few years later, Pierre Daix, who had in the meantime come to his senses, that is, anti-communist, bitterly admitted that David Rousset was the first to have got it right.

After the dual fall of Communism and Nazism, it became clear that battling violence meant battling dissimulation. This is what Alexander Solzhenitsyn explained in a text written on 12 February 1974, the day he was expelled from the USSR:

> violence intrudes into peaceful life ... as if it were carrying a banner and shouting: 'I am violence ...'. But violence quickly grows old. And it has lost confidence within itself, and in order to maintain a respectable face it summons falsehoods as its allies. ... And the simplest and most accessible key to our self-neglected liberation lies right here: personal non-participation in lies. Though lies conceal everything, though lies embrace everything – not with any help from me.[12]

How long did it take for the West to admit the reality of the Gulag and the evil nature of Communism in all its guises, Castroist, Soviet, Maoist, Polpotist? Almost forty years after the Second World War! How long did it take for the criminal nature of Putin's regime to be recognized, despite all the evidence? More than twenty years after he came to power, and he still has a great many supporters in France! How many attacks, atrocious murders and serial massacres did it take to link terrorism to political Islam as a religion that has been infected with extremism and could well destroy itself from within?[13] Many well-meaning people continue to deny this link for fear of being suspected of racism. Today, as in the past, the truth takes a while to sink in. Either it is unimaginable, like the death camps under the Nazis, or it disturbs the intellectual comforts of the time, the compromises that democracies make with dictatorships. The truth is inaudible until it bursts forth, appalling and tragic, leaving us with feelings of shame and disgust. It's an adrenalin rush that catches one off-balance and blurs perceptions. Such intense horror (murder, carnage, mass torture) strikes home outrageously. How could I not have known?

The camera revolution?

In the 1980s, an innovation led us to believe that we were entering another dimension. Cameras would make it possible to record any abominations and thus embarrass regimes that, under cover of secrecy, were eliminating undesirables and erasing their disappearance down to the last traces. Images would finally reveal the unspeakable, and we would enter a reign of transparency. The argument was reinforced by the fact that autocrats, wary of camera operators and reporters, would only tolerate authorized filming. It's true that a television advert or a short video is more likely to raise awareness than a long newspaper article. But the image can go two ways: it can shock as well as anaesthetize when there is one after another. A new regime was installed: the reign of habitual over-exposure. Every evening, new images bring us new horrors: earthquakes in Syria and Turkey, exhumations of mass graves in Ukraine, civil war in Sudan, pogroms in Israel, mass destruction in Gaza, ethnic cleansing in Armenia; one shocking abomination is replaced by another. That's how the cycle works: today's event cancels yesterday's; every tragedy is subject to the principle of attrition.

The right to interfere optically, which preceded the right to interfere altogether, far from moving us, ends up putting us to sleep. Misfortune delivered *en masse* to our homes overloads us and wears us down. Daily life is hard enough, so why inflict on ourselves images of people a long way away madly killing each other? Every day, via the media, we absorb the idea that people are a quantifiable commodity – so common that they can be easily squandered, unless they are close to us. As much as we value individual life in the West, we perceive the globe as an overpopulated space whose proliferation threatens the planet's equilibrium. The ideal of every individual's inherent dignity comes up against this realization about the multitudes. Where numbers triumph, morality capitulates.

For Plato, evil was ignorance; for the moderns, from the Marquis de Sade onwards, it is an ecstatic release [*jouissance*], and the will to inflict harm. The good man, said Plato, is content to dream of evil deeds; the evil man commits them. Reversing an age-old tendency towards secrecy, some torturers revel in the real-time exhibition of murder. Crime out in the open on social networks, killings on Instagram or X (ex-Twitter) shared by thousands of followers. It's street fights or lynchings broadcast live by gangs who want to show off their exploits and terrorize their enemies. It was ISIS, followed by Hamas, who first invented mass murder in stereo, on a GoPro re-broadcast on every screen. Not only does it destroy everything Christian, Yazidi or Kurdish, take control of memory and archives, burn churches and temples, but it also spectacularly displays its crimes as a source of pride. These new-generation jihadists have invented a parlour game: the enjoyable massacre, the nonchalant slaughter on a loop on TikTok or Instagram, slapping each other on the backs. Dragging corpses behind a four-wheel drive shouting with delight, playing football with a severed head, decapitating God's enemies to put everyone in a good mood, with the accompaniment of a rousing musical score – this is what we might call *genocidal enthusiasm*. Just as Lévi-Strauss distinguished between the raw and the cooked, we must distinguish between the cold, bureaucratic Nazi death machine and the bloodthirsty fervour of jihadism. One is meticulous and diligent, the other messy and involved. Allah's fanatics go about their work in the same way as the Hutu extremists who cut up their enemies with machetes and rested in the evening: they fall upon the enemy bodies, crushing, burning and mutilating them. There is no hierarchy in this killing: it's the democratization of mass murder to cries of 'Allahu Akbar'. On 7 October 2023, a young man from Hamas called his parents from his victims' phones. He shouted with joy like a student who had just learned that he had passed his exams: 'I'm in Mefalsim (a kibbutz), I killed ten Jews with my own hands. Their blood is on my hands.' His father encouraged him: 'May Allah bring you peace ... kill, kill, kill!' 'Be proud of me, Father.'[14] Killing Jews is exhilarating: that's what Russell Rickford, a professor at Cornell University in the United States and a great supporter of Black Lives Matter, also proclaims. At a demonstration, he was delighted by the pogrom of 7 October and wanted to share his intoxication: 'It was exhilarating! It was exhilarating! It was energizing! I was exhilarated!'[15] This staunch anti-racist truly embodies what Marek Edelman called 'Hitler's posthumous revenge' in relation to the Serbian militias in 1993. When will the far left rehabilitate the Führer? In Germany on 7 October, demonstrators wearing Palestinian keffiyehs handed out sweets to passers-by to celebrate the good news. Hamas, for its part, skilfully plays both sides, terror and pity. It prides itself on raping, beheading and burning women and the elderly, and makes the videos available to the general public, but it uses the deaths of Palestinian children during bombardments to incite pity in the international community and to hasten the condemnation of Israel.

Showing everything terrorizes spectators and galvanizes followers. The jihadists want to frighten *kouffars* and infidels, but they also want to recruit new candidates for mass crime. On 14 July 2016, when the prisoners at Fleury-Mérogis heard the news of the Nice massacre, a lorry driven by a Tunisian jihadist that ran down eighty-six people,[16] they celebrated loudly for hours.[17] ISIS has broken new ground in the history of barbarity, or rather it has taken advantage of new technologies to gather copycats. It does not discourage; it recruits. The late Yevgeny Prigozhin, former head of the Wagner militia, publicly killed a deserter from his private army with a sledgehammer as an example to others. To this apprenticeship in rape and torture, Hamas has added the 'prayer of gratitude', with its leaders prostrate before the television in Doha broadcasting the spectacle of the massacres committed by its troops. The Third Reich death bureaucrats, cold servants of extermination, are opposed to the joy of Allah's sadists who dismember, cut up, disembowel and smash with a gusto that nothing can assuage. These evildoers put their hearts into their work. They must destroy the body and the face of the enemy who never existed. Genital mutilations, necrophilia, paedophilia, one after the other, according to a precise roadmap. The Hamas productions are reminiscent of that specific category of horror film for teenagers known as the 'slasher': the multiple, almost mechanical killings as established by John Carpenter's *Halloween* movies. In the *Einsatzgruppen*, the shooters were allowed cigarette breaks and some got drunk on the evening of their killings to erase the horror of what they had done.[18] But our madmen of God are lustful, irritable, mass murderers. Methodical extermination on the one hand, chaotic extermination on the other, to borrow a distinction from Léon Poliakov.[19] But many find extenuating circumstances for

Hamas: it is weak, powerless in the face of one of the most powerful armies in the world, according to Angela Davis.[20] The oppressed have every right, including the right to break the elementary rules of human decency. The great massacres today are carried out in the name of justice, the oppressed, morality and God. Violence can no longer simply say, I kill out of pleasure. It argues that an earlier offence has been committed, demands reparation and temporarily authorizes slaughter. Brutes begin by exposing their wounds, summoning their dead to better perpetrate mass murder in return. Before sharpening their knives, they declare themselves victims in order to obtain absolution.

Some despots also use past killings in all good conscience to intimidate the survivors. Recep Erdogan, a great denier of the Armenian genocide, brought up the 'survivors of the sword' when referring to Armenians and Christians in May 2020. He was not expressing remorse but, on the contrary, pride. They were targets who deserved to be eliminated.[21] To insult the survivors is to threaten them with the same fate if they raise their heads. The neo-Sultan does not bother to deny his crimes; he claims them, glories in them and promises to do it again (Turkey is only 0.2% Christian, compared with 20% at the beginning of the twentieth century). Ferocity no longer needs to be disguised; it can simply be put on full display.

The torturer's pleasure

'The rose is without "why"', said the seventeenth-century German mystic Angelus Silesius, celebrating the Creator's bounty. *Hier ist kein warum*, said a guard to a thirsty Primo Levi, as he snatched an icicle hanging from the roof that he wanted to suck.[22] There is no why in hell. Evil has no reason, like the rose. It is pure delight to destroy. It is committed by ordinary people, as Hannah Arendt said, who transgress one taboo after another, perfectly legally. What is a torturer? A free man or woman who mutilates and murders as they please, because they are allowed to. Germaine Tillion, a sociologist who was deported to Germany, had already noted this:

> Even so, it was this team of average people, all recruited from the traditional German bourgeoisie, educated, practising hygiene and clean linen, and even speaking foreign languages, who ran, without protest, such a highly criminal and original enterprise as Ravensbrück.[23]

There's no need for a vocation: a favourable environment, the guarantee of impunity and a good salary can encourage an ordinary person to inflict abuse with particular refinement.

There are as many books about great murderers as about their victims, no doubt because the former permit themselves things that the common man does not. The novelist Neige Sinno, who was continuously raped by her stepfather from the age of seven to fourteen, wanted to know what was going on in his mind. And what she discovered, both in her own case and in the literature, astounded her: her abuser wanted to be loved![24] As Jean Hatzfeld explains in relation to Rwanda, executioners generally have no scruples. 'Is it possible that of all categories of war criminals, the perpetrator of genocide winds up the least traumatized?'[25] Questioning them does not shed any light on the mystery of evil. Hans Frank, Governor General of Poland, architect of the Final Solution in a huge part of the Reich, and a talented pianist, was proud to have been identified by *The New York Times* at the beginning of 1943 as 'War Criminal No. 1'.[26] It was boasting, Hannah Arendt tells us, that was Eichmann's downfall. He too wanted his fifteen minutes of fame and he betrayed himself! Among the most remarkable monsters of the twentieth century was the Khmer Rouge leader Duch (1942–2020), who was responsible for the S21 torture and extermination centre near Phnom Penh. Interviewed for months by the film-maker Rithy Panh, himself a genocide survivor, he revealed himself to be a meticulous being, driven by an almost sexual excitement to destroy and disperse his prisoners.[27] What's more, he had a 'full-throated' laugh, so happy he was to kill, to extract confessions, to do his job properly. Mass murder was a huge orgasmic release for him.[28] Not for a moment did he show any repentance. Depending on his rank in the hierarchy, the executioner is an executor. He does a paid job and nothing angers him more than to see one of his 'clients' commit suicide. This was the case with Mala Zimetbaum, who escaped from Auschwitz, was recaptured and sentenced to death. On the gallows, she managed to cut her wrists with a razor blade, much to the fury of the SS officer on duty, who shouted: 'You want to be a heroine? You want to kill yourself? That's what we're here for! That's our job.'[29] But role usurpation is always possible: the *Einsatzgruppen* who took part in the Shoah in the USSR during Operation Barbarossa, when one and a half million Jews were shot and thrown into pits, were able to access psychological support after their work. Himmler, in order to spare them bouts of animal-like self-pity, chose to reverse their guilt: 'Instead of saying: What horrible things I did to people!, the murderers would be able to say: What horrible things I had to watch in the pursuance of my duties, how heavily the task weighed upon my shoulders!'[30] They had thus suffered more than the children, women and elderly people shot at point-blank range.[31] Victim reversal is a real acrobatic art.

A *declaration of love to gangsters*

Criminals and serial killers fascinate a certain left-wing intelligentsia as long as they are on the right side of history. It was the poet-thief Jean Genet who best cast this kind of spell. Forging a legend of a miserable childhood in public care and an enemy of the bourgeoisie, he was first bewitched by the Nazi superman, and was allegedly the lover of a French SS officer. Jean Genet was celebrated as a saint and martyr by Jean-Paul Sartre and revered by the entire chic left, from Foucault to Derrida. As the historian Ivan Jablonka[32] has revealed, breaking with a long tradition of idolatry, Genet was a bitter anti-Semite and a genuine fascist who made 'poetry' out of the Oradour massacre and Hitler's 'craziest banditry'. He exalted 'the battalions of blond warriors who fucked us in the ass on 14 June 1940' and the Stuka pilots who 'laughed as they sowed death'.[33] Later, he would choose the Palestinian cause out of simple hatred of Israel.[34] And the fervour went beyond provocation. The same could be said of the rebellious thief and gangster Pierre Goldman, himself suspected of murdering two pharmacists, a figure of the extreme left who ended up being killed in a mysterious way and of whom Alain Krivine, founder of the (Trotskyist) *Ligue communiste révolutionnaire*, said: 'He screwed up, but he's family.' The same goes for Jacques Mesrine, the recidivist criminal disguised as Robin Hood, celebrated by publisher Gérard Lebovici; or the terrorist Mohammed Merah, the murderer of Jewish children in a Toulouse school in March 2012 and praised by Houria Bouteldja.[35] There is also the novelist Virginie Despentes, who at the time of the *Charlie Hebdo* massacre sang a declaration of love to the Kouachi brothers:

I was also the guys who went in with their weapons. The ones who had just bought a Kalashnikov on the black market and had decided, in their own way, the only way available to them, to die on their feet rather than live on their knees. I also liked those who made their victims stand up and say who they were before shooting them in the face ... I loved them in their clumsiness – when I saw them, weapons in hand, spreading terror by shouting 'we have avenged the Prophet' and not finding the right tone to say it. Bad action film, bad gangsta rap. Right down to their heroic act, something that didn't work. There were two days like that of such intense shock that I got high on loving everyone – in a powerful radius.[36]

So it goes with bourgeois rebels. They denounce the established order as a crime, but they lyricize crime as a rebellion against the bourgeois order. Marguerite Duras, for example, writing in *Libération* on 17 July 1985 about the Grégory affair, subjectively declared Christine Villemin guilty of killing her child but 'sublime, necessarily sublime' because she was a victim of male domination.[37]

The Great Barbarians even hypnotize their enemies. When Stalin died, the entire French National Assembly went into mourning. Its President, Édouard Herriot, called for a minute's silence in memory of Hitler's conqueror. Tributes were paid throughout France. The Communist daily *L'Humanité* proclaimed that all the peoples of the world were in mourning, in their immense love for Stalin. *Le Monde* was not to be outdone:

Stalin will undoubtedly be remembered as the man who reconciled Russia and the revolution, to the point of making them inseparable. ... The pursuit of this happy formula has also enabled man to win some of his most magnificent victories over nature.[38]

Who remembers that *Le Figaro*, then headed by Jean d'Ormesson, ran the headline on the death of Mao Tse-tung in September 1976: 'China, Mao's widow'? It's the ultimate triumph of Evil when your adversaries celebrate you as a blessing.

FASCIST OR TOTALITARIAN?

Which insult has the greatest symbolic density? Stalinist? The term has an old-fashioned ring to it. Poet Louis Aragon was called a Stalinist scoundrel on 10 May 1968 by the politician Daniel Cohn-Bendit, but he didn't seem to mind. The epithet tends towards the bureaucratic. Totalitarian is too obscure and no longer makes sense to younger generations who have lost their historical references. It's an abstract word. As the Hungarian writer Imre Kertész explains, when Jean Améry (alias Hans Mayer), a former Auschwitz deportee, found himself faced with enemies: 'It was not totalitarianism that beat him with a horsewhip and hung him by his shackled wrists but Lieutenant Praust, who happened to speak a Berlin dialect.'[39] Only 'fascist' sounds hurtful enough as an insult. If the left uses and abuses this insult, it's because it hurts and forces the other party to defend itself. Anti-fascists can respectably go about reviving the golden era of the Resistance. And the French say 'facho' as an attenuating diminutive that indicates a penchant for evil without having the reprobative charge of fascist.

When it comes to evil, National Socialism gets the gold medal. For although the crimes of Communism have been toned down, Hitler enjoys the immortal status of Absolute Ignominy. With all his exemplary atrocities, he can be played in any key. He is imbued with a superlative intensity. In the comparison between Auschwitz and the Kolyma Gulag, the former wins out. And who, apart from specialists and historians, knows anything about Kolyma? Anyone who criticizes Communism is suspected of excusing fascism. Anyone who criticizes fascism is suspected of indulging Stalinism and its various variants. It's a dizzying double bind when you hate both systems equally. Collective memory has made up its mind: the Gulag remains the blind spot of totalitarianism, always less serious than Auschwitz, even though they were two sides of the same coin. Future generations will have to work out how to think about these two sides of barbarism together.

What is fascism? asked Romain Gary. A certain way of hating. But the spectrum is too narrow, because that way of hating covers several regimes: one can hate with the same intensity in the name of race, class, the true God, the nation, the Earth. Barbarity is now a hybrid of several types of past horrors. Our lexicon is still too poor to describe it. 'If you want a picture of the future, imagine a boot stamping on a human face – for ever' (George Orwell).[40]

CHAPTER 10

Healing the past?

> What shall we do, Nicolas?
> Bury the dead and mend the living.
>
> ANTON CHEKHOV, *PLATONOV*

A new ambition runs through Western modernity: reparation, over the long-term, for past wrongs inflicted. This was the fond hope that Walter Benjamin had of redeeming all the tears of the vanquished, while the Messiah himself weeps over the damaged souls, hoping that redemption will spring from his tears.[1] Failing to invent the future, we prefer to revive a past seen as an abyss of mud and blood, a huge wound to be healed. But the near present also hurts us – just think of the 2015 Bataclan attack in France. How can we integrate this horror into a coherent narrative, to mend the wrongs? Through justice, which pacifies and channels pain and grief. By testifying in court, the victims recounted, to attentive ears, their suffering and 'put their burden to rest'.[2] The fact that the trial was able to take place, some years after the events, was already a relief and a miracle. True reparation lies first and foremost in the exercise of justice itself. But the handicapped will remain so, the dead will not return, and the trial will find it hard to stitch the traumas with its suturing threads. The verdict will appease the injured or their loved ones, but it will be judged too moderate by some and too severe by others. The mad desire to right all wrongs, to heal time's scars, can only fail. What has happened has happened, and it will not go away.

Can money alleviate grief?

For several decades now, the *Conseil d'État* has accepted that mental pain and various emotional disorders, including the fear of being afraid, can be accounted for, ignoring the adage that 'there is no price for tears'. However, since the terrorist attacks, tears do have a price, on a scale even, depending on whether you have lost an eye, an arm, a leg or, more tragically, a loved one, a spouse or a child.[3] And since the Guarantee Fund for Victims of Acts of Terrorism [*Fonds de garantie des victimes d'actes de terrorisme*] was set up in France, more or less penny-pinching negotiations have been taking place among victims, survivors and Fund representatives, who are anxious to keep disbursements low. Claimants, or rather their lawyers, overplay their misfortunes, sometimes with the humiliating feeling of 'begging for money'.[4] In 2020, just over 45 million euros were paid out in 'compensation and arrears of terrorism incomes', and in 2019 just over 50 million euros.

Money is a necessary step in dealing with suffering. Depending on what you have lost, a loved one or a body part, the amount of compensation will vary. For every injury suffered in a mass killing, an accident or a disaster, there is a figure, a budget line that varies according to the degree of involvement of the people involved. The heights of argumentation that lawyers on both sides can reach are as much a convention as they are a useful diversion from the felt damages. Money is not enough, but it is indispensable. The American mother of a 9/11 victim, who was awarded $3 million by the compensation fund, replied: 'I've got a better idea. Keep the money and bring my son back.'[5] In the case of the Bataclan attacks, a lump sum is awarded to directly affected victims, around 30,000 euros; for indirect victims, it is calculated according to their degree of proximity to the victims: 17,500 euros for a spouse, 12,500 for children under the age of 25, 7,500 for brothers and sisters, and so on.[6] But as long as we are negotiating, we are quantifying the misfortune, deferring it with abstract figures.

Financial compensation for torture, abductions and disappearances, as was the case in Morocco with the creation by Mohammed VI in 2004 of the Equity and Reconciliation Commission, remains a half-measure if it is not accompanied by real reforms and a willingness to punish the guilty parties (no torturer in this case was charged or even named, and the violations of rights continued).[7] When an organization, in this case the *Mouvement International pour les Reparations* (MIR) founded by Garcin Malsa, demands the payment of 240 billion euros in compensation 'to the people of Martinique' for slavery, something tells us that this may be an unreasonable demand.[8] The claimants themselves do not seem convinced of the validity of their demands. Requiring the living to pay through the nose for a distant crime committed by possible ancestors – some French citizens are the product of immigration, recent or more distant – can only elicit a shrug of the shoulders. There is a lot of talk these days about a 'black debt' in the form of monetary reparations. It's a fascinating subject, and one that excites the interest of many lawyers.[9] In July 2023, the Court of Cassation rejected a claim for compensation from 'descendants of slaves' who were demanding recognition of the 'transgenerational trauma' caused by the slave trade.[10] If slavery is to be considered a crime against humanity, the Taubira law of May 2001 had already achieved this by enshrining it in the Criminal Code. In France, the judges are only considering moral reparation, even though many economists, including Thomas Piketty, are calling for the Haitian case to be reopened, because France imposed a disproportionate tax on the young independent republic to compensate the planters.[11] The case is not without merit.

The issue of restitution is crucial, but who are the debtors? The spectrum is too narrow if it only considers Western countries. We are forgetting other players: African kings who practised slavery themselves and sold their subjects or prisoners to European or Arab slave traders. Then there is the Arab-Muslim world, carrying out the slave trade at least until the 1980s, and which has recently reappeared in Libya. We also forget that, until and including the nineteenth century, 'whites' were captured by the barbarians, particularly in Corsica, and sold on the oriental markets: 'slave' comes from 'Slavic'. ISIS has reintroduced this pigmentary privilege in its slave markets in Raqqa and Mosul by singling out light-skinned, blue-eyed captives. Should we introduce a time limit, or take this phenomenon back to the origins of humanity? Some would like to put their own price on the crimes of the past, setting up retrospective tribunals. What happens if you yourself are a descendant of slaves and slave-owners, as the historian Frédéric Régent discovered,[12] or like the 'decolonial' activist Françoise Vergès, whose great-great-grandmother owned a mere 121 slaves in 1848 on Réunion Island?[13]

This type of claim is insatiable. Once the sum has been paid, if it was, it would have to be topped up by supplements, and the flagellation would continue for ever and ever, while new atrocities were being committed by the living. Similarly, when the city of San Francisco proposed, in a vast plan to 'repair systemic racism', to allocate $5 million to each African-American (15 March 2023) but also to guarantee a minimum annual income of $100,000 dollars for each eligible black adult, a house in San Francisco for $1 per family and this for 250 years, we realized we had a hoax on our hands. Will we have to deduct from this price of the blood shed by the Americans, the 620,000 who died during the Civil War, to abolish slavery? Why, moreover, only African-Americans, and not Native Americans or every minority that makes up American society, since each has suffered in one way or another? Following this logic, every Huguenot descendant in France could demand compensation in memory of St Bartholomew's Day and Catholic persecution, every working-class family in Europe could demand compensation for belonging to those exploited by capitalism, crushed in the class struggle. If we're going to straddle the epochs, why not go back to the dawn of time?

We think of repair in the same mechanical way as a car taken to the garage or a doctor setting a broken leg, or a damaged elbow. We 'rebuild' ourselves after a bereavement, but those who have lost a loved one will never be the same again. It's not true that 'what doesn't kill you makes you stronger', as Nietzsche famously put it. Recovering from cancer does not mean regaining your former integrity. You can survive a heart attack, but your heart muscle will still be weakened. It is about going through an ordeal that will mark you for life and leave your body fragile. Every human life is based on flaws that nothing can fill, and 'there are no spare parts for speaking beings'.[14] There are train wrecks from which we never recover, which we continue to live with and which eat us up from the inside. The loss is irremediable, and every existence is a series of mourning experiences that we endure and take on in spite of ourselves. There is never a return to 'biographical innocence', to use Georges Canguilhem's phrase. 'It happened, therefore it can happen again; that is the core of what we have to say', said Primo Levi.

If the money is an enormous step forward, it is because it rules out revenge and paralyses aggression. Its neutrality puts an end to quarrels. But the exchange of goods is only a stage before the exchange of blows according to Claude Lévi-Strauss; it does not erase animosity. Money pays off a debt, but it's not a sure thing; it doesn't stop grudges. These are the limits to the market: profit does not erase conflicts or the memory of past humiliations. The gentle commerce extolled by Montesquieu can also exacerbate rivalries and fuel war, if men are driven not just by their interests but by also their passions. Many people who have received compensation refuse to cash it in, or immediately pass it on to others as if it scorched their fingers.[15] Agreeing to an amount, however high, settles nothing unless it is accompanied by a collective word of forgiveness that gives meaning to the process. Money doesn't fix things, but there can be no fixing without money – that's the paradox.

Duty to remember or duty to history?

Our era is being driven by someone who keeps their eyes stubbornly fixed on the rear-view mirror instead of looking ahead. We would so much like things not to have happened the way they did! To keep yesterday's injustices at bay, we piously pretend to retain them in memory. The duty to remember was coined by Primo Levi, as we have seen, to encourage survivors to bear witness to their experience in order to convince incredulous contemporaries. Robert Antelme similarly spoke of the lack of comprehension between the American soldiers who liberated Dachau and the skeletal inmates covered in lice and sick with typhus. They were unable to communicate because they were speaking to each other from two different planets.[16] But over the decades, this duty to remember has become an official cult, a sort of religion of retrospectivity. The respect due to the dead has been transformed into compulsive commemorations that must take account of all those who disappeared yesterday in order to prevent the horror returning. As early as 27 January 2020, in a speech at the Shoah Memorial, Emmanuel Macron declared with Christ-like pathos: 'The memory of horror must not fade. The Shoah must not heal. It must remain a living wound in the side of our Republic.' If it does heal, 'the underground evil will emerge once again'. Really? Commemorating does not prevent the return of evil, as the explosion of anti-Semitism in Europe in autumn 2023 proved. On the contrary, the more we talk about the genocide of the Jews, the more we stoke the rage against them and the desire to kill them again. Like his predecessors, President Macron has used and abused the official remembrance industry. In truth, no one can forget the Shoah, which survives as much through the work of historians as through the animosity of competing groups. Erasure is impossible, but who owns it is up for grabs. We keep the name of the catastrophe as an empty shell, but we expel the Jews and Gypsies in order to take their place.

We have a one-sided view of history, reducing it to massacres and killings and forgetting its riches, its masterpieces. We combine amnesia with hyperamnesia, ignorance of traditions with a maniacal scrupulousness about yesterday's atrocities. Our temporal glasses blind us in two ways: we are no longer heirs but vigilantes delegated by the court of the present to judge the crimes of the past. What's more, evoking the outrages of yesteryear blinds us to those of today. We have thus missed the birth of ISIS, the horrors of the Great Lakes region east of the Congo, Russia drifting towards totalitarianism. Historical consciousness inevitably reads the present only in terms inherited from the past. It is only the fear of the past that mobilizes us, and when the fear of the present arises, our eyes are dry and our brains turned off. The duty to remember serves above all to codify an agreed narrative: it is most often the imposition of an official history in which the roles are distributed in advance, the West guilty and the other peoples innocent. The time of colonialism and slavery is then frozen in an eternity of denunciation. The duty to remember brandished by some is met by the duty to repent on the part of others. The educational virtues of reminiscence are celebrated less than the punitive virtues of indictment. If memory condemns and castigates, history desacralizes, explains and reconciles. It also refrains from judging, disavowing what Claude Liauzu called 'the tyranny of official chronicles'.[17] Charles Péguy distinguished between memory, which is vertical, and history, which is horizontal, and even said they were at right angles. The former is an emotional depth that comes directly from the past, while the latter smooths out and reviews the facts. One burns and strikes, the other soothes and unfolds.[18] The main debt we owe to the peoples we have enslaved, apart from the official recognition of these persecutions, is the will to encourage the spread of democratic regimes everywhere or to speed up the attrition of dictatorships. It means not remaining silent when these same regimes fall into oppression or arbitrariness (and we know how embarrassed France is to criticize the excesses of Algerian or African governments in the name of the 'colonial debt' that seals our lips). The fear of repeating yesterday's mistakes makes us too indulgent towards contemporary abominations.

While substantial compensation can alleviate harm, there are crimes that cannot forgiven, as expressed by Vladimir Jankélévitch, a French philosopher and Jew of Russian origin; there are killers who cannot be redeemed and who must be locked up without any hope of redemption. They have gone so far in their abjectness that they have lost any prospect of returning to the human community. Even death would be too good for them; there will never be an equivalent to the suffering they have inflicted. The Enlightenment did not set out to repair History but to change it, to pull it out of the dark abyss of obscurantism. Now we are less interested in inventing the future than in erasing, sanitizing and disinfecting the past.

There is only one way to make amends for the crimes of the past, and that is to prevent their repetition in the present. All the rest is verbiage and resentment. For example, how many anti-slavery activists remain silent about today's serfdom, which leaves them cold. You don't hear them talk about ISIS, Libya or Qatar, only about Nantes, Bordeaux or London. There are two uses of memory:[19] a memory of saturated narcissism that recites the endless list of butcheries, assassinations and deportations of which our ancestors were guilty, and which is taken as an end in itself, and a vivid mobile memory that keeps the source of indignation alive, keeps us sensitive to all injustices. The former forgets nothing of what was so as not to see what is. The second refuses to be complicit in today's ignominy.

The fact remains that there is something very profound in Ernest Renan's words, that those who wish to make history must forget history. The inability to forget, the gymkhana of almost daily commemorations, is truly a European madness. We must abandon the idea of a long-term reparation of past wounds, even financial ones. The tortured and oppressed will not be avenged; no amount of financial compensation will erase the horror. Historical truth is what history's martyrs deserve, not a desire for unlimited tinkering on the part of their descendants. We cannot make our contemporaries pay for the crimes of their forebears, or open the bottomless vault of butchery and murder to extract rage and hatred. Just as we can't wake the dead and the tortured and cast them at humanity's doorstep.

The living can be repaired by grafting, cosmetic surgery, ablation or correction.[20] City centres that were destroyed can be rebuilt identically. One can restore a site, a forest, replant a burnt area, clean up a lake or a gulf, reconstitute extinct species by cloning, but not erase a dark period in history. The past cannot be annulled or regenerated, except ephemerally through grand spectacles or re-enactments of historic battles; it must be taught. It has the dual characteristic of being both finished and unfinished. It's not set in stone, it's in constant motion. 'No one knows what yesterday will be made of', we used to say in jest during the Stalinist era, when the authorities rewrote history every year or air-brushed photographs to their heart's content. But by always wanting to inject fury and wrath, we are setting up a veritable civil war of memories that are incompatible with each other, making it impossible to establish a common chronology, since there will always be groups who, in the name of their beliefs or their suffering, do not recognize themselves in it.

Memory is not always virtuous, nor is forgetting always harmful. There comes a time when you have to let the dead bury the dead and take their pain with them. There is always a risk in valuing yesterday's tears to the detriment of today's ambitions. Forgetting is the only way to make room for newcomers and lighten the burden of debts. This is the power of resurrection for generations to come. As Maurice Blanchot said of Robert Antelme's long ordeal in Buchenwald, man is the indestructible who can be infinitely destroyed.[21] But he can also be indefinitely revived. Yesterday's abominations can plunge us into endless despondency or spur us on to rebuild better societies.

TERROR AND ANNIHILATION

If there is one thing we learn from concentration camp literature, it is that the torture or the confinement did not sanctify the victims. In Primo Levi's book, the SS reduced the crowd of prisoners to a grey, amorphous mass who stole, denounced and occasionally killed for a piece of bread. Apathetic, vulnerable, exhausted by typhus or cholera, tainted by dysentery and hunger, they were debris crushed by a machine of death, awaiting the end like a liberation. Charlotte Delbo, interned at Auschwitz in 1943 and then transferred to Ravensbrück in 1944, tells the story of a spring Sunday in the camp:

> All the women were seated in the dust of the dried mud, a miserable swarm that made one think of flies on a dung heap. Probably because of the smell ... so dense and fetid. ... The stink of diarrhea and corpses. Above this stink a blue sky. And in my memory spring was singing.[22]

The camps were laboratories for the degradation of the human species. Bruno Bettelheim recounts that some inmates, mimicking the SS, enjoyed hitting each other to test their endurance.[23] Worse still, following the example of the Nazis, they eliminated unfit new arrivals as soon as they entered the camp.[24] When Auschwitz was liberated by Soviet troops in February 1945, Primo Levi described it as a huge frozen latrine

where starving zombies – subhumans in Nazi termi-
nology – vegetated. The characters in Isaac Bashevis
Singer's 1978 Nobel Prize-winning novel, most of
whom were former deportees, were not ennobled by
the camp experience. It turned them into scoundrels,
debauchees, hooligans and pimps.[25] The beatings and
humiliations didn't make them any better. The author
does not shy away from pointing out their pettiness
and meanness, without being judgemental or hostile.

It was the perversity of the Nazi and Stalinist
systems to break the very people they were preying
on, to make them loathe themselves. The 'aristocrats'
had to distinguish themselves from the lice-ridden
prisoner mob and eliminate them without remorse.
And the prisoners had to internalize their imminent
death. Primo Levi:

> With the adaptable, the strong and astute individuals,
> even the leaders willingly keep contact, sometimes even
> friendly contact, because they hope later to perhaps
> derive some benefit. But with the musselmans,[26] the
> men in decay, it is not even worth speaking ... one
> knows that they are only here on a visit, that in a few
> weeks nothing will remain of them but a handful of
> ashes in some near-by field.[27]

Extreme misfortune accelerates decay and does
not allow for any optimistic take on the suffering
that might give people an uplifting boost. It does
not educate people; it makes them desperate and
bitter. This is a far cry from the edifying vision of
Solzhenitsyn, who saw the Gulag as the workshop for
the regeneration of the Slavic world. On the contrary,
there was a great temptation to passively succumb to
the blows in order to attain the final deliverance.[28]

Even after liberation, confidence in existence had died: 'life was returned to me/and here I am in front of life/as though facing a dress/I can no longer wear'.[29]

Those most tortured never thought of themselves as victims, but rather as mutants. In their way of surviving such abjection, they speak to us from deep inside some accursed distant planet. There is a point where misfortune is no longer possible, where sadness and tears have become a luxury for healthy people. This is the scandalous ending to Imre Kertész's book, in the very last lines of his account of Auschwitz: 'For even there, next to the chimneys, in the intervals between the torments, there was something that resembled happiness. ... Yes, the next time I am asked, I ought to speak about that, the happiness of the concentration camps.'[30] Primo Levi recounts how his experience of the camps enriched him: 'onto my brief and tragic experience as a deportee has been overlaid that much longer and complex experience of writer-witness, and the sum total is clearly positive in its totality, this past has made me richer and surer'.[31] Auschwitz was his university and his hell. And in 1954, Bruno Bettelheim wrote to a friend: 'Now that all that has fortunately been behind me for fifteen years, I can admit it: the year I spent in concentration camps did me good.'[32] Primo Levi eventually committed suicide, as did Bruno Bettelheim, Jean Améry and several others.

Reconciliation, with whom and how?

On 20 December 2022, Dutch Prime Minister Mark Rutte, against the advice of his party, apologized to the descendants of Surinamese and Antilleans living in the Netherlands. He himself hesitated for a long time before revealing the darker side of slavery, abolished only in 1873 in the monarchy. But Mark Rutte's prevarications did not convince those concerned, who saw in his speech not the expression of sincere repentance but rather what Gustave Flaubert called 'the oblique genuflection of a pious person in a hurry'. A few months later, on 1 July 2023, the King of the Netherlands, Willem-Alexander, completed this gesture in a more solemn manner. So here Mark Rutte is joining a long line of heads of state that began with Willy Brandt kneeling before the Warsaw Ghetto memorial on 7 December 1970, and continued with President de Klerk's solemn apology to Nelson Mandela in 1994 during the handover of power at the end of apartheid. What was then something quite fruitful, helping to move a political process along, gradually became a mechanized ritual devoid of meaning. Better to say nothing than to overdo requests for forgiveness.

To take a current example, it is likely that the Russians and Ukrainians will only resume dialogue once Moscow's troops have been driven out of the occupied territories and take the blame for their actions. This is unlikely to happen for a long time, if ever. The USSR, having imploded from within because of Gorbachev's decisions as General Secretary of the Communist Party in 1989, never had to look back on its barbarity as Nazi Germany did. There was no Communist version of Nuremberg imposed by the victors and the Stalinist abscess was never lanced from within, only blamed on 'personality cults'. For reconciliation to happen, the aggressor must be defeated militarily and enter into a long process of self-examination. They have to officially ask for forgiveness and will not have too many years to reflect on their crimes.

When de Gaulle and Adenauer met in Reims Cathedral on 8 July 1962, the Third Reich had been defeated for seventeen years. Adenauer had been resisting Nazism since 1933 and de Gaulle had led the Free French in London. Both heads of state were Catholics by culture, and Reims was a symbolic choice. The city had been martyred in the First World War and Clovis was baptized there. The two men shaking hands not only strengthened the construction of Europe but also, after all the blood that had been spilled, sealed a new brotherhood. We should remember how the leading French politician Léon Blum, imprisoned in Buchenwald in 1943 as a possible bargaining chip, a 'temporary tenant of a vast slaughterhouse' and certain of being shot at any given moment, pleaded in letters to his son in 1944 for an unconditional reconciliation with Germany.

There are other types of reconciliation. Asphyxiation, for instance, as in Algeria, when to quell the civil war of 1991–2002 they decreed the abolition of the past with a ban on talking about it under penalty of prosecution for 'anyone who dares to instrumentalize the national tragedy'. In return, former terrorists were given government jobs.

South Africa is another example of accord with its Truth and Reconciliation Commission based on Bantu *Ubuntu* – the humanity of all – and Christian forgiveness. It promised impunity to apartheid criminals in exchange for the truth, on the model of transitive, non-punitive justice. Confident in the fact that 'even the worst racist has the capacity to change', as Desmond Tutu said, this form of fraternization relies on the intimate transformation of the criminal rather than on vindictiveness. This avoided the pitfall of sterile revenge, which produces counter-revenge, or the public humiliation of a section of the national community.

The term 'transitional justice' – coined in 1992 by the jurist Ruti Teitel[33] – is used to describe the political process of organizing a way out of a dictatorship, a bloody regime or a war: an attempt is made to move from the hell of mass crime to the purgatory of cohabitation in order to rebuild a political community. Similarly, the aim of 'restorative justice' is not so much to punish criminals or murderers as to bring them face to face with their victims and together in the presence of the police, social services and sometimes the families involved.[34] Inspired by traditional societies, this kind of reconciliation complements traditional systems of prevention and punishment, provided that the offender acknowledges his or her wrongdoing and that the offence is not an unforgivable crime. Not everyone has John Paul II's generosity of spirit. He forgave his would-be murderer, Mehmet Ali Ağca, after an assassination attempt on 13 May 1981 in Rome.

Finally, there is reconciliation by decree: fraternize or I'll put you in prison. In Paul Kagame's post-genocide Rwanda, the aim was to affirm the unity of the people, but under the iron grip of the all-powerful ruling party. This compulsion to build bridges under the iron fist of the State forbade 'ethnic divisionism' and the 'trivialization of genocide' on pain of imprisonment or re-education.[35] The victims were forced to live side-by-side with their former executioners, while the Hutus were constantly reminded that they were, and remain, on the wrong side of history. In Rwanda, as in South Africa, the result is still precarious. In the latter case, 'the truth was not measured but manufactured. To be charitable, we can say that the truth was negotiated. It was this truth that rescued South Africa from a revolutionary abyss. It is also the very same truth that will hover as a spectral figure over the country's uncertain future', said Ebrahim Moosa, professor of Islamic studies, in 2000.[36] Since then nothing has really contradicted this prediction. All these policies of conditional forgiveness sketch out the outlines of a possible redemption without actually achieving it. There are some half-open doors that the government closes, like the Memorial association founded by Sakharov in 1989 and dissolved in December 2021 by the Russian Supreme Court because it 'created a false image of the USSR'. The work of exposing offences was brutally interrupted when Stalin was rehabilitated.

Even in the young nations of the South, in Africa and Asia, the skeletons are spilling out of their cupboards, not to mention ISIS, Hamas and al-Qaeda. Shortly after they are born, these new homelands stain their glorious legends with multiple acts of violence. The last half-century has taught us that there are no innocent peoples post-independence. And history itself is moving in two diametrically opposed directions. While one part of humanity – mostly the democracies – is developing institutions to punish mass crime, the new carnivores – Turkey, Iran, Russia, China and Afghanistan – are flourishing. The West is renouncing imperialism, while former empires want to revive their former glory.[37] One part of humanity wants to embark on a process of exorcism from its evil ways, while the other shamelessly plunges in. *Crime and punishment go hand in hand, the former always outnumbering the latter.* Abjection and cruelty will never cease to horrify us; evil abounds, incredibly inventive in its manifestations. There are still too many bereavements to cope with, not to mention those caused by war or reprisals.

If there is one lesson that Europe can offer the world, it is the way in which its member nations, recruited from bloodshed and slaughter, have come to terms with each other while on the brink of the abyss, proving that the bitterest legacies can be overcome. We can't halt the tragedies of history, but we can limit them as much as possible. We can reflect on the metaphor of Penelope undoing her day's weaving at night. The accounts will not be settled, the debts forgiven, or the memories appeased. It will always be preferable for an international institution, such as the Criminal Court, to separate the victims from the aggressors and recognize the former as having official status, enshrined in law, and the latter as having the possibility of making amends if they are sincere. 'Condemn the sin and forgive the sinner', as the Gospels say. On condition, however, that the sinner acknowledges his or her wrongdoing and genuinely wants to make amends.

A RUN OF BAD LUCK

In their *Journal*, the Goncourt brothers tell of a woman who, on a stagecoach journey, tells one of her friends, whom she has not seen for a long time, the poignant story of her family. Her father had been shot, her mother had drowned, her husband had died in a fire. All she had left was a child living in Egypt, who was recently bathing in the Nile in a playful and carefree mood, when a crocodile started moving in on him. But the woman couldn't go any further with her story. The passengers, horrified at first, didn't wait for the end, didn't wait for the crocodile to open its terrible jaws and swallow the child. Suddenly they burst into thunderous laughter. Enough is enough. There's a limit to everything.[38]

There are individuals who, in any situation, infallibly choose the path of disaster. They have an uncanny ability to fail at everything they undertake. This extraordinary propensity to 'create their own misfortunes', as Paul Watzlawick said, calls for admiration. Their lives soon collapse in a heap, reinforcing the inevitability of it all. If, by chance, they come across a fellow sufferer, they embark on a mad competition, ostentatiously bragging about all the bad luck that has come their way. No one has the right to beat them on this ground. They want to stay locked in the dungeon of their despair. And if they fall ill, they amass the most dreadful pathologies, each becoming an encyclopaedia of morbidity. These chronic sufferers are threatened by only one thing, a momentary appearance of happiness. Life holds out its arms to them, inviting them to surrender to it, to love. For a moment, they are on the borderline of a good mood. But it's too late, because joy has to be cultivated. All they have sown is bad luck and negativity; they have to bow their heads and resolve to carry on.

CHAPTER 11

The hero, an ambiguous antithesis

The glory of great men is the heritage of a free country.
After their death, all the people inherit it.

MADAME DE STAËL

There is no hero without an audience.

ANDRÉ MALRAUX, *MAN'S HOPE*

When Odysseus, in the eleventh canto of the *Odyssey*, arrives on the shores of Hades, the realm of the dead, he meets the shade of the dead Achilles. He has a great admiration for this hero who chose a short life and won undying glory in battle. But Achilles' reply shocks him: 'Odysseus, you must not comfort me/for death. I would prefer to be a workman,/hired by a poor man on a peasant farm,/than rule as king of all the dead.'[1] The dead are an indistinct, amnesiac rabble, for Hades is the realm of oblivion. Only the living can still sing the praises of the departed hero. Without them, there is only confusion and chaos. Odysseus, stunned by this revelation, flees the teeming crowd of the dead forever, to return to the world of the living. This brief apologue says it all. If being a hero means risking your life in the service of a higher purpose, there is an immediate objection. Is it worth throwing your hat in the ring? Wars are a production line of heroes. The aura of the supermen is brought down to the popular level to justify collective death, like the parade of the Immortals in Russia, where demonstrators march with portraits of their ancestors killed between 1941 and 1945, anxious to display the moral supremacy of the great Slavic people over the rest of humanity. Heroic morality knows only one simple binary: 'us and them, friend and foe, courage and cowardice', as Tzvetan Todorov writes.[2]

What victimhood has over heroism is that victimization can be democratized, while heroism cannot. Heroism remains the preserve of a succession of elites, whereas victimization turns a private drama into a collective epic. But heroism has been corrupted by states, by cold monsters that have turned soldiers into human cattle for dubious causes. Downgraded to duty, heroism has become the alibi for authoritarian regimes and has morphed into a killing machine. The absolute hero, as Max Scheler[3] saw it, would be a robot who would go to his death in a mechanical way, or like a cyborg we would say nowadays. He would be a monster, a martyr like the shahibs of radical Islam trained to die for a Moloch God thirsty for mass graves. Bloody fools, but fools all the same.

The demolition of the hero under the Ancien Régime

When Louis XIV established absolute monarchy and invited the French nobility to Versailles in 1682, he not only divided a turbulent aristocracy, he also transformed fierce warriors into courtiers and gossipy little marquises, of which Saint-Simon was the brilliant chronicler. The great lords went from rebels to flatterers, from swordsmen to jesters. The 'destruction of the hero' of Paul Bénichou[4] coincided in Europe with the questioning of the chivalric ideal in the seventeenth century, the point at which the Ancien Régime began to weaken. Cervantes, with the figure of Don Quixote, had anticipated this decline: a scruffy, idealistic knight who thought he was taking on giants but was only charging at windmills. Nobles ceased to be demigods who dazzled and amazed; their desire for prestige was a form of sublimated self-interest that Pascal and La Rochefoucauld called pride or vanity. Honour degenerates into a base pantomime, like furious little roosters whose self-esteem is wounded and who demand justice in duels. Oversize heroes, puffed up only with their own self-importance, as in Corneille's plays. Men who dream what they should be, not what they are.[5] These strong-willed creatures are driven by an appetite for glory, making spectacles of themselves, showing their triumphs to all and sundry.

A new anthropology was to emerge from the French Revolution, giving rise to two major types: the bourgeois, the man of order and work, and the anti-bourgeois, the artist, the revolutionary, the outlaw, anxious to undo what the former had built. La Rochefoucauld battled against the aristocracy from the point of view of the future commoners; Nietzsche in turn fought the commoners, the man of the herd, in the name of a vanished aristocracy that he dreamed of resurrecting with the will to power. His 'magnificent *blonde brute*, avidly rampant for spoil and victory'[6] was to give rise to a new individual and new gods. But unbeknownst to him, his great lords would wear the runes of the SS and the uniforms of the Wehrmacht. The last tragic episode in the heroism of the Ancien

Régime was the mounted charge of the French cuirassiers at Reichshoffen on 6 August 1870, cut to pieces by the Prussian artillery.

There are at least two kinds of heroes, those who want to replace the ordinary man with a superior type, and those who put their exceptional courage at the service of others, like Joan of Arc, according to Michelet and Péguy, both Saviour of France and Saint capable of caring for wounded Englishmen, profoundly vulnerable and valiant, a unique conjunction of the worldly and the spiritual.[7] 'Only great hearts know how much glory there is in being good', observed Saint François de Sales. But look also at Simone Weil, deported to Auschwitz, stateswoman, bringing fundamental emancipation laws for women, who combined the two figures of victim and heroine. Jacques Julliard rightly said that 'she pulls us neither to the left nor to the right, but upwards'.[8] Human beings only achieve their essence by surpassing themselves. They brave death so that the lives of those in danger may triumph. They combine audacity and freedom to lead them towards the Good.

Heroes by chance

If one must suffer to be a victim, but act to be a hero, then we cherish above all the transformation of anonymous people into exceptional individuals, through some accident or rescue. They act without thinking, almost by instinct. There are the everyday supermen and superwomen, firefighters or police, who take real risks for others and fight against fire, floods, earthquakes, hostage-taking. But this is their job, almost a service. The ordinary person who jumps into the water to save someone who is drowning, or who goes up to rescue a child from a burning building, stirs our admiration because they impulsively put everything on the line. They have forgotten spontaneous selfishness to come to the aid of a stranger. They are supermen or women by accident, not through professional bravery. If they hadn't done it, what would they have had to lose? No one would blame them. But for just one moment, someone else's life was more sacred than their own. It makes absolutely no sense, but it is the height of generosity. There are circumstances that awaken an audacity in all of us that we never knew existed. It's that god of the moment, the Greek *kairos*, that decides everything on a whim and separates the cowardly from the brave.

But heroism is more than simple courage; it is a narrative and a social construct, almost a reconstruction of the event.[9] Courage is a state of mind and an education, especially at a time when what Monique Castillo calls 'the culture of discouragement' prevails.[10] Everything is being done today to disarm future generations through the cult of fear. In the 1970s, the German philosopher Hans Jonas, an icon of the Greens, stressed the 'heuristic' virtue of fear as a tool for knowledge and insight into the destructive potential of our technical instruments.[11] As in Thomas Hobbes's *Leviathan* (1651), we need to create a new political order out of human impotence, bending mortals under the yoke of terror. In view of climatic and planetary disaster, Hans Jonas himself, like a whole section of the ecology movement, proposed a 'benevolent tyranny' of enlightened people.

If courage is fear overcome, it is a revelation for oneself and for others. There are singular individuals who, at certain periods in history, have shown exemplary bravery: Georges Clemenceau, Louise Michel, Nadezhda Mandelstam, Albert Camus, Jean Moulin, Charb, etc., 'these well-tempered souls' as Manuel Valls described them in a book devoted to these great figures.[12] It takes more than valour at certain times; it takes an admirable and clear-sighted view of history. No one can define courage, but everyone knows what cowardice is. Courage is not intrepid bandits or hooligans, with their derring-do; rather it implies an impulse of the heart, a form of generosity, as the etymology reminds us. Above all, it implies a legend corroborated by time. The hero, writes Marek Edelman, is not only the fighter who took up arms against Nazism, but also the young girl who climbed into the death wagon so as not to let her mother go off alone to Treblinka, prepared to endure the ordeal with her.[13] Just as the saint is not content to do what is Good, but does what is Best, the hero attempts the impossible and succeeds.

This was the case of the police commissioner, assisted by his teammate, who decided, against the advice of his superiors, to enter the Bataclan theatre on 13 November 2015, shooting a terrorist to stop the carnage. Both of them, certain of dying, briefly phoned their respective partners, but emerged unharmed. Arnaud Beltrame, a senior police officer and fervent Christian, was murdered by a terrorist on 24 March 2018 in Carcassonne while voluntarily taking the place of hostages in a supermarket in Trèbes. He died of his wounds in hospital and was honoured by the entire nation. Ukrainian film-maker Oleg Sentsov was released from Putin's jails after a vast international campaign on his behalf. Enlisted in the Special Forces at the start of the war, he found a soldier in a trench near Bakhmut in July 2022 with his head smashed by a bullet. He hoisted him onto his shoulders, brought him back to the rear and saved him. Another Ukrainian combatant, Oleksandr Matsievsky, was filmed smoking a cigarette. Taken prisoner in April 2023 by the Russians, who demanded that he renounce his homeland, he looked his executioners straight in the eye and cried out 'Long live Ukraine' before falling to the gunfire. Heroes and saints alike transform their acts into great feats and awaken the best in all of us.

We can glean just as many admirable gestures from the course of recent history. Lassana Bathily, the Malian employee of the Hyper Cacher store in Vincennes, saved several people during the hostage situation on 9 January 2015. Mamoudou Gassama, an illegal immigrant from Mali, climbed four floors of a Paris building on 26 May 2018 to rescue a child clinging to a balcony. Psychoanalyst and philosopher Anne Dufourmantelle was struck down by cardiac arrest after rescuing a friend's son from drowning at Pampelonne beach near St Tropez in July 2017. The child was ten and she fifty-three. She sacrificed herself out of the goodness of her heart. In April 2023, a thirteen-year-old schoolboy in Michigan (USA) got behind the wheel of his school bus after the driver collapsed. He managed to park the vehicle on the side of the road.

In June 2023, a young Frenchman in Annecy, Henri d'Anselme, 'the man with the rucksack', stood between some children and a murderer trying to stab them. A Bedouin taxi driver and an Israeli Arab, Youssef Zyadney, alerted on the morning of 7 October 2023, saved around thirty young revellers from the Hamas massacre. Not to forget either the Righteous of the Second World War who, in France at least, saved three quarters of the Jewish community: 'They were men or women, old or young, rich or poor ... they could not explain why they acted as they did.'[14]

And what would we have done in their place? This kind of action is more instinctive than reflective, and springs from the intersection of chance and decision. You can't put it off; you have to act in the moment. Reaching for a drowning person, coming to the aid of a woman threatened with rape, sheltering fugitives hunted down by killers: a spark can ignite in the most trivial situations and lift us to greatness. But it's a greatness that has no future and is often forgotten, even if it raises our collective profile. All heroes are unique points of intersection in the life of humanity and make us proud to be part of it. They inspire a healthy imitation in everyone. There could be no social life without these tiny stories that inspire admiration. For the saint, as for the hero, according to Henri Bergson, it is enough to appear and shine forth to make a name for oneself. They inspire such an aura of devotion and intelligence that ordinary people are captivated by them. The former revives established religion, the latter takes common humanity to new heights.

Some heroines combine heroism and exemplarity, such as the demonstrators in Iran or Afghanistan who refuse, at the cost of their lives, to bear the yoke of the bearded men (the journalist Narges Mohammadi was awarded the Nobel Peace Prize in 2023, infuriating the Tehran authorities). Or the Peshmerga fighter Asya Ramazan Antar, dubbed the 'Kurdish Angelina Jolie' for her resemblance to the American actress, who was killed in a clash with Islamic State jihadists. And the young Pakistani Christian Malala Yousafzai, who was shot in the head by the Taliban because she supported education for girls, and who was awarded the Nobel Peace Prize at the age of seventeen. These people, through their admirable acts, create authority: etymologically, they augment us, extending the bounds of what it means to be human.

Heroism, admirable when it is solitary, becomes problematic when it is required of an entire people enlisted under the banner of propaganda. Heroism is the fallback position of any totalitarian regime that wishes to sacrifice thousands of men simply for the power of a leader or a party. The result is no longer armies of soldiers but, as in Russia, cohorts of puppets trained to kill, their fear dulled by alcohol or amphetamines. Ukraine itself is caught up in the inconsistencies of state gallantry: it wants to make heroes of the people, including ordinary civilians, and popularize dead soldiers. It is erecting Walls of Heroes, as in the Kiev fresco on the walls of St Michael's monastery, with thousands of photos of soldiers fallen at the front since the 2014 Donbass war. No soldier is forgotten: their name, their portrait and their qualities are displayed among their brothers and sisters in-arms. You are still with us, that's what these permanent wall displays say.

Every hero is irreplaceable when he or she acts; he or she was the indispensable person at the crucial moment. 'No man is a hero to his valet', said Hegel, 'not because the hero is no hero but because the valet is – a valet with whom the hero has to do, not as a hero, but as a man who eats, drinks, and dresses.' Not everything that diminishes giants makes dwarfs grow. When the vulgate rules, tall poppies should not appear. There is no passion more democratic than that of belittling the great, casting them down from their pedestals after having adored them (de Gaulle and Churchill are good examples). The fall of idols is an occasion for collective rejoicing when the drive forwards gives way to exhaustion, when people are tired of worshipping and subject their ephemeral gods to a levelling morality to bring them back into the fold. This is the ambivalence of modern societies; they revere the extraordinary as much as they try to democratize it, to reduce it to the lowest common denominator. There is a deep-seated grudge against heroes for being higher than we are. Aristocratic culture under the Ancien Régime offered everyone examples of valour and admiration. Democratic culture increases the rivalry. If someone casts a shadow over me I have an urge to belittle them, in the name of equality and a common mediocrity.

If they are not just in the service of some chance opportunity, exceptional people strive for excellence. Because they 'expand the frontiers of human possibilities', as Karl Jaspers said,[15] they extract us from our constrictions and open us up to a wider dimension of ourselves. They put at risk what is most dear to us all: our biological life. The leap from heroism to greatness is a rare one in history. De Gaulle, the hero of 18 June 1940, who raised France to the rank of a power resisting Nazism, went on to become a head of state, a decolonizer and the founder of the Fifth Republic. Charismatic people, whether men or women, multiply talents and skills. They stimulate the potential for intelligence and generosity in everyone. Heroes, like the great philosophers or heads of state, do not belong to their time, they belong to all ages. They are the summits (of thought, science, political art) that lift us above our tiny worries, our petty concerns. They take us where we never thought we would go.

But be careful, too much of the sublime can spoil things. While the hero is the antithesis of the victim, everyday life is only held together by anti-heroes. There is also self-sacrifice, courage and madness in the gesture of a nurse who inserts a drip, washes a sick patient, empties a basin, or in the devotion of parents and teachers who feed, protect, educate and guide their offspring. Community life is only held together by this invisible cement, this almost animal instinct that binds human beings together in the warm bath of benevolence and care for the most disadvantaged.

CHAPTER 12

Is this how men live? (Louis Aragon)

> If you can meet with Triumph and Disaster ...
> Or watch the things you gave your life to, broken,
> And stoop and build 'em up with worn-out tools ...
> You will be a man my son.
>
> Rudyard Kipling

How does one cope with bereavement and loss? Consoling a friend stricken with a terminal disease, offering words of comfort? Recovering from a mugging or a broken relationship? Whenever misfortune strikes us, we feel helpless and dazed, deprived of both a response and the appropriate language. We all have our own strategies. Some shut themselves away and bury their grief deep down, while others sound the alarm, call on their loved ones and demand their attention. Old hands recall previous crises, reminisce about how they overcame the shock and were able to calm down again. Younger ones, devastated, ask for help from their elders, relying on their examples to regain hope. The intolerable is the multiplication of one evil after another, 'Because misfortunes never come singly. Misfortunes intermarry; they beget children, as in the Book.'[1] Disgraces seem to accumulate without end and we have to remove one after the other to prevent the Hydra from producing other heads that will savage us and finish us off.

Going through hell and back?

Age makes us more tolerant of the hardships that come our way, because they are part of the order of things. As time goes by, there is more death in our make-up than life, friends slip away, the body becomes more fragile, and falling ill is not a shock but the norm, up to a point. Being in good health after the age of sixty means moving from one illness to another, provided none is debilitating. Pathologies only tell us one thing, and that is to fight them before they strike us down. All suffering is bearable if it has already been recounted and experienced by others; if it is part of our shared experience. But our capacities to bear it are unequal: the same crucible that grows some, annihilates others, purifies the former and brings down the latter. We resist evil, not to defeat it, but to put off the inevitable surrender.

When we look at borderline situations, hostage-taking, comas, serious accidents, cataclysms, we always ask ourselves: *How did they get through that hell?* Jean-Paul Kauffmann, for three years hostage to a terrorist group in Lebanon where he experienced the trauma of travelling rolled up in a carpet; the journalist Olivier Dubois kidnapped in the Sahel and held for 711 days; the journalist Florence Aubenas kidnapped in 2005 in Baghdad for 157 days in extremely harsh conditions. What kept Olivier Dubois going? Studying the Quran to understand his kidnappers, sport and his cooking skills. He asked his jailers for a pressure cooker to improve the camp's rather crude cuisine, and prepared cakes, doughnuts and bread stuffed with dates. At first, his guards refused to eat with a reprobate, but after tasting one of his cakes, they asked for more. This captivity was, according to him, the longest reportage ever made.[2] French-Colombian MP Ingrid Betancourt, who was held prisoner for six years by Farc, a group of far-left drug traffickers, was able to hold on thanks to her faith. Florence Aubenas was mistakenly imprisoned, along with her guide Hussein Hanoun, by a Sunni group opposed to the American presence in Iraq. She told of her captivity in a cellar four metres long by two metres wide and one and a half high, without hearing a single sound apart from water dripping in the rusty pipes. For the first few days of her detention, bound hand and foot, lying on a bed, she was allowed twenty steps a day and a maximum of eighty words of conversation with her jailers. As for Jean-Paul Kauffmann, hostage of Hezbollah, he recited to himself, from the depths of his filthy dungeon, the 'tables of Bordeaux law', the founding text that has ranked Bordeaux wines since 1855. Ironically, his torturers considered alcohol to be an abomination. It was the memory of aromas that kept him going: 'And sometimes, in the deep, dark well, the miracle happened: the cedar and blackcurrant flavours of Cabernet Sauvignon, the plum aromas of Merlot.'[3] For him, the ultimate test 'is not suffering but Time. Suffering keeps you busy. But Time, without measure or end, is the cruellest torment, the greatest trial for the captive. It is a club. You constantly have to duck not to get it in the face.' And the Israeli hostages, captives of Hamas, how did they hold out, before some of them were executed or tortured, not forgetting the women, the sex slaves of their captors?

In a beautiful book written to exorcize his captivity, *La Maison du retour* [The House of Return], an account of his purchase of a dilapidated building in the Landes, Jean-Paul Kauffmann described his years in prison as a failure:

> Being caught, experiencing humiliation and fear, experiencing the exceptional stupidity of your jailers every day, always getting the short end of the stick, there's nothing to boast about: it's not an accident but a failure. You take a turn for the worse, you drag your family and loved ones into this shipwreck. Being a survivor is not a victory either. It's a catch-up session.[4]

And if 'in the depths of my bottomless pit, reading worked like a spell',[5] the spell was over. He was no longer hooked. He compared himself to Borges, who went blind but continued to buy books. It was in the trees, which he was now planting and caring for, that he sought his 'lost presence': emotion was stronger in front of a plant than in front of a printed book. So there are calamities from which we never recover, exorcisms that fail. The former hostage says he was devastated, a prisoner of irrepressible melancholy. But it was still in a very literary book that he expressed how tired he was of literature. And in the case of Florence Aubenas, whose composure and humour was always unfailing, she refused to take on the role of victim, even though her release gave rise to a quasi-national celebration, with French President Jacques Chirac welcoming her in person on the tarmac at Villacoublay in June 2005: 'I am the opposite of the unfortunate victim looking for a panic station. I feel more like I'm starting to piss people off.'[6] The entire work of psychotherapist Bruno Bettelheim, a former Buchenwald captive, autism specialist and theorist of 'extreme situations', is a reflection on survival: did the deportees manage to escape the horror of the concentration camp or are they still haunted by the torture they endured? The author gives a double yes to this question. Both hypotheses are equally true: psychic dislocation and possible reconstruction. The miraculous are guilty of an unforgivable crime: to have survived, to have had this scandalous and prodigious opportunity. 'I live because a friend, a comrade, died in my place', said Elie Wiesel. In fact, Bruno Bettelheim ended up killing himself on 13 March 1990, anniversary of the day the Nazis entered Vienna, his home town, although we do not know whether this was motivated by chronic depression or nightmares from his past.

To recover or to resign?

The trouble with unhappiness is that it burdens you with its presence and you miss out on the world. As long as it is there, insolent and imperious, we are no longer with others, or merely grudgingly. There are at least two ways of being a victim: passively, shut away in your injury as if it were a fortress, and actively, where you come together with others to share a common destiny. Victims' associations (for road accidents, terrorist attacks, medical errors) are there to influence the authorities to prevent future tragedies. The seriously injured, the disabled and the traumatized, strengthened by their shared weaknesses, want first and foremost to return to a normal life. Against terrorism, paedophilia, feminicide and genital mutilation, these groups play an essential role in influencing the passing of preventive legislation.[7] Anonymous men and women, wounded in their flesh, want to bring their suffering into the public arena and demand recognition. These new players are shifting the threshold of intolerance for everyone and forcing society to take note. What used to be a matter of misfortune, the usual trials and tribulations of life, now falls into the category of the inadmissible. Here, as elsewhere, in the world of work, people are fighting not to allow themselves to be reduced to their misfortune, to change the way they look at disability, for example. We take serious notice of public figures (Bernard Tapie, Florent Pagny, Jean d'Ormesson, Axel Kahn) suffering from a serious illness and who teach us lessons in patience and courage. Each illness or change gives rise to specific responses, to *coalitions of the aggrieved* where a double task of mutual aid and exchange is played out. People from all walks of life and all origins are drawn together by the same trauma and decide to fight it together. By inserting their private dramas into a collective chapter, each patient becomes both the pupil who learns from the others and the teacher who teaches them how to use medical and legal knowledge.

The model for this type of therapy is Alcoholics Anonymous, founded in 1935 and popularized in France by Joseph Kessel. It is based on the principle of a twelve-step programme of recovery within a supportive fellowship, the treatment being summed up in the famous prayer: 'My God, give me the serenity to accept the things I cannot change, the courage to change the things I can and the wisdom to know the difference.' A magnificent message evocative of Stoic philosophy, but without a trace of resignation. *Misfortune is a fact, and there's no need to make a faith of it.* We'll never get to the bottom of it, we can only arrange temporary cease-fires with it. If we have to be cured of the desire to cure everything, it is absurd to bow down to modifiable fates on the grounds that the battle is lost in advance. We can cure certain ills, but not misfortune itself, which is diabolically clever at reinvention. The fact that not everything is possible does not mean that nothing is permissible; and each generation takes up the fight again with new weapons, knowing that the elimination of one scourge is immediately followed by the appearance of a new one. The more we battle the trials of life, the more there is no solution to human misfortune.

A way out of victimization?

Contemporary citizens, rising up against their suffering, have the choice of brooding over their shame or reconstituting themselves, shedding the robes of martyrdom to enter the orders of the free. It is likely that our era will not be able to decide between these two options. Claiming the banner of the persecuted is also a business, let's not forget: both our difficult childhood and our victorious restoration are up for sale. Entire careers have been built on this theme. 'Those who refuse to fight are more grievously wounded than those who fight', said Oscar Wilde. As it happens, wisdom is the always difficult marriage between acquiescence and revolt, patience and stubbornness. When you have reasons to live, you have reasons to suffer and to fight for what you love. The writer Cioran recounts with some mischief that one day his mother, seeing him despondent, said: 'If I had known, I would have had an abortion.' Instead of being affected by this, the young man, as he was then, received this admission as a liberation. He was the result of chance, not necessity.[8]

It is not the victim condition that one has to extract oneself from, but victimization mentality. The fate of the victims themselves lies in their own hands. We have no right to tell them what to do, neither in forgetting nor in remembering. The fact remains that many are rebelling against what has become an actual status. Such is the case of Samantha Geimer in Los Angeles. Roman Polanski forced himself on her sexually when she was thirteen and a half after her mother had left her alone with the film-maker. Asked by a journalist what she thought of Adèle Haenel's statement to *The New York Times* on 24 February 2020: 'Distinguishing Polanski [at the César Awards] is spitting in the face of all victims. It means raping women isn't that bad', she replied:

> I completely disagree. Asking all women to bear the brunt not only of their attack but also of everyone else's indignation for all eternity is spitting in the face of all those who have recovered and moved on. ... No one has the right to tell a victim what to think and how to feel. When you refuse to let a victim forgive and move on to satisfy your own need to hate and punish, you only hurt them more deeply. A victim has the right to put the past behind them, and an abuser also has the right to rehabilitate and make amends, especially when they have admitted their wrongdoing and apologised.[9]

This is an unusual comeback, and an embarrassment for those who want to trade in women's pain. In 2009, Samantha Geimer requested the American courts to drop proceedings against the Franco-Polish director, and said she had recovered. She leads a happy life. Against the current trend towards grief, she refuses to turn her disgrace into an honorary title. Take also the writer Tristane Banon, who had been attacked by Dominique Strauss-Kahn. In *La Paix des sexes* [The Sexes at Peace], she denounced the 'drumbeat of victimhood':

> I'm a woman, not a victim. I was a victim, but these things pass. When the status of victim tends to become an added value, an ennoblement that some women want to acquire at all costs, just as one seeks to achieve social status, I think, on the contrary, that to make a heroine of the victim rather than wanting to respect her, is to kill the warrior in her, murder the creator, put a value on submission, ban women from being equal to men.[10]

Or, again, the essayist and journalist Peggy Sastre, who was also raped. She decided, as a personal choice, not to lodge a complaint, on the principle that 'evil people only have as much power over us as we give them'.[11]

> Because I kept saying that my rape hadn't done anything to me … once I realized that the guy wasn't listening to my refusal and that any more resistance would have put me in danger, I simply waited it out. I was told to 'let go', to express my anger, my rage, my pain that, how could I not, it was 'staring me in the face'. I could only pathologically 'repress' it.

Taking part in therapy sessions where the counsellor pushes her to 'emotional outbursts' to explode into tears and trembling, she rebels and refuses to add her case 'to the flock of softened-up crazies'.

None of these women is setting an example. They sketch out another path, the desire to turn the page and continue to live a normal life. Others, like the aforementioned Neige Sinno, who was raped by her stepfather from the age of seven, are haunted by the experience.[12] 'Literature didn't save me; I'm not saved', she explains in a beautiful book in which she wants to bear witness, after Christine Angot's novels, for all those who have gone through the nightmare of incest. The alternative remains open, and it's not for us to judge. But where there are wounds there are also resurrections. We can choose to scratch at our wounds, to lock ourselves in them like in a prison or to let them close up. Two philosophies of misfortune clash within us: one is a source of despair, the other of rebirth. With the first we writhe in misery, the second summons up confidence, for the will to take responsibility for ourselves in the future. Even after the worst affliction, it's a question of rediscovering our capacity for new enterprises when fear makes our ambitions shrivel up.[13] Similarly, after a tragedy, we can restore lost integrity, engaging in a 'constructive recapitulation', in the words of Henri Bergson, rather than endlessly brooding over the abject and the gloomy. There is always a second act in life, even if our ghosts still haunt us sometimes. You have to find a way out of the Shades, between despondency and hope. The demons can catch up with us; it's an inner battle that knows neither victor nor vanquished. Beyond doubt and dread, only what increases our energy is worth celebrating.

Revenge or forgiveness?

Forgiveness, or rather the impossibility of forgiveness, was a lifelong philosophical obsession of Vladimir Jankélévitch. In a famous book, (*L'Imprescriptible*, 1986) he wrote: 'Pardoning died in the death camps'.[14] A former member of the Resistance, hunted down by the Vichy police and incapable of forgetting, let alone granting amnesty, he forbade his students to quote any twentieth-century German philosophers. He was furious that relations with Germany were being normalized at the cost of a certain amnesia:

> When the guilty are fat, well nourished, prosperous, enriched by the 'economic miracle,' a pardon is a sinister joke. No, a pardon is not suitable for the swine and their sows.[15]

A German philosophy professor, Wiard Raveling, who had not taken part in the crimes, nevertheless openly asked Jankélévitch for forgiveness in a letter sent in 1980. He admitted that he had not slept well and remained horrified by the crimes committed in the name of his people. Jankélévitch was moved and replied that he had been waiting for such a letter 'for thirty-five years', from someone who had accepted the abomination without having participated in it. None of his German colleagues or philosophers had ever apologized to him. And he concluded his reply by inviting Raveling to his home on Quai aux Fleurs, near Notre Dame, not to talk about atrocities but to play the piano together with his daughter and son-in-law. Nothing was forgiven, but a hand was extended.[16]

'You will not have my hatred', exclaimed the husband of a Bataclan victim.[17] The statement came as a shock. It can be understood in two ways: as an anticipated surrender in the face of barbarity, or as a refusal to give the killers an importance they do not deserve, once they have been eliminated. Revenge reduces us to the level of those we punish, but to avoid feeding this obscure feeling, our aggressors must first be brought to their knees. We may be able to wage war without hatred, as author and politician André Malraux suggested, but we cannot wage it without the will to destroy the enemy by any means necessary. It's hard to imagine the Allies landing on the beaches of Normandy with messages of love for the Nazis, or French soldiers fighting ISIS by proffering roses. As long as the murderers, the henchmen and the cutthroats are alive, there can be no forgiveness. Of course revenge is despicable, but not having it implies the enemy is out of action. Nothing was uglier than the settling of scores after the Liberation, when some people used the anti-fascist struggle as an excuse to pursue personal enmities. It's hard not to think here of Pierre Dac's painfully ironic comments:

The Resistance fighters of 1945 are among the most glorious and valiant fighters of the Resistance, those who deserve the most esteem and respect because, for more than four years, they courageously and heroically resisted their ardent and fervent desire to join the Resistance.[18]

Primo Levi had already addressed the problem of hatred as a primary desire for revenge, for the pain inflicted on a real or supposed enemy. 'Hatred', he said, 'is personal, directed against a person, a face ... yet our persecutors had no names, they had no faces, they were distant, invisible, inaccessible ... the Nazi system ensured that direct contact between slaves and masters was reduced to a minimum.'[19] How can you hate an impersonal machine that has no face? 'Hatred is a barrier to free thought. I do not accept hatred', said Joseph Kessel in his book on the Resistance, *Army of Shadows*, first published in 1943. Like suffering, hatred leaves us welded, by an unbreakable bond, to those we want to kill and hurt again, even to the point of killing or hurting their loved ones afterwards. It creates a humanity of clones who resemble each other to the extent they want to annihilate each other.

What breaks the omnipotence of evil is the democratic system, which allows disagreement to be expressed without dooming opponents to elimination. It came about because of human weakness and wickedness, which it can possibly remedy by limiting the power of an individual or a group. But what destroys cruelty's appeal is the small change of goodness, which is the secret heart of the Christian metaphysical tradition. If Good alone is powerless in the face of Evil, the only way out for humankind is 'The private kindness of one individual towards another; a petty, thoughtless kindness; an unwitnessed kindness. Something we could call senseless kindness. A kindness outside any system of social or religious good.'[20] Primo Levi, too, was saved by the generosity of one of his fellow prisoners, Lorenzo: 'an Italian civilian worker brought me a piece of bread and the remainder of his ration every day for six months; he gave me a vest of his, full of patches; he wrote a postcard on my behalf to Italy and brought me the reply. For all this he neither asked nor accepted any reward, because he was good and simple and did not think that one did good for a reward.'[21] Vassili Grossman went on to say that goodness will save the world: 'The powerlessness of kindness, of senseless kindness, is the secret of its immortality. It can never be conquered. The more stupid, the more senseless, the more helpless it may seem, the vaster it is. Evil is impotent before it.'[22] On the scales of ignominy, goodness weighs nothing and yet it alone is remembered. Executioners must not be given undue importance once they have been erased or imprisoned. The only concern is to prevent them from having children, since hatred is fertile and travels in malleable brains, which become its hosts and propagators. Let us not forget the arid hatred, the dry hatred that runs in the veins of the petty shopkeepers of memory, pursuing a pitiless revenge into past centuries. The cohort of the righteous does not make the monstrosities of Nazism any less abominable, but at least evil did not have the last word.

Finally, there is also generosity on the part of the victims when they put their own misfortune to one side and observe the solidarity of the rejected, bear witness for others, Jews for Tutsis, Armenians for Kurds, Christians for Uighurs, and attest that no other community leaves them indifferent. This solidarity among the rejected is the highest manifestation of human altruism.

The cancer of hatred

It is always dangerous for a state, especially a democratic one, to give in to vindictiveness rather than respond proportionately, even in the case of severe aggression. The United

States of America knows all about this, having embarked on a series of wars for twenty years after 11 September 2001, all of which were lost, by instigating a state of exception and comprehensive surveillance of the citizens. To defend civilization with the weapons of barbarism is to install the barbarian at the very heart of civilization, at the risk of blurring the boundary between the two. Nietzsche wrote: 'Beware that, when fighting monsters, you yourself do not become a monster.'[23] American democracy could be permanently scarred by these pointless and brutal expeditions, which have tarnished the image of the United States for decades. This is what Joe Biden reminded the Israeli government of the day after the pogrom of 7 October 2023, when Prime Minister Benjamin Netanyahu had only the word revenge on his lips. The American President called for violence focused solely on destroying Hamas and not on punishing civilians in Gaza or the West Bank. Israel cannot behave like Putin's Russia or Bashar El Assad's Syria.

It is preferable for vendettas to remain in the realm of fiction or to be confined to those underworld groups known as gangs or mafias, based on unconditional allegiances, mob loyalties, just like power in Moscow. An international order based on the same kind of allegiances would be a return to the law of the jungle and chaos. 'Revenge is a second suffering that corrodes your energy. You can't get out of it. It's a fatal passion. Even when it's sated, it never lets you rest', wrote Jean-Paul Kauffmann.[24] Not everyone has the greatness of soul of Mirabeau, who forgave offences because he forgot them. Bossuet, a good prelate fascinated by the sword and greatness, celebrated in the victory of the Prince of Condé at Rocroi (19 May 1643 against the Spaniards) 'the pleasure of victory combined with that of forgiveness'. The most beautiful revenge is that in which one triumphs without humiliating the other. There is a bitter pleasure in retaliation that makes the person who wronged you pay a blood tax, leading to an endless payback cycle over several generations in clan societies. That kind of retaliation is also a dead end.

There is a way of forgiving that disarms resentment without absolving the aggressor. Take the case of the Resistance fighter Noëlla Rouget, who was deported to Ravensbrück and who, on her return from the camps, obtained a pardon from General de Gaulle for her persecutor, Jacques Vasseur. This zealous collaborator of the Gestapo in Angers, responsible for 230 deaths and 310 deportations, had tortured her. They corresponded, but he never expressed the slightest regret. In this particular case, isn't *forgiveness the best form of revenge*, given that this woman was able to get the better of her torturer? He was now her thing; she was no longer his plaything. Salman Rushdie, who survived forty years in hiding and an assassination attempt, prefers to tell stories and leave his enemies to their fury rather than dwell on his fate. Greatness of the soul comes through breaking the cursed chain of revenge, interrupting the race to resentment. Granting forgiveness is an act of grace for the offender on condition that he or she is no longer in a position to do harm. There are requests for clemency that are shocking, such as the one made by Pope Pius XII to the Nuremberg Trials concerning Hans Frank, the 'General Governor' of Poland who was directly or indirectly responsible for the deaths of 3 million people.[25] This request amounted to complicity rather than Christian charity.

In forgiveness, we speak to the wicked in the language of restitution, we shame them for their actions and, above all, we reconcile with ourselves by passing from rage to appeasement. Instead of dwelling on the abomination, one assimilates it. Sometimes, in a gesture of incredible audacity, the survivors try to understand what happened:

like the moving dialogue between the father of a jihadist and the father of a Bataclan victim, Azdyne Amimour and Georges Salines.[26] One condemned his son's actions outright, while the other was mourning his twenty-eight-year-old daughter who was killed on 13 November 2015. Both were trying to break down 'the walls of mistrust, misunderstanding and sometimes hatred that divide our society' and were committed to combating radicalization. But this collaboration drove the father of another victim crazy, Patrick Jardin, who also lost his daughter that evening. 'They accuse me of being hateful and it's true, Mr President, I am hateful and what disgusts me most are the parents of victims who are not hateful. The man who wrote a book with the father of one of the terrorists makes me want to vomit.'[27] Let's be careful not to judge, those of us who did not lose a wife, child or husband that night and who would probably be driven to distraction if it had happened to us.

But the height of sanctity (or madness) comes from those who have decided to love their enemies and bless in advance the blows that will be dealt them. This was the attitude of the monks of Tibérine in Algeria in 1996, and in particular that of the Trappist prior Christian de Chergé, who, refusing to leave that country, saw his eventual assassin as his future friend: 'for this life lost, I give thanks to God. In this "thank you," which is said for everything in my life from now on, I certainly include you, my last-minute friend who will not have known what you are doing ... I commend you to the God in whose face I see yours. And may we find each other, happy "good thieves" in Paradise, if it please God, the Father of us both.'[28] To treat one's murderer as a friend, and above all to forgive him in advance for his fatal act, is too rare a self-sacrifice not to be emphasized. It's a Christian excess. The Czech philosopher Jan Patočka also spoke of 'praying for the enemy' and celebrated 'the love of those who hate us'. But praying for one's persecutors was also the attitude of those condemned at the Moscow trials, who praised their executioner and shouted 'Long live Stalin!' at the foot of the scaffold. This submission was not due to Bolshevik perversity alone, but to a subservient mentality. To end up desiring what the tyrant wants is the ultimate stage of servitude. The space between loving one's enemies and consenting to the unspeakable is as thick as a cigarette paper. It's such a fine line that separates the admirable from the detestable!

WHAT IS A GOOD DEATH?

According to the ancient Greeks, a good death was a blessing, the crowning glory of a short life in which combat promised immortality. Since humans, unlike the gods, are ephemeral, the warrior had to transform his death into an imperishable good. 'He dies young whom the gods love', said Menander.[29] Soldiers can choose between glory and a short life, or a long life without glory. Youth is made to be mown down; the death of old men is pitiful. 'To die is a beautiful thing when you have fallen on the front line as a man with heart.'[30] This is at least one lesson that Christianity retained from Greece, since Jesus died at the age of thirty-three. It's hard to imagine the Son of God being crucified at seventy or eighty. But the body of the warrior riddled with arrows radiates a brilliant beauty, provided that his enemies have not insulted him by lacerating him or throwing dirt on him to defile him. There is no such thing as a balding or greying hero; gallant acts are all about escaping decrepitude. In Ukraine, a lieutenant in the Azov Brigade explained:

'We know that our lives are destined to be short but brilliant.'[31] In the *Iliad*, to die young is to belong to a chosen minority, to persist through the brilliance of one's name, to remain memorable and not lost in 'the obscure crowd of combatants who fell beneath the walls of Troy'.[32] True death is silence and oblivion. And for us, modern citizens, what is a good death? A swift and painless departure, an end that is chosen rather than endured? We can also heroically offer our demise to someone weaker than ourselves. Like the historian Marc Bloch: when he was about to be shot by the Nazis on 16 June 1944, alongside other Resistance fighters, he is said to have helped a trembling young teenager who asked him, 'Is this going to hurt?' 'No, son, it won't hurt', he replied, before being the first to fall, shouting 'Vive la France!'

Conclusion

So, first of all, let me assert my firm belief
that the only thing we have to fear is … fear itself –
nameless, unreasoning, unjustified terror which
paralyses needed efforts to convert retreat into advance.

Franklin D. Roosevelt, 1933

To put it bluntly, oppressed peoples or groups have only one right, but it is a sacred one, the right to be oppressed no longer. And we have only one duty towards them, to assist them if their existence is threatened. But the fact of having been dominated or discriminated against does not confer any metaphysical superiority of one category of human beings over any other. The idea that they are always right, even when they turn to violence, is untenable. No minority is immune to barbarity, no minority has acquired a kind of metaphysical grace as a result of the misfortunes it has endured that would exempt it from accountability. So let's have done with those angelic peoples, especially in the global South, who forbid others to judge them and feel that they are owed everything by virtue of the outrages perpetrated in the past.

Not all the humiliated have the same interests. It is impossible to unite them under the same banner, to bring them together singing the 'Internationale'. Evil is plural; if we must remain on the side of those who suffer, each concern is unique and requires an appropriate response. How can we avoid the demonic reversibility that turns today's victim into tomorrow's persecutor? How can we escape the unforgiving metronome that has marked history's rhythm for two centuries? Once the oppressor has been brought down and reparations have been made, those emerging from their outcast state must take on the responsibilities that freedom implies, to submit to the moral and legal constraints that apply to everyone. It means, in the end, acknowledging time's discontinuity. The transferral of grievances is broken.

The victims are our ambassadors in the land of darkness, which they have traversed with quite admirable courage. Just as healing has its own timetable, setbacks can be put to good use, which is the art of turning disaster into advantage. Never has Sartre's phrase, 'what we do with what has been done to us', better defined the problem. We are not only the products of our history and our environment, we also have a margin for play that is called freedom and enables us to escape from determinism. We are also the junctions where curses branch off, where hatred and anger are extinguished. We are the descendants, but even more the ascendants who are inaugurating a new history. It is like the miracle of childhood, which begins the human adventure afresh on new foundations and does not retain the fury or anger of the elders. All we can wish for the younger generations is that they are not indebted, and free themselves from our old grudges. The past should not weigh down upon their shoulders like a giant. Step to one side and it slips away, leaving them to breathe freely.

To get away from this state of institutionalized suffering, one has to break the adherence to the self, and not be shut away among those little groups of self-proclaimed martyrs who are intoxicated by their condition to the point of hypnosis. It is not the harm suffered that is irreversible, but the harm inflicted on others, the only harm we cannot forgive ourselves for. The sacredness of misfortune makes it impossible to escape from its cursed circle. It blazes, unalterable, trapping us forever in its funereal glow. In the West, the cult of hedonism and the disorderly gold-rush towards happiness are paradoxically accompanied by a subterranean idolatry of suffering. You can be seriously ill, recovering from a serious illness or a dreadful event, and still love, hope and work. The greatness of a good life lies in wiping out the disappointments and humiliations, leaving them behind in the black hole of the past, the better to look forward to a future full of the unexpected and the surprising. There are too many imaginary victims and too many forgotten unfortunates in our societies, too much official whining: our political life is an endless book of complaints, a catalogue of groans even though we live better than most other nations.

For too long, we've been bottle-fed despondency and acquiesced to powerlessness. Isn't it time for a paradigm shift? Despite what the apostles of decline say, history is not written and the future is not closed. It is not inevitable that democracies, victorious in 1989, will disappear, battered by new obscurities, or that the great battles for emancipation will sink into dogmatism and acrimony. To call oneself a victim by title rather than a victim of chance is to give up in advance, to weaken one's immune defences, to bow one's head. Instead of exalting that which makes us human, the domestication of our fears, we espouse the sole concern of survival, cowering in isolation with the shutters all closed. Recognition of the fragility of each individual must not kill off the spirit of resistance. We are at war and today we need thoughts that exalt energy and zeal. Victimization leads to fatalism. The stupid repetition of our problems prevents us from distinguishing between the transformable, which depends solely on our will, and the immutable, which does not depend on us.

All lives encounter misfortune, bereavement, illness and suffering, but they are also full of joy, wonder and beauty. Some people believe they have been ennobled by the blows and insults they have received. We can also be ennobled by the astonishment, the pleasure, the amazement of living among people, our fellow human beings and those who are different from us. To live is always to be reborn into a new self, to escape one's previous identities, like a snake shedding its skin, to be defined neither by one's antecedents nor by the setbacks one has experienced. Cicero remarked that the misfortune that we believe to be insurmountable never ruins all possibilities of fulfilment. There is no night so dark that a ray of light cannot filter through. We don't know in advance what we can bear, and we're surprised that we've come through certain trials without flinching. We forget the great pains but not the great pleasures: the former pass, the latter can begin again *ad infinitum*. Life goes on, even after the worst vicissitudes: this simple phrase keeps us going. Cruelty kills but does not break us, like the cafes and restaurants hit by jihadist bombs that reopen soon afterwards. Composure is one of the faces of heroism.

Three times in recent history, Europe and France have stood firm: the repeated Islamist attacks, the Covid cataclysm and the war of aggression in Ukraine prove that the plaintive citizens of the old West are still capable of picking themselves up again. It's not the virulence of our adversaries that we need to fear, it's the hatred we have for each other. We have a choice: to remain part of History and defend ourselves, or to leave it and fade away. Defeatism is the holiday home of privileged people; it is the sigh of a fat cat purring in comfort. Brought up, cradled and cajoled as we were in the prosperous post-war world, are we capable of facing up to the challenges of climate change, the return of war and terrorist barbarity? Are we going to bemoan the harshness of the times, or are we going to face up to them? Who will teach future generations the *courage to endure*, to face setbacks head-on, without faltering, whining or failing? Men and women must learn to resist the seduction of panic. That, quite simply, is what being human is all about.

We need to be prepared for hard times, if only to avoid them. We are stronger than we think; our enemies weaker than they think. But our greatest enemy is within us: it's called panic, self-hatred and complacency in the face of misfortune.

Notes

Introduction: Thucydides and Jesus Christ

1 Cited in Jean-François Braunstein, *La Religion woke*, Paris: Grasset, 2022, p. 25.
2 Kimberlé Crenshaw (born in 1959), a lawyer and activist, invented the concept of intersectionality in 1989.
3 Peter Boghossian, James Lindsay and Helen Pluckrose coined the term in 2017–18 to criticize what they saw as an impoverishment of academic work around race, gender, sexuality and fat people.

Chapter 1: 'One day all will be well, so runs our hope'

1 Voltaire [1756], 'Poem on the Lisbon Disaster, or examination of this axiom: All is well', in *Toleration and Other Essays by Voltaire,* trans., with an introduction, by Joseph McCabe, New York: G.P. Putnam's Sons, 1912, p. 262.
2 Frédérique Leichter-Flack, *Pourquoi le mal frappe les gens bien*, Paris: Flammarion, 2023.
3 'Do not think of those who have been killed in God's cause as dead. They are alive, and well provided for by their Lord.' Sourate Al-Ahram, Quran, quoted by Atmane Aggoun, 'Le martyr en Islam', *Études sur la mort*, 130/2, 2006, pp. 55–60.

4 Roselyne Rey, *The History of Pain*, Cambridge, MA: Harvard University Press, 1995.

5 Jan Synowiecki, *Échos des lumières*, Paris: Nouveau Monde, 2022.

6 Karl Marx [1849], *Wage Labour and Capital*, New York: International Publishers, 1933, p. 30.

7 Odo Marquard, *Skepsis und Zustimmung*, Leipzig: Reclam, 1994, pp. 99–109, cited in Byung-Chul Han, *La Société palliative*, Paris: PUF, 2022, p. 47.

8 Alain, *Alain on Happiness*, trans. Robert D. and Jane E. Cottrell, Evanston, IL: Northwestern University Press, 1989.

9 Ibid., p. 10.

10 Ibid., p. 249.

11 Philippe Ariès, *Western Attitudes Toward Death from the Middle Ages to the Present*, trans. Patricia M. Ranum, London: Marion Boyars, 1974, p. 51.

12 Catherine Rollot, 'Comment les adeptes de la "mort positive" réenchantent le passage de vie à trépas', *Le Monde*, Supplement 15, May 2023.

13 An advertising campaign in the Paris metro to promote palliative care shows an ecstatic family surrounding a terminally ill grandfather, with a caption telling us that the nurse has become his buddy! The triumph of cool agony! *SFAP Osons vivre avec les soins palliatifs*, March 2023.

14 Marjorie Philibert, 'Se faire "composter" après sa mort, une façon de réduire son empreinte écologique', *Le Monde*, 12 November 2023.

15 Critically applied to the X and Y generations, this concept comes from the book *I Find That Offensive* by Claire Fox (London: Biteback, 2016), a former communist activist.

16 Friedrich Nietzsche, *Beyond Good and Evil*, trans. Helen Zimmern, New York: The Modern Library, 1917, p. 151.

17 Frank Furedi, *Therapy Culture: Cultivating Vulnerability in an Uncertain Age*, London: Routledge, 2003, p. 19. Furedi also sees a sign of this change in mentality in the different attitudes among survivors of deportation, who try to remain stoic, and their children, who, although less directly affected, are much more emotional.

18 Nathalie Zajde, *Guérir de la Shoah*, Paris: Jacob, 2005, p. 243.
19 Jean-François Laé, *L'Instance de la plainte. Une histoire politique et juridique de la souffrance*, Paris: Descartes et Cie, 1996, p. 218.
20 Rey, *History of Pain*, p. 63.
21 Etienne Bonnot de Condillac, *Oeuvres philosophiques*, Paris: Presses universitaires de France, 1947, p. 172.
22 *Naked and Afraid*, Discovery Channel, March 2023.
23 As quoted in Michel Dacorogna and Marie Kratz, 'Living in a stochastic world and managing complex risks', ESSEC Working Papers WP1517, ESSEC Research Centre, ESSEC Business School, 2015.

Chapter 2: All kinds of awful

1 Piotr Smolar, 'Le fentanyl, la drogue qui ravage les États-Unis', *Le Monde*, 9 January 2023.
2 Gérald Bronner, *Les Origines. Pourquoi devient-on qui l'on est ?*, Paris: Autrement, 2023; Arnaud Lacheret, *Les Intégrés. Réussites de la deuxième génération de l'immigration nord-africaine*, Bordeaux: Le Bord de l'eau, 2023.
3 According to DARES (Directorate of Research, Economic Studies and Statistics), immigrants are concentrated in what are known as 'demanding' occupations, comprising 39% of domestic workers, 22% of cooks, 28% of caretakers and 27% of unskilled construction workers. *Le Point*, 12 October 2021. The more difficult a job, the more likely it is to be held by an immigrant.
4 Cicéron, *Devant la souffrance*, Paris: Arléa, 1996, p. 36.
5 Here I take up a theme already developed in my *The Temptation of Innocence: Living in the Age of Entitlement*, New York: Algora, 2000.
6 In *The Two Sources of Morality and Religion*, Henri Bergson evokes the magnificent and impossible gesture of the Declaration of the Rights of Man. Trans. Ashley Audra and Cloudesley Brereton, London: Macmillan, 1935, pp. 243–4.

7 Tina Yong, 'The rise of "trauma essay" in college applications', November 2023, YouTube TED Talks.
8 Danuta Kean, 'The pornography of misery memoir', *Daily Mail*, 9 October 2007.
9 John Crace, 'How to write a misery memoir', *The Guardian*, March 2008. In his book *A Child Called 'It'* (London: Seven Dials, 2019), the American Dave Pelzer details the scandalous abuse he suffered at the hands of his alcoholic mother. Two subsequent books extend this harrowing story. Pelzer's three books – all recollections of his childhood – provoked considerable controversy, including doubts about the veracity of the claims.
10 Friedrich Nietzsche, *On the Genealogy of Morals*, trans. Walter Kaufmann and R.J. Hollingdale, Third Essay, Section 9, New York: Vintage Books, 1989, p. 113. A literal translation from the French edition (*Généalogie de la morale*, Paris: Gallimard, p. 169), as used by the author, reads: 'disease *inoculators* seem to us today to be more useful than any healer or "saviour"' [Trans.].
11 Nietzsche, *On the Genealogy of Morals*, p. 123.
12 Marcel Proust, *The Guermantes Way*, trans. C.K. Scott Montcrieff, New York: Random House, 1925, p. 399.
13 Georges Canguilhem, *The Normal and the Pathological*, trans. Carolyn R. Fawcett, New York: Zone Books, 1991, p. 196.

Chapter 3: Suffering produces laws

1 Christine Lazerges, 'Le renforcement des droits des victimes par la loi No. 2000-516, 15 June 2000', *Archives de politique criminelle*, No. 24, 2002/1. In France, it was the 'Laurent Atthalin' ruling of 8 December 1906 that inaugurated victims' rights. It was the law of 15 June 2000 that really strengthened victims' desire for reparation, protection of their dignity and image, and compensation.
2 Laé, *L'Instance de la plainte*, p. 150. Repealed in 2016, it became article 1240 of the Civil Code.

3 Ibid., pp. 87–8.
4 Ibid., p. 167.
5 Amnesty International, 'World leaders' neglect of refugees condemns millions to death and despair', 15 June 2015.
6 Louis Chaigne, *Paul Claudel: The Man and the Mystic*, trans. Pierre de Fontnouvelle, New York, Greenwood Press, 1961, p. 48.
7 Sigmund Freud, 'Some character-types met with in psycho-analytic work', in *Writings on Art and Literature*, Stanford, CA: Stanford University Press, 1997, p. 155.
8 Élisabeth Badinter, *Fausse route*, Paris: Odile Jacob, 2003.
9 Prince Harry, with J.R. Moehringer, *Spare*, New York: Penguin Random House, 2023.
10 Raphaëlle Leyris, in *Le Monde des livres*, 22 September 2023.

Chapter 4: The one-upmanship of martyrdom

1 Yascha Mounk, *France Inter*, 18 December 2023, interview with Léa Salamé and Nicolas Demorand.
2 Cited by Braunstein, *La Religion woke*, pp. 88–9.
3 On this theme, see Eugénie Bastié's book *La Dictature des ressentis*, Paris: Plon, 2023.
4 Le DDV (*Le Droit de Vivre* – an antiracism journal), 1 May 2023, has an excellent article by this university professor at Nanterre against the new censors.
5 Célia Laborie, *Le Monde*, 12 June 2023.
6 Véronique Lorelle, 'Quand la signalétique des toilettes fait la chasse aux préjugés', *Le Monde*, 22 March 2023.
7 Cited by Caroline Eliacheff and Daniel Soulez Larivière, *Le Temps des victimes*, Paris: Albin Michel, p. 291.
8 Danielle Harling, 'Girl awarded $800k after taking McDonald's to court over chicken nuggets', *Yahoo Life*, 21 July 2023.
9 Richard Prasquier, 'Un clivage générationnel', *Actualité juive*, 31 November 2023.

10 'M. Le Pen n'aime pas l'art contemporain', *Le Monde*, 20 January 1993.

11 In Toulouse, on 16 December 2019, a group of 'anti-capitalists' attacked a living nativity scene made up of children, choristers and musicians, to cries of *Stop aux fachos*. Anne-Sophie Chazaud, 'L'esprit de Noël au temps des "antifascistes incultes"', *Le Figaro*, 16 December 2019.

12 In a tweet, Mathilde Panot criticized the President for paying tribute to the Pétain of 1914–18. In 2018, during the commemoration of the armistice of the First World War, Macron described Marshal Pétain as an eminent strategist of the Great War who was later led astray by dubious choices. Which is exactly the truth.

13 Louis-Ferdinand Céline, *Castle to Castle*, trans. Ralph Manheim, New York: Carroll & Graf, 1987, p. 61.

14 Inspired by Rimbaud's 'I am of an inferior race from all eternity', the expression 'to avenge one's race' is ambiguous. For Rimbaud, race does not mean skin colour but his position in society, that of a marginal and exiled poet. On the other hand, the expression 'to avenge one's race' was used unabashedly by the Vichy propagandist Philippe Henriot, a supporter of the Third Reich, when, in a 1944 speech against the comedian Pierre Dac, 'born Isaac André', he exclaimed that Georges Mandel, Minister of the Interior, had declared war on Germany to 'avenge his race'. It should be noted that Ernaux's political commitments are almost all directed against the State of Israel, and that she has also defended the 'native' Houria Bouteldja, a fervent anti-Semite.

15 *Le Monde*, 21 December 2022. We mustn't play down the pressure from the ultras of French identity.

16 François Héran, 'I do not deserve a Samuel Paty murder', *Marianne*, 24 November 2021. According to François Héran, Samuel Paty was 'very embarrassed, and for good reason' (Samuel Paty had shown his pupils a drawing by Coco depicting Mohammed in a prayer position that some considered obscene). 'There are cartoons that are completely contextualized, based on criticism and reaction to an event. And then there are some that are an outrage for the sake of

an outrage, such as ass-fucking drawings.' It is worth noting that Héran repeated the word *enculade* over and over again in his public appearances.

17 *La Chaîne Info,* 1 November 2021.

18 'Pologne: Tollé à propos d'un slogan se référant au nazisme de manifestants anti-vax', *Le Figaro*, 15 December 2021.

19 Giorgio Agamben, *Le Monde*, 24 March 2020, interview with Nicolas Truong.

20 René Girard, *La Route antique des hommes pervers*, Paris: Grasset, 1985.

21 Beginning in the 1980s, this theory is both constructivist – race is a socio-legal construct – and anti-egalitarian, criticizing the racial colour-blindness that ignores skin colour. It marked the triumph of Malcolm X over Martin Luther King. Although purporting to be progressive, this doctrine, with its obsession with pigmentation and latent anti-Semitism, is the Anglo-Saxon version of the Nuremberg racial laws of 1936. We saw this in October 2023, after the barbaric attack by Hamas in southern Israel, when various LGBT and feminist groups in America and Europe came out in favour of Hamas against the Jewish state and played down the importance of the pogrom of 7 October 2023. Ironically, these same groups in Gaza or the West Bank would be thrown off buildings or liquidated.

22 Johann Michel, *Devenir descendant d'esclave*, preface by Jean-Luc Bonniol, Rennes: Presses universitaires de Rennes, 2015.

23 'As the son of a cleaning lady', Gérald Darmanin, *RTL*, 18 October 2022. As it happens, it was Camus who set the ball rolling against Sartre, his bourgeois rival, recalling his working-class origins and his illiterate, inarticulate mother. The philosopher Michel Onfray followed suit, recounting the life of his father, a farm labourer, and his mother, a cleaning lady. In 2023, Didier Éribon published *The Life, Old Age and Death of a Woman of the People*, trans. M. Lucey, *Granta*, 166, 2024, in which he recounts the life of his mother, a cleaning woman and factory worker who was forced to move to a nursing home in her old age. Since

at least Jules Vallès, the identification of the poor with the figure of the virtuous poor has become a literary genre in its own right in France, like that of actors' sons or daughters in show business.

24 Robert Hughes, *Culture of Complaint: The Fraying of America*, Oxford: Oxford University Press, 1993.

25 Shelby Steele, 'A negative vote on affirmative action', *The New York Times Magazine*, 13 May 1990, Section 6, p. 46.

26 For example, Glenn C. Loury, 'Don't judge Blacks by a different standard', *City Journal*, Fall 2022; John McWhorter, *Woke Racism: How a New Religion Has Betrayed Black America*, London: Swift Press, 2023; Thomas Chatterton Williams, *Self-Portrait in Black and White: Unlearning Race*, New York: Norton, 2019.

27 Cicero, *Cicero's Tusculan Disputations*, trans. A.P. Peabody, Boston: Little Brown and Co., 1886, p. 108.

Part Two (title)

1 I refer here to my *The Temptation of Innocence*, New York: Algora, 2000, Part 3: 'Victimist Competition', pp. 213ff. On this theme see also Jean-Michel Chaumont, *La Concurrence des victims. Génocide, identité, reconnaissance*, Paris: La Découverte, 2010; and Guillaume Erner, *La Société des victimes*, Paris: La Découverte, 2006, a reflection on consensual compassion.

Chapter 5: The thieves of suffering

1 This controversy is recounted in the excellent book by Franco-British jurist Philippe Sands, *East West Street: On the Origins of Genocide and Crimes Against Humanity*, London: Orion, 2017. See in particular p. 385.

2 Ibid., p. 380.

3 Galia Ackermann and Stéphane Courtois, eds., *Le Livre noir*

de Vladimir Poutine, Paris: Perrin/Robert Laffont, 2022, p. 338.

4 Charlotte Delbo, *None of Us Will Return*, Boston: Beacon Press, 1978, p. 6.

5 'Le jour d'après', YouTube, 13 April 2020. https://www .youtube.com/watch?v=JB75qjw0XSI

6 Paul Ricœur, *Time and Narrative*, vol. 3, Chicago: University of Chicago Press, 1988, p. 187.

7 In 2015, the *Conseil d'État* and the *Conseil constitutionnel* noted that 'war crimes are not of the same nature as crimes against humanity; impunity from the latter would affect the entire international community', and that imprescriptibility must remain exceptional. *Brief of the Conseil d'État*, 1 October 2015, No. 390 335.

8 Jacques Sémelin, 'From massacre to the genocidal process', *International Social Science Journal*, 54/174, 2002, pp. 433–42.

9 There is a good summary account of this in Chaumont's *La Concurrence des victimes*, pp. 126ff.

10 Cited in ibid., p. 112.

11 Tzvetan Todorov, *Memory as a Remedy for Evil*, trans. Gila Walker, Kolkata: Seagull Books, 2010.

12 Iannis Roder, *Sortir de l'ère victimaire. Pour une nouvelle approche de la Shoah et des crimes de masse*, Paris: Odile Jacob, 2020.

13 Rosa Amelia Plumelle-Uribe, *White Ferocity: The Genocides of Non-Whites and Non-Aryans from 1492 to Date*, trans. V. Popper, Dakar: Codesria, 2020, p. 1.

14 Aimé Césaire, *Discourse on Colonialism*, trans. J. Pinkham, New York: Monthly Review Press, 1972, p. 36.

15 Ibid., p. 36.

16 I refer the reader to my *The Tears of the White Man: Compassion as Contempt*, trans. W.R. Beer, New York: The Free Press, 1986; *Un coupable presque parfait. La construction du bouc émissaire blanc*, Paris: Grasset, 2020; and *The Tyranny of Guilt: An Essay on Western Masochism*, trans. S. Rendall, Princeton, NJ: Princeton University Press, 2012.

17 PIR, 'Pour une lecture décoloniale de la Shoah', with Enzo Traverso, Ramon Grosfoguel and Youssef Boussoumah.

18 See Richard J. Golsan, *Justice in Lyon*, Toronto: University of Toronto Press, 2022, p. 217.

19 Houria Bouteldja, *Whites, Jews, and Us: Toward a Politics of Revolutionary Love*, trans. R. Valinsky, South Pasadena, CA: Semiotext(e), 2017, pp. 59, 113.

20 Joëlle Fiss, *The Durban Diary: What Really Happened at the UN Conference against Racism in Durban (2001)*, New York: American Jewish Committee, 2008, p. 7.

21 Achille Mbembe, 'On Palestine', Foreword in Jon Soske and Sean Jacobs, *Apartheid Israel: The Politics of an Analogy*, Chicago: Haymarket Books, 2015, p. vii.

22 Etymologically, the Nakba refers to the expulsion of 750,000 Palestinians after the creation of the State of Israel in 1948. In the years that followed, almost a million Jews were in turn expelled from Arab countries. As Richard Prasquier writes, 'It is a question of positing the Nakba as the archetypal crime, of making it the "real" Shoah and of denying the Jews the slightest geographical anchorage in a land to which they are nonetheless attached by their entire history and all their traditions.' The Palestinian calendar of victimhood is supposed to erase that of Israel. https://world.hey.com /richard.prasquier

23 The Protestant refugee aid organization Cimade, which is close to the ultra-left, wanted to make the Nakba a major event in May 2023. In February 2013, Cimade boycotted a ceremony honouring the Jewish victims of Nazism in the name of the duty to remember, as Israelis today behave more or less like the Nazis, but on a lesser scale, according to them. 'But we are not anti-Semitic', they felt obliged to add in a letter to CRIF (Representative Council of French Jewish Institutions).

24 Achille Mbembe, 'The society of enmity', *Radical Philosophy*, Nov./Dec. 2016, p. 24.

25 *Le Canard enchaîné*, D.H. and C.L., 'Des taxis parisiens interdits aux Juifs', cited in *Tribune juive*, 23 November 2023.

26 X, 4 December 2023.

27 *Libération*, 8 October 2023: 'Are you aware that hundreds of Palestinians have also been killed, @libé? Whole families massacred? Not the right skin colour perhaps?' Mona Chollet is probably not aware that Israel is a multi-racial society where Ashkenazim from Central Europe, Moroccan, Iraqi, Iranian and Yemeni Jews and Falashas from Ethiopia live side by side.

28 *La Méridienne.info*, 11 October 2023, blog by Mona Chollet. The author reveals her preference for a two-state solution.

29 Bernard Lewis, *Le Retour de l'islam*, Paris: Gallimard, Folio histoire, 1985, p. 250.

30 Goethe Institut, 'The specters of comparison', May 2020. https://www.goethe.de/ins/us/en/kul/art/stp/deb/22019616.html

31 Luis Sepúlveda, *Une sale histoire*, Paris: Métailié, 2005, p. 44.

32 As Guillaume Meurice, a 'humorist' on *France Inter*, put it, Benjamin Netanyahu is 'a Nazi without a foreskin', 30 October 2023.

33 For example, Didier Fassin, a professor at the Collège de France, published an article in the online *AOC* on 1 November in which he expressed alarm at the 'spectre of genocide' in Gaza and compared the actions of the Israeli army with those of the German generals in Namibia at the beginning of the twentieth century, who wiped out the Hereros. This military undertaking was a kind of dress rehearsal for the Shoah. Denying the legitimacy of the State of Israel as a mere colonial entity, he blamed the descendants of the Holocaust for the Holocaust they were about to commit against the Palestinians.

34 François Azouvi, *Le Mythe du grand silence*, Paris: Fayard, 2012, and in Folio Gallimard, 2012, 2015 with an unpublished afterword.

35 Imre Kertész, *The Holocaust as Culture*, trans. T. Cooper, Kolkata: Seagull Books, 2011.

36 In 1773, the Marquis de Pombal banned black slaves from entering France and abolished the hereditary transmission of

slave status. The actual abolition of slavery took more than a century.

37 Benoît Vitkine, 'Portrait d'une Russie soumise et violente', *Le Monde*, 16–17 April 2023, based on the documentary 'Russie, un peuple qui marche au pas' by Ksenia Bolchakova and Veronika Dorman, *France 5*.

Chapter 6: Putin, or the petty civil servant of crime

1 Archduke Otto von Habsburg (1912–2011), heir to the Austro-Hungarian Empire, was one of the few Austrian leaders to refuse the Anschluss and leave his country when Hitler came to Vienna.

2 Dobrica Cosić, 'Le temps du réveil', interview with Daniel Salvatore Schiffer, *L'Âge d'homme*, 1992, p. 30.

3 Ministère de l'Information de Belgrade, 1992, p. 5.

4 'Moscou compare l'Occident à Hitler', *VOA Afrique*, 18 January 2023. https://www.voaafrique.com/a/moscou -compare-les-actions-de-l-occident-contre-la-russie-%C3 %A0-celles-d-hitler-contre-les-juifs/6923341.html

5 On the attitude of Ukrainian nationalists towards the Jews, see the excellent dossier in the May 2023 issue of *K* magazine, and in particular the article by Boris Czerny, 'The Shoah as a keystone for Ukraine's entry into the European Community'. https://k-larevue.com/en/the-shoah-as-a- keystone-for-ukraines-entry-into-the-european-community/

6 On this abominable period, read Michaël Prazan's excellent *Einsatzgruppen. Les Commandos de la mort nazis*, Paris: Points Histoire, 2010.

7 Vassili Grossman, *Tout passe*, Paris: Le Livre de Poche Biblio, Preface Linda Lê, p. 13. See also the English edition, *Everything Flows*, New York: New York Review Books, 2009.

8 Grossman, *Everything Flows*, p. 184.

9 Mavcé, a naive painter and member of the Bosnian Serb Assembly, quoted by Véronique Nahoum-Grappe in 'Poétique et politique: Le nationalisme extrême comme système d'images', *Tumultes*, 1994.

10 Ackermann and Courtois, *Le Livre noir de Vladimir Poutine*, p. 400.

11 Vladimir Zhirinovsky, *Un bond final vers le sud*, 1993, p. 123, translation by the Foreign Affairs Committee of the French National Assembly.

12 See Ackermann and Courtois, *Le Livre noir de Vladimir Poutine*. During the second war in Chechnya, he threatened to 'flush terrorists right down the toilet', and in 2008, during the Georgian crisis, he threatened to hang President Saakashvili 'by the balls'.

13 A group of professional crooks who abide by the laws of the underworld that emerged in the 1930s and waged the Suka war in the Gulag after 1945. Varlam Shalamov recounts these bloody clashes in his book *Sketches of the Criminal World: Further Kolyma Stories*, New York: New York Review Books, 2020.

14 Ackermann and Courtois, *Le Livre noir de Vladimir Poutine*, citing Yves Hamant, 'With Putin, slang codes a particular lifestyle', pp. 107ff. Putin and Lavrov speak the code of honour of the underworld, a highly hierarchical world as in a caste system, and Russian diplomats follow suit. On 13 February 2022, the Russian ambassador to Sweden declared: 'Excuse my language. The sanctions? We shit on them', ibid., p. 118.

15 For a refutation of this position, see Philippe de Lara, 'Le problème russe', *Telos*, April 2023.

16 Giuliano da Empoli, *The Wizard of the Kremlin*, trans. W. Wood, London: Penguin/Random House, 2022.

17 Ackermann and Courtois, *Le Livre noir de Vladimir Poutine*, p. 47.

18 Ibid., p. 390.

19 Paul Morand, *L'Europe russe annoncée par Dostoïevsky*, Geneva: Pierre Cailler, 1948.

20 Video, January 2023: Soloviev addresses Chechen troops, assuring them that they are engaged in a holy war.

21 George Steiner, *The Portage to San Cristobal of A.H.*, London: Faber and Faber, 1981.

22 Vassili Grossman, *Life and Fate*, trans. R. Chandler, New York: Harper and Row, 1983, p. 397.

23 Derek Offord, 'Russian intellectual life in the 1840s and 1850s', in *Portraits of Early Russian Liberals: A Study of the Thought of T.N. Granovsky, V.P. Botkin, P.V. Annenkov, A.V. Druzhinin, and K.D. Kavelin*, Cambridge Studies in Russian Literature, Cambridge: Cambridge University Press, 1985, pp. 1–43; Grossman, *Everything Flows*, p. 180.

24 The American journalist Roger Cohen shed considerable light on the mental state of Russian society in a very long article in *The New York Times* on 7 August 2023, 'Putin's forever war'.

25 François Musseau, 'Dans le camp du mensonge', *Libération*, 17 June 2005.

26 Javier Cercas, *L'Imposteur*, Arles: Actes Sud, 2015.

Chapter 7: Towards a generalized 'gynocide'?

1 Andrea Dworkin cited by Lynne Segal, 'Does pornography cause violence?', in Pamela Church Gibson and Roma Gibson, eds., *Dirty Looks: Women, Pornography, Power*, London: BFI Publishing, 1983, p. 12.

2 Cited by Katie Roiphe, *The Morning After*, Boston: Little, Brown and Co., 1993, p. 141.

3 Marilyn French, *The War Against Women*, London: Hamish Hamilton, 1992. Marilyn French's first book, *The Women's Room* (1977), sold 20 million copies worldwide.

4 French, *The War Against Women*, p. 179.

5 Pauline Bart and Susan Brown-Miller, quoted by French in *The War Against Women*, p. 193.

6 Frédérik Detue, 'Le défi testimonial d'Adèle Haenel', *Ligne de crête*, 11 December 2019.

7 Véronique Nahoum-Grappe and Marie Ladier-Fouladi, 'En Iran et en Afghanistan, un crime contre la moitié de l'humanité', *Le Monde*, 9 March 2023.

8 Cited in Frédéric Martel, *The Pink and the Black: Homosexuals in France since 1968*, trans. J.M. Todd, Stanford, CA: Stanford University Press, 1999.

9 In her 'Letter from Paris', published shortly after the Bataclan

attacks, Judith Butler denounced the collective grief of the French people and worried only about one thing, the risk of France sliding into a police and militarized state. *Libération*, 19 November 2015. English version: https://www.versobooks.com/en-gb/blogs/news/2337-mourning-becomes-the-law-judith-butler-from-paris

10 Esther Benbassa, *Libération*, 5 April 2016.

11 In *Le Monde* on 13 September 2019, Céline Parisot, president of the *Union syndicale des magistrats*, contested the term 'feminicide' and opposed the gendering of crimes, which would contravene the universality of the law. Opposing her, Pierre Farge, a lawyer at the Paris Bar, insisted, on the contrary, that this crime should be written into the Penal Code as it stands.

12 Novelist Claire Berest put it nicely: 'Women kill their husbands to get rid of them, men kill their wives to keep them', 23 August 2023, on *C à vous* TV talk show.

13 Source: Ministère de l'Intérieur, no date.

14 Alice Maxence, 'Féminicides, l'ennemi intime', *Franc-Tireur*, 8 March 2023.

15 Silvia Federici, *Witches, Witch-Hunting and Women*, Oakland, CA: PM Press, 2018.

16 In Canada, the first mass murder took place in Montreal in 1989 when Marc Lépine, certain that feminists had ruined his life, killed fourteen women and wounded nine others and four men in the École poly-technique. This supposedly first mass feminicide elevated Marc Lépine to hero status among Incels. In 2014, there was also the Isla Vista massacre in Santa Barbara, when Elliot Rodger, aged twenty-two, killed six people and injured fourteen others, leaving a manifesto in which he confessed his hatred of women. Other acts of Incel terrorism followed, mostly in North America: 1 October 2015 in Oregon, nine dead, eight injured; 23 April 2018 in Toronto, ten dead, fourteen injured; in Tallahassee, Florida, on 2 November 2018, etc.

17 In France, the proportion of people sentenced to prison for sexual violence was 5.5% in the early 1980s, peaking at 25% in 2001 and falling to 10.1% in 2022. Statistics from the Ministry of Justice, 1980, 2022, Prison Administration.

18 The term *emprise* entered the law for the first time on 30 July 2020 in article 226-14 of the Criminal Code.

19 Catharine MacKinnon, *Le Viol redéfini: Vers l'égalité, contre le consentement*, Paris: Flammarion, 2023.

20 See Sabine Prokhoris, *Le Mirage #MeToo*, Paris: Cherche-Midi, 2021.

21 Ivan Jablonka, *Des hommes justes*, Paris: Seuil, 2019.

22 Camille Froidevaux-Metterie, 'Le nouveau venu qui se rêvait pionnier', *Libération*, 23 October 2019.

23 Judith Butler, *Gender Trouble: Feminism and the Subversion of Identity*, New York: Routledge, 1990, p. 30.

24 'Le Prince de la Belle au bois dormant est-il un prédateur sexuel?', *France Culture*, 5 December 2017.

25 Vincent Tournier, 'Blanche Neige, réveille-toi!', in *Après la déconstruction*, Paris: Odile Jacob, 2022, pp. 217ff.

26 Mona Chollet, *Beauté fatale*, Paris: La Découverte, 2015, p. 287.

27 '"Picasso abusait des femmes, comme Harvey Weinstein", selon l'artiste Olafur Eliasson', *Le Figaro*, 17 February, 2020.

28 Butler, *Gender Trouble*, p. 3.

29 See Prokhoris, *Le Mirage #MeToo*.

30 Quoted by Charles Krauthammer, 'Defining deviancy up', *The New Republic*, 23 November 1993, p. 24,

31 Susan Faludi, *Backlash: The Undeclared War against American Women*, New York: Crown, 1991, p. 104.

32 Source: https://www.justice.gouv.fr. Convictions for sexual violence, updated 23 May 2023. Overall, 15% of complaints result in a sentence, and 70% of cases handled by the justice system are dismissed. Most rapes are committed within the family against minors.

33 *Le Monde*, 9 March 2020. Petition signed by Frédérique Baulieu, Delphine Meillet, Corinne Dreyfus-Schmidt, Marie Dosé, etc.

34 Marie Dosé, 'Éloge de la prescription', *L'Observatoire*, 2021, p. 93.

35 Erner, *La Société des victimes*.

36 Dosé, 'Éloge de la prescription', p. 93.

37 The statute of limitations is twenty years for felonies, six years for misdemeanours and one year for minor offences. War crimes and terrorist offences are subject to a thirty-year statute of limitations, while sexual offences are subject to a thirty-year statute of limitations after the victim has reached the age of majority. The victim can therefore take legal action up to the age of forty-eight; in Dosé, 'Éloge de la prescription', p. 13.

38 Margarete Buber-Neumann, *Under Two Dictators: Prisoner of Stalin and Hitler*, London: Pimlico, 2008.

39 Barbara Necek, *Femmes bourreaux. Gardiennes et auxiliaires des camps nazis*, Paris: Grasset, 2022, pp. 10–11.

40 Ibid., pp. 103–4.

41 Ibid.

42 Hasna Hussein, 'Les Veuves noires de Daech', *Contre-discours radical*, 3 November 2019.

43 Soren Seelow, 'Comment juger les "revenantes" de l'État islamique. La justice antiterroriste aux prises avec les stéréotypes de genre', *Le Monde*, 11 April 2023.

44 As noted by Eliacheff and Larivière, *Le Temps des victimes*, pp. 103–4.

45 Charlotte Harpur, 'Kheira Hamraoui was beaten with an iron bar', *The New York Times*, 4 November 2023.

46 According to *Tétu* magazine, 12 July 2019, citing figures from the AGIR association, in 2014, 11% of gays and lesbians and 20% of bisexuals said they had experienced domestic violence.

47 'En Occident, les combats militants secondaires ont pris le pas sur l'essentiel', *Le Point*, 25 May 2023.

48 Brittany Wong, 'The "Barbie" movie is ending relationships left and right', *Huffington Post*, 31 July 2023.

49 Ryan Bort, 'Florida schools are slashing Shakespeare to comply with DeSantis agenda', *Rolling Stone*, 8 August 2023.

50 Madame Figaro.fr, 'La comédienne Typhaine D, créatrice d'une grammaire ou "la féminine l'emporte sur la masculine"', 30 October 2023. *Hommage* contains the word for 'man', *femmage* contains 'woman'. *J'espère* is

'I hope', but it incorporates the word for father, *père*, for which the unlikely substitute in this case is *mère*, mother [Trans.].

51 Owen M. Fiss, 'What is feminism?', *Arizona State Law Journal*, 26/2, 14 November 1994, pp. 413–28.

Chapter 8: Decolonize the decolonizers?

1 'Finie l'Afrique dominée, place à l'Afrique souveraine', *Le Monde*, 26 January 2023.
2 El Hadj Souleymane Gassama (aka Elgas), *Les Bons Ressentiments. Essai sur le malaise post colonial*, with a preface by Sophie Bessis, Marseille: Riveneuve, 2023.
3 Philippe Bernard speaks of 'changing our approach to Africa' and that 'We would do well to see current events as a new phase in decolonisation', in his article 'Afrique: "Il serait trop facile de ne voir que 'la main de Moscou' dans ce spectaculaire congédiement de la France"', *Le Monde*, 4 February 2023.
4 Nicolas Bancel and Pascal Blanchard, 'La question du passé colonial est le dernier "tabou" de l'histoire de France des xixe et xxe siècles', *Le Monde*, 31 October 2023. When you read the article, you realize that it is a call for tenders: the two authors are candidates for the post of director of a major museum of colonization.
5 Such is the case of the Spaniard Gloria Oyarzabal, who, travelling in Africa with a growing unease about her 'white woman's privilege', decided in her photos to 'deconstruct' – to use the current easy commonplace – the stereotyped images born of colonialism in order to engage in a dialogue 'around gender, race, colonialism'; in Emmanuelle Lequeux, 'La plasticienne espagnole Gloria Oyarzabal décolonise les corps féminins', *Le Monde*, 29 January 2023.
6 Jean-François Bayart, *Les Études postcoloniales, un carnaval académique*, Paris: Karthala, 2010.
7 Under the leadership of Achille Mbembe, the Innovation

Foundation for Democracy in Africa was launched on 6 October 2022 in Johannesburg with a French endowment of 50 million euros for five years. The initiative was launched in 2017 by Emmanuel Macron to lead to more peaceful Franco-African relations. For now, anti-French sentiment fanned by propaganda from Moscow is reaching fever pitch. The foundation is chaired by the philosopher Souleymane Bachir Diagne.

8 Something I noted in *The Tears of the White Man*.

9 Coumba Kane, 'Fatou Diome: "La rengaine sur la colonisation et l'esclavage est devenue un fonds de commerce"', *Le Monde*, 25 August 2019. The decolonization of thought had already been done by thinkers such as Aimé Césaire or Frantz Fanon, noted Diome: 'After all their efforts, are we still wondering how to liberate ourselves?'

10 Aimé Césaire, *Discourse on Colonialism*, trans. J. Pinkham, New York: Monthly Review Press, 1972, p. 10.

11 Johann Michel, *The Reparable and the Irreparable: Being Human in the Age of Vulnerability*, trans. N. Carter, Lanham, MD: Lexington Books, 2023, p. 181.

12 Daniel Rivet, 'Le fait colonial et nous: Histoire d'un éloignement', *Vingtième siècle, Revue d'histoire*, No. 33, 1992, pp. 130, 138, quoted in P.A. Taguieff, 'L'imposture décoloniale', *L'Observatoire*, 2020, p. 135.

13 Jean Birnbaum, *Un silence religieux: La gauche face au djihadisme*, Paris: Seuil, 2016.

14 Kamel Daoud, 'Emmanuel Macron-Kamel Daoud, les coulisses d'une conversation', *Le Point*, 11 January 2023.

15 https://www.olivierabel.fr/2017/08/07/le-pardon-briser-la-dette-et-loubli/

16 Cited by Maroun Eddé, *La Mémoire coupable*, Paris: Bouquins, 2022, pp. 137–8.

17 Xavier Driencourt, 'Les Algériens se rient de notre naïveté', *Le Point*, 25 May 2023.

18 Cf. Pascal Bruckner, 'Introduction', in *An Imaginary Racism: Islamophobia and Guilt*, trans. S. Rendall and L. Neal, Cambridge: Polity, 2018.

19 Quoted in the excellent article by Barbara Lefebvre, 'Pourquoi

comparer les musulmans d'aujourd'hui avec les Juifs d'hier est inacceptable', *Figaro Vox*, 3 July 2017, republished 13 December 2021.

20 Edwy Plenel, *For the Muslims: Islamophobia in France*, London: Verso, 2016, p. 15 (eBook).

21 *France Info*, 3 November, 2023.

22 According to Interior Minister Gérald Darmanin, since January 2023, 1,762 anti-Semitic incidents have been recorded in France, compared with 564 anti-Christian incidents and 131 anti-Muslim incidents. *Le Figaro*, 18 November 2023.

23 Claude Lévi-Strauss, *Tristes Tropiques*, Paris: Plon, Terre humaine, 1955, pp. 466–7. Quotation not in English edition [Trans.].

24 Edward Saïd, *Orientalism*, New York: Pantheon, 1978.

25 Part of this quotation can be found in Enzo Traverso, 'La fabrique de la haine. Xénophobie et racisme en Europe', *Contretemps: Revue de Critique Communiste*, 17 April 2011. https://www.contretemps.eu/la-fabrique-de-la-haine -xenophobie-et-racisme-en-europe/

26 Charles de Saint Sauveur, 'Les étudiants juifs s'inquiètent de la montée d'un antisémitisme d'extrême gauche', *Le Parisien*, 28 September 2023.

27 Braunstein, *La Religion woke*.

28 Alvin H. Rosenfeld, *The End of the Holocaust*, Bloomington: Indiana University Press, 2013.

29 The Abraham Accords are two peace treaties signed under the aegis of President Donald Trump between Israel and the United Arab Emirates on 13 August 2020 and Israel and the Sultanate of Bahrain on 11 September of the same year. Morocco joined on 24 November 2022, much to Algeria's dismay. It is generally accepted that these treaties, designed to ward off the Iranian threat, were to the detriment of the Palestinians, who were abandoned by their Arab brothers. Saudi Arabia suspended the signing of this agreement following the Gaza war in October 2023.

30 Interdisciplinary report written by independent researchers and submitted to DILCRAH (Delegation to Combat

Racism, Anti-Semitism and Anti-LGBT Hate), July 2023. The report dismisses the hypothesis of systemic racism from the outset, but highlights a shortage of supervisory staff, acknowledges that some police officers have gone off the rails and recommends training 'in social and ethno-cultural diversity'; Antoine Albertini, *Le Monde*, 19 July 2023.

31 Arnaud Lacheret, *Les Intégrés*, Bordeaux: Le Bord de l'eau, 2023.

32 Emmanuel Brenner, ed. with Georges Bensoussan, Iannis Roder, Barbara Lefevre and Sophie Ferhadjian, *Les Territoires perdus de la République*, Paris: Fayard, 2002.

Chapter 9: Barbarism as a cover-up?

1 Primo Levi, *The Drowned and the Saved*, trans. R. Rosenthal, London: Michel Joseph, 1988, p. 121.

2 Marek Edelman, *The Ghetto Fights*, London: Bookmarks, 1990.

3 Ibid., p. 50.

4 Ibid., p. 55.

5 Marek Edelman, *Mémoires du ghetto de Varsovie*, Paris: Liana Levi, 2002, with a Preface by Pierre Vidal-Naquet, p. 74. (Quotation not in *The Ghetto Fights* [Trans.].)

6 Todorov, *Memory as a Remedy for Evil*.

7 Grossman, *Life and Fate*, p. 213.

8 Ibid., p. 21.

9 Grossman, *Everything Flows*, p. 153.

10 Thomas Wieder and Jérôme Gautheret, 'Ukraine: The suppressed tragedy of the great famine of 1932–1933', *Le Monde*, 12 May 2022.

11 Thomas Wieder, 'David Rousset dénonce les camps soviétiques', *Le Monde*, 7 January 2001.

12 Alexander Solzhenitsyn, 'Live not by lies'. https://archive.org/details/LiveNotByLies/page/n1/mode/2up

13 Abdelwahab Meddeb, *La Maladie de l'islam*, Paris: Le Seuil, 2005.

14 'Les images insoutenables du pogrom', *Le Point*, 26 October, 2023.

15 Marc Weitzmann, 'France's nightmare is yours now', *Tablet Magazine*, 31 October 2023. https://www.tabletmag.com /sections/news/articles/the-global-pogrom

16 Emmanuel Carrère, *V13, Chronique judiciaire*, Paris: Éditions P.O.L., 2022, p. 142.

17 Ibid., p. 42.

18 Christopher R. Browning, *Ordinary Men: Reserve Police Battalion 101 and the Final Solution in Poland*, London: Penguin Books, 1992, pp. 65, 69.

19 Ibid.

20 'Of course, Hamas's violence against civilians cannot be justified, but there is no comparison because the Israeli military is one of the most powerful forces in the world. There is a huge disproportion and the civilians of Gaza have no weapons, they don't know how to protect themselves' (Radio France, interview with Sonia Devillers, 20 November 2023).

21 Gatestone Institute, Uzay Bulut, 18 May 2020.

22 'Here there is no why' [Trans.].

23 Necek, *Femmes bourreaux*, p. 180.

24 Neige Sinno, *Sad Tiger*, trans. N. Lehrer, New York: Seven Stories Press, forthcoming 2025.

25 Jean Hatzfeld, *Machete Season: The Killers in Rwanda Speak*, trans. L. Coverdale, New York: Picador, 2006, p. 200.

26 Sands, *East West Street*, p. 242.

27 Rithy Panh, with Christophe Battaille, *The Elimination: A Survivor of the Khmer Rouge Confronts His Past and the Commandant of the Killing Fields*, trans. J. Cullen, London: The Clerkenwell Press, 2013. See also François Bizot, *The Gate: A Memoir*, New York: Knopf, 2004.

28 Panh, *The Elimination*, p. 133.

29 Cited in Tzvetan Todorov, *Facing the Extreme: Moral Life in the Concentration Camps*, trans. A. Denner and A. Pollack, New York: Henry Holt, 1996, p. 64.

30 Hannah Arendt, *Eichmann in Jerusalem: A Report on the Banality of Evil*, New York: Viking, 1963, p. 106.

31 Browning, *Ordinary Men*.

32 Ivan Jablonka, *Les Vérités inavouables de Jean Genet*, Paris: Seuil, 2005.

33 Quoted by Éric Conan, 'Genet démasqué. Ni saint ni martyr, mais pronazi!', *L'Express*, 17 January 2005.

34 For more on this theme, see Éric Marty's excellent book *Jean Genet, post-scriptum*, Paris: Verdier, 2006.

35 'Mohamed Mehra is me and I am him. I am of the same origin and the same condition. We are postcolonial subjects. We are natives of the Republic', Printemps des quartiers populaires, 2012, Bagnolet. https://www.infolibertaire.net /mohamed-merah-houria-bouteldja-et-la-compassion-a-deux -vitesses/

36 *Les Inrocks*, 17 January 2015.

37 'No man in the world can know what it's like for a woman to be taken by a man she doesn't desire. The woman penetrated without desire is in the murder. The cadaverous weight of virile pleasure over her body possesses the heft of the murder she doesn't have the power to commit – the weight of madness'; Marguerite Duras, 'Sublime, forcément, sublime, Christine V', trans. A. Slade, *Janus Head*, 9/1, 2006, pp. 8–18, p. 14.

38 'L'homme et son heritage', *Le Monde*, 25 February 2003.

39 Imre Kertész, *The Holocaust as Culture*, trans. T. Cooper, London: Seagull Books, 2011, p. 68.

40 George Orwell, *1984*, New York: Signet, 1949, p. 203.

Chapter 10: Healing the past?

1 Catherine Chalier, *Traité des larmes*, Paris: Albin Michel (Spiritualités series), 2003, pp. 195ff.

2 Frédéric Bibal cited in Carrère, *V13, Chronique judiciaire*, p. 299.

3 See Mathieu Delahousse, *Le Prix de nos larmes*, Paris: L'Observatoire, 2022.

4 Ibid., p. 134.

5 Ibid., p. 90.

6 Ibid., pp. 172–3.

7 Pierre Hazan, 'The nature of sanctions: The case of Morocco's Equity and Reconciliation Commission', *The International Review of the Red Cross*, 90/870, 2008, p. 400.

8 Cited in Michel, *Devenir descendant d'esclave*, pp. 283ff.

9 On the material consequences of the Taubira law, see Julien Vincent, 'L'argent de l'esclavage, débat sur une compensation historique', *Le Monde*, 2 June 2023.

10 *Le Figaro*, 5–6 July 2023. The Fort-de-France Court of Appeal had already rejected this request on the grounds that the facts were time-barred. The Court of Cassation pointed out that the statute of limitations had begun to run on the day 'when civilized nations recognized the concept of crimes against humanity with the Universal Declaration of Human Rights of 10 December 1948'. Lastly, it established that 'none of the individuals had produced any documents establishing that they individually suffered damage that could be directly and definitely linked to the crimes suffered by their ancestors who were victims of the slave trade and slavery'.

11 After 1804, France forced its former colony to pay compensatory indemnities of 150 million francs at the time, which hampered the island's economic development; Marie Slavicek, 'Haïti: Comment la France a obligé son ancienne colonie à lui verser des indemnités compensatoires', *Le Monde*, 23 May 2022.

12 Frédéric Régent, *Les Maîtres de la Guadeloupe. Propriétaires d'esclaves, 1635–1848*, Paris: Tallandier, 2019.

13 https://en.wikipedia.org/wiki/Fran%C3%A7oise_Verg%C3%A8s

14 Hélène L'Heuillet, 'Le désir de réparation, sens et limites', *Sens-Dessous*, 30/2, 2022, pp. 101–10. https://doi.org/10.3917/sdes.030.0101

15 'For our part, we say to the Germans: keep your indemnities, crimes cannot be bought … there is no reparation for the irreparable' (Vladimir Jankélévitch, *L'Imprescriptible*, Paris: Seuil, 1986, p. 59). We know that in the 1950s Menachem Begin launched violent diatribes against the very idea of

financial negotiations 'with the murderers of our parents' (Pierre Hazan, *Judging War, Judging History: Behind Truth and Reconciliation*, trans. Sarah Meyer de Stadelhofen, Stanford, CA: Stanford University Press, 2010, p. 28).

16 Robert Antelme, *On the Human Race: Essays and Commentary*, trans J. Haight, Evanston, IL: Northwestern University Press, 2002.

17 Claude Liauzu, 'Violence et colonisation', *Histoire Coloniale et Postcoloniale*, 15 August 2005. https://histoirecoloniale.net/violence-et-colonisation-par-claude-liauzu/

18 Charles Péguy, *Clio*, 1913.

19 The first person to denounce the abuse of memory was Tzvetan Todorov in his book *Les Abus de la mémoire*, Paris: Arléa, 1992. See also Todorov's 'The uses and abuses of memory', in Howard Marchitello, ed., *What Happens to History: The Renewal of Ethics in Contemporary Thought*, New York: Routledge, 2001, pp. 11–39.

20 Maylis de Kerangal, *Réparer les vivants*, Paris: Folio Gallimard, 2014.

21 Antelme, *On the Human Race*.

22 Charlotte Delbo, *Auschwitz and After*, trans. R.C. Lamont, New Haven, CT: Yale University Press, 2014, p. 111.

23 Bruno Bettelheim, *Surviving, and Other Essays*, New York: Knopf, 1979, p. 80.

24 Ibid., p. 79.

25 Isaac Bashevis Singer, *Meshugah*, trans. by the author and N. Wachtel, New York: Farrar, Straus & Giroux, 1994. The books' main character is the prostitute Myriam, who received gifts stolen from murdered Jewish girls by the Nazis.

26 In the language of the camps, the 'Muslims', 'muselmänner' in Yiddish, were prisoners so weakened and resigned, too submissive to survive, that they were doomed to death.

27 Primo Levi, *If This Is a Man; The Truce*, trans. S. Woolf, London: Vintage, 1996, p. 94.

28 Buber-Neumann, *Under Two Dictators*, p. 223.

29 Delbo, *Auschwitz and After*, p. 240.

30 Imre Kertész, *Fatelessness*, trans. Tim Wilkinson, New York: Vintage, 2004, p. 262.

31 Levi, *If This Is a Man*, p. 398.
32 Nina Sutton, *Bruno Bettelheim: The Other Side of Madness*, London: Duckworth 1995, p. 120.
33 Hazan, *Judging War, Judging History*.
34 See Dosé, 'Éloge de la prescription', pp. 78–80. Also Eliacheff and Larivière, *Le Temps des victimes*, pp. 279–80. A film that came out in 2023, *Je verrai toujours vos visages*, dealt specifically with this process.
35 See Susan Thomson, 'The politics of national unity and reconciliation in Rwanda: Everyday resistance to an imposed public face', *Genèses*, 81/4, 2010, pp. 45–63.
36 Ebrahim Moosa, 'Truth and reconciliation as performance: Spectre of eucharistic redemption', in Charles Villa-Vicentio and Wihlelm Verwoerd, eds., *Looking Back. Reaching Forward. Reflections on the Truth and Reconciliation Commission*, Cape Town: Cape Town UP/Zed Books, 2000, pp. 113–22, p. 116.
37 On this point, see the persuasive book by Bernard-Henri Lévy, *L'Empire et les cinq rois*, Paris: Grasset, 2018.
38 Cited by Deszö Kosztolanyi, *Kornél Esti*, trans. B. Adams, New York: New Directions, 2011, ch. 11.

Chapter 11: The hero, an ambiguous antithesis

1 Homer, *The Odyssey*, trans. E. Wilson, New York: Norton, 2018, p. 295. See discussion by Jean-Pierre Vernant, *Mortals and Immortals*, Princeton, NJ: Princeton University Press, 1991, p. 83.
2 Todorov, *Facing the Extreme*, p. 12.
3 Max Scheler, *Le Sens de la souffrance*, trans. Pierre Klossowski, Paris: Aubier Montaigne, 1938.
4 Paul Bénichou, *Man and Ethics: Studies in French Classicism*, trans. E. Hughes, New York: Anchor Books, 1971.
5 Philippe Sellier, *Le Mythe du héros*, Paris: Bordas, 1970.
6 Friedrich Nietzsche, *The Genealogy of Morals*, trans. H.B. Samuel, New York: Boni and Liveright, 1918, p. 23. Emphasis in the original.

7 Jules Michelet, *Jeanne d'Arc* [1841], cited in Sellier, *Le Mythe du héros*, p. 173 for Michelet and p. 176 for Péguy.

8 Jacques Julliard, 'À Simone Veil: Ce que nous lui devons', *Marianne*, 30 June 2017. https://www.marianne.net /politique/simone-veil-ce-que-nous-lui-devons

9 Marc Tourret, 'Qu'est-ce qu'un héros?', *Inflexions*, 1/16, 2011, pp. 95–103.

10 Monique Castillo, 'Le courage qui vient', *Inflexions*, Civils et militaires series, 1/22, 2013, pp. 35–24, p. 36.

11 Hans Jonas, *The Imperative of Responsibility: In Search of an Ethics for the Technological Age*, Chicago: University of Chicago Press, 1985.

12 Manuel Valls, *Le Courage guidait leurs pas: 12 destins face à l'Histoire*, Paris: Tallandier, 2023.

13 Ibid., p. 20.

14 Raul Hilberg cited in François Azouvi, *Le Mythe du grand silence: Auschwitz, les Français, la mémoire*, Paris: Epilogue, 2015, p. 556.

15 Karl Jaspers, ed., *Les Grands Philosophes*, trans. Jeanne Hersch, Paris: Presses Pocket, p. 23.

Chapter 12: Is this how men live?

1 Charles-Ferdinand Ramuz, *Terror on the Mountain*, trans. M. Stansbury, New York: Harcourt, Brace & World, 1967, p. 66.

2 Interview with Olivier Dubois, *Libération*, March 2023.

3 Jean-Pierre Perrin, 'Portrait: Le reclus', *Libération*, 27 January 1997.

4 Jean-Paul Kauffmann, *La Maison du retour*, Paris: Nil Éditions, 2007, p. 268.

5 Ibid., pp. 248–50.

6 *Elle*, 27 June 2005.

7 Take, for example, Les Orchidées rouges [The Red Orchids], an association founded in 2016 by Marie-Claire Moraldo, a Franco-Ivorian activist who has herself been circumcised. It campaigns against genital mutilation, forced marriage and

gender-based violence, and for the professional retraining of women.

8 The story is told by Boris Cyrulnik in his book *Un merveilleux malheur*, Paris: Odile Jacob, 1999, p. 38.

9 Peggy Sastre, *Slate*, 22 February 2020. What she said enraged the lynch mob.

10 Tristane Banon, *La Paix des sexes*, Paris: Éditions de l'Observatoire, 2021.

11 Peggy Sastre, 'Affaire Polanski: Pourquoi il faut entendre la parole de Samantha Geimer et Emmanuelle Seigner', *Le Point*, 12 April 2023.

12 Sinno, *Sad Tiger*.

13 Between 1995 and 1997, American psychiatrists in San Diego created a new nomenclature, ACEs (adverse childhood experiences), in which they correlated physical, psycho-logical or sexual violence suffered in childhood with obesity and addiction problems in adulthood.

14 Vladimir Jankélévitch, 'Should we pardon them?', trans. A. Hobart, *Critical Inquiry*, 22/3, 1996, pp. 552–72, p. 567.

15 Ibid., p. 567.

16 Jean-Jacques Lubrina, *Vladimir Jankélévitch. Les dernières traces du maître*, Paris: Le Félin, 2009, pp. 187–95.

17 Antoine Leiris, *Vous n'aurez pas ma haine*, Paris: Fayard, 2016.

18 https://www.historia.fr/guide-culture-loisirs/expositions -sorties/pierre-dac-du-tac-au-dac-2064618

19 http://clioweb.free.fr/dossiers/39-45/primolevi.htm

20 Grossman, *Life and Fate*, p. 408.

21 Levi, *If This Is a Man*, p. 10.

22 Grossman, *Life and Fate*, p. 410.

23 Nietzsche, *Beyond Good and Evil*, p. 87.

24 Perrin, 'Portrait: Le reclus'.

25 Sands, *East West Street*, p. 358.

26 Azdyne Amimour and Georges Salines, *Il nous reste les mots*, Quebec: Robert Laffont, 2020.

27 Cited by Carrère, V13, *Chronique judiciaire*, p. 97.

28 Johann Christoph Arnold, 'Christian de Chergé: A story of forgiveness', *Plough Magazine*, 10 January 2015. https://

www.plough.com/en/topics/life/grieving/christian-de-cherge
-a-story-of-forgiveness

29 Jean-Pierre Vernant, *L'Individu, la mort, l'amour: Soi-même et l'autre en Grèce ancienne*, Paris: Folio, 1996, pp. 42, 43.

30 Tyrtaeus, Fr 6, 1–2, cited by Jean-Pierre Vernant, 'La belle mort et le cadavre outrage', in Gherardo Gnoli and Jean-Pierre Vernant, eds., *La Mort, les morts dans les sociétés anciennes*, Paris: Éditions de la Maison des sciences de l'homme, 1990. https://books.openedition.org/editionsmsh/7734?lang=en

31 Rémy Ourdan, 'Un an après la bataille de Marioupol, la brigade ukrainienne Azov retourne au combat sur le front de Zaporijia', *Le Monde*, 11–12 June 2023.

32 Vernant, *L'Individu, la mort, l'amour*, p. 88.